TRIALS AND TRIBULATION

TRIALS
and
TRIBULATION

THE STORY OF R.A.F. GRANSDEN LODGE

CHRIS SULLIVAN

Copyright © 2015 Chris Sullivan

The moral right of the author has been asserted.

Apart from any fair dealing for the purposes of research or private study, or criticism or review, as permitted under the Copyright, Designs and Patents Act 1988, this publication may only be reproduced, stored or transmitted, in any form or by any means, with the prior permission in writing of the publishers, or in the case of reprographic reproduction in accordance with the terms of licences issued by the Copyright Licensing Agency. Enquiries concerning reproduction outside those terms should be sent to the publishers.

Matador
9 Priory Business Park,
Wistow Road, Kibworth Beauchamp,
Leicestershire. LE8 0RX
Tel: (+44) 116 279 2299
Fax: (+44) 116 279 2277
Email: books@troubador.co.uk
Web: www.troubador.co.uk/matador

ISBN 978-1784622-336

Front cover: Detail from a photograph, taken by S.A.C. Graham Taylor, of the R.A.F.'s Battle of Britain Memorial Flight Lancaster PA474 as it prepares for takeoff on a mission to drop poppies over the newly unveiled Bomber Command Memorial in London on 28th June 2012 (Ministry of Defence)

British Library Cataloguing in Publication Data.
A catalogue record for this book is available from the British Library.

Printed and bound by CPI Group (UK) Ltd, Croydon, CR0 4YY
Typeset in 11pt Adobe Garamond Pro by Troubador Publishing Ltd, Leicester, UK

Matador is an imprint of Troubador Publishing Ltd

MIX
Paper from
responsible sources
FSC® C013604

*For my family and friends -
and for those who took off,
but never came back.*

CONTENTS

Prologue	ix
Laying Foundations	1
Special Duties	16
The Snoopers	37
Pathfinders	58
Lancasters and V-Weapons	80
The Battle of Berlin	104
Invasion	132
Night Strikers	163
The Final Push	196
MANNA, EXODUS and Cook's Tours	223
After the Bombers	244
Epilogue	269
Acknowledgements	275
Glossary	278
References	284
Appendix: The Units	296
Index	299

PROLOGUE

Wartime airfields can be very atmospheric places. When standing at Gransden Lodge at dusk, one can easily imagine a huge Lancaster bomber taxying out onto a runway for takeoff, perhaps with one of the tense and apprehensive young airmen on board exchanging a farewell wave with a friend in the small knot of chilly people who have gathered to wish good luck to the departing crew. On a foggy, frosty January day, if you walk around the airfield's perimeter track, it's hard not to feel sympathy for the long-suffering ground crews, dropping their tools and cursing under their breath as, with freezing hands, they would have worked on the bombers parked in the open nearby to ready them for their next mission. But pause near the old control tower on a warm summer's day, surrounded by the scents of the countryside and the song of the skylarks, and it's possible to conjure up a happier scene, imagining that you can just overhear, through the tower's open windows, the voices of the men and women inside laughing and chatting as they work, perhaps discussing their romantic liaisons of the previous evening or planning their next day's leave in Cambridge.

In the early 1990s, the gliding club of which I am a member moved to Gransden Lodge. This gave me the opportunity to spend a lot of time around the airfield investigating, and indulging in flights of fancy like those I've mentioned above. Even then,

TRIALS AND TRIBULATION

twenty years and more ago, there was not much that was left on the old airfield site that could provide some link to the lives of the hundreds of men and women who had lived and died there during its relatively brief operational life. However, it was still just possible to find the odd piece of tangible evidence from those times – perhaps a broken cosmetic bottle, or a fragment of a coffee cup carrying a 1944 date stamp – that made that physical connection.

As I walked and wondered, I soon began to realise that I really wanted to understand more about what I was seeing, so I began researching the airfield's history, and eventually this book was the result. In it I've tried to record not only the events that took place, but also to try to give a flavour of what is was like to live on a bomber airfield during wartime. Its title aims to reflect some the differing uses to which the airfield has been put over the years, such as a base for secret wartime radar trials, and, of course, to acknowledge the trials and tribulation facing bomber crews setting off to meet whatever fate awaited them.

Some of the major sources of information for this book were the original archive documents of the time, and as is inevitable when dealing with any subject that has a specialised vocabulary, abbreviations and acronyms are rife. Some of the more common are explained in the glossary, but one that will occur frequently is 'O.R.B.'. This refers to an Operations Record Book, which was a document kept both by individual units and operational stations, and was intended to form a historical record of the activities of the organisation in question. The level of detail recorded in these Operations Record Books can vary widely, but in general they are an extremely useful source of information, and will be quoted extensively, along with other official documents. Since they were written at the time by people close to the events, they give a unique insight into how

PROLOGUE

people perceived, and felt about, what was going on around them. Such extracts from official sources, held at the U.K. National Archives, appear in an appropriate typewriter-like typeface thus:

```
New Year's Day passed very quietly on the
Station. A special meal was had by the Airmen and
the Officers somewhere along the lines of the
Christmas dinner.
```

A reference to the document in which an extract can be found (for example, [AIR 27/1790]) follows each one. I have tried to honour the sometimes eccentric punctuation, spelling and grammar of the sources that have been quoted, as well as using the German name of locations in that country wherever possible. Extracts from books, letters and other publications and documents appear like this:

> *"In the early days of flying over enemy territory we did carry bombs when joining a Bomber Command stream, ..."*

I may not have succeeded, but I have attempted to record all the missions carried out from Gransden Lodge – for overnight operations, the date given is that on which it was recorded, though sometimes the aircraft may have taken off in the early hours of the following morning. More importantly, I have tried to note all the individuals or aircraft crews that went missing while serving at the airfield. Because of this, some sections of this book may read like a litany of 'this many aircraft attacked

TRIALS AND TRIBULATION

this target on this date, and these crews were lost'. I have endeavoured to make this reporting as interesting as possible, but where I have failed, I hope the intent behind it is sufficient justification.

Any errors and omissions are all mine.

LAYING FOUNDATIONS

Gransden Lodge airfield is located on the borders of Bedfordshire and Cambridgeshire, approximately 11 miles (18 km) almost due west of Cambridge, and lies between the village of Longstowe and the adjoining villages of Great and Little Gransden.

The story of the airfield itself begins in 1940, but the villages in the immediate neighbourhood have a history going back many centuries. In fact, aerial photographs of the area near Caxton church (1.5 miles/2.5 km north-east of the airfield) show evidence of settlement during prehistoric times. In the Domesday Book of 1086, Little Gransden is recorded as *Grantenden*, meaning *Granta's valley*, and its manor had only eleven 'peasant households'. At the same date, Longstowe was called *Stou* (or *Place*, probably meaning *Holy Place*), but by 1268 it had become known as Longstowe. It, too, had a tiny population of just seventeen villagers in Domesday. A medieval manor house stood on the site of the present Longstowe Hall, which was built by the Cage family sometime after 1571 to replace it. The Hall is still occupied today, though it was extensively modified in the 19th and 20th centuries.

In the early 21st century a pilot who had flown from Gransden Lodge some 60 years earlier made an audio record of those times and his part in the events that had taken place there. He described the region where the airfield was to be built as being absolutely

TRIALS AND TRIBULATION

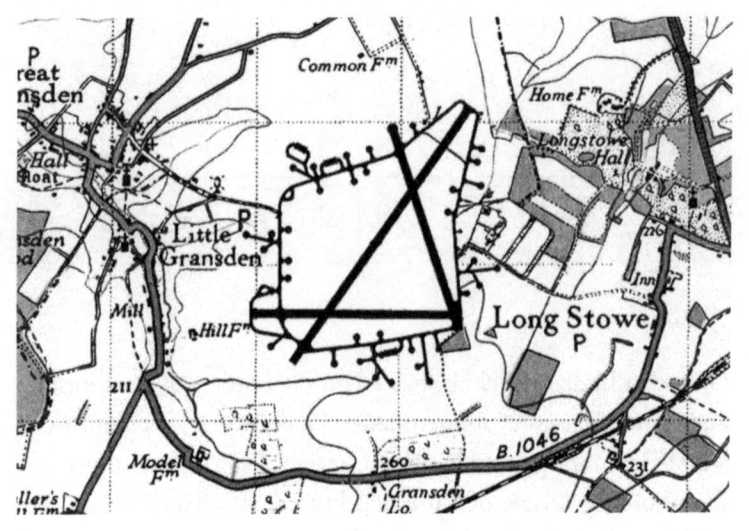

The location of the airfield, showing the 1944 layout (Map © National Library of Scotland – overlay by the author)

unspoiled, and just, one would imagine, as it had been at the turn of the 20th century. The impact that the creation of an airfield would have had on such a rural area can easily be imagined, but this was something that happened in many places and to many communities throughout the U.K. during World War Two.

The name of the airfield seems to be derived from that of a farm in the locality, although confusingly, different maps show two farms labelled Gransden Lodge within a very short distance of each other. One farm, which still exists, is to the south of the airfield, and the other, sometimes known as Lodge Farm, was just on the northern edge of the area to be occupied by the new airfield. Quite why the airfield was not named after one of the nearby towns or villages, the usual practice, is not clear.

The new airfield at Gransden Lodge was planned as a satellite airfield. When the R.A.F.'s new Expansion Period airfields were being built in the 1930s, it was clear that despite secrecy and attempts at camouflage, any potential enemy would have little

LAYING FOUNDATIONS

difficulty in locating them through aerial reconnaissance, and once identified, they were vulnerable. Satellite airfields were designed to mitigate this vulnerability. Built within easy reach of their parent airfield, they existed so that operations could continue should the parent airfield be attacked, with the aircraft being diverted there and fuel and munitions being brought in by road.

The airfield is located about 7 miles (11 km) east of its parent of Tempsford, itself built as a satellite of Bassingbourn, which is approximately 6 miles (10 km) to the south of Gransden Lodge. Bassingbourn was, incidentally, the base of the Boeing B-17 bomber 'Memphis Belle', made famous in two films.

Tempsford, like its satellite airfields, was part of the R.A.F.'s No. 3 Group when it opened in late 1941, and within months it began its role as a base for special duties units. These included radio and radar investigation and development units, and perhaps most famously, Tempsford was the base from which the agents of the Special Operations Executive, the 'Joes', were flown into and out of occupied Europe. Gransden Lodge's fairly isolated location also made it suitable as an airfield from which to carry out similar clandestine operations.

Another station that appears often in Gransden Lodge's story is Graveley. This airfield, built at around the same time as Gransden Lodge and located about 6 miles (10 km) to the north, was also intended to be a base from which special duties could be carried out. As we will see later, it was also to be the place where a pioneering aid to safer operational flying was first installed. The plan at this time was that No. 3 Group should centralise all its special duties units at Tempsford, Gransden Lodge and Graveley, under Tempsford's control.

This much we know, but, given the huge investment of money and effort that went into the wartime airfield building program, detailed information on airfield construction can be surprisingly difficult to obtain. Perhaps it was the sheer scale of the undertaking that meant that the volume of records generated was just too large to keep in the archives. As an example of the size and cost of this immense building program, in 1942, which was the year when the construction of airfields was at its peak, a new bomber airfield was being brought into service *every three days*, and the average cost of each airfield was over £500,000. That sum was just for the runways etc. for the airfield, before any buildings or services were taken into account. To put these numbers into perspective, the £500,000 cost of building such an airfield would be equivalent to around £18 million today.

The village of Little Gransden nestles in a slight valley, and it was the higher, flat land to the east of the village, which is of heavy clay and so hard to drain and once formed the village common, that was requisitioned in 1940 in order to build Gransden Lodge airfield. At some point the requisitioned land was purchased by the Air Ministry; exactly when this happened is not clear, but it was apparently before 1946. The construction of the station was contracted out to the building firm of John Laing and Son, and must have commenced (or at least have been in an advanced state of planning) by November 1940 at the latest. From the start, the construction of the new airfield would have caused disruption to the lives of the inhabitants of the surrounding villages.

Among the scanty sources of official information available relating to the period of the airfield's construction are the maps that were drawn at various dates to record the assignment of satellite airfields to parent stations, and the allocation of airfields to the R.A.F.'s Groups. The station distribution map dated 14th November 1940 shows both Tempsford and Gransden Lodge,

LAYING FOUNDATIONS

though Bomber Command's Order of Battle for that date mentions neither of them. However, in a table attached to the R.A.F.'s monthly aerodrome return for November 1940, the hope was expressed that Tempsford would have runways ready by January 1941, with buildings ready by March of that year, and that Gransden Lodge would have two runways ready for use by February 1941.

The plan of the general layout of the airfield to which we must assume Laing and Son would have been working is shown below, and it differs markedly from the form that it would finally take. It is interesting to note just how sparse the airfield area was, with no provision for hangars or hardstandings for parking aircraft – probably understandable if the airfield was only intended as a satellite – and the rather peculiar way in which the runways did not extend all the way to the perimeter tracks. This feature was not unique to the airfield, and another example can still be seen at R.A.F. Syerston in Nottinghamshire, which opened in December 1940, where at least one of the surviving runways was also constructed to this pattern. The main runway at Gransden Lodge was planned to be 1,400 yards (1,280 m) long, with the other two at 1,100 yards (1,005 m). The cluster of buildings at the top of the plan is marked as 'Gransden Lodge', the farm previously noted as sometimes being known as Lodge Farm.

The Expansion Period airfields such as Bassingbourn were built with a certain amount of comfort for the inhabitants in mind, and the living and domestic accommodation was, in general, fairly centralised and close to the locations where their daily work would have been carried out. When war came, it became clear that it was much safer to disperse the living accommodation away from the airfield site itself, in order to reduce the danger to station personnel if the airfield was bombed. To this end, many (but not

TRIALS AND TRIBULATION

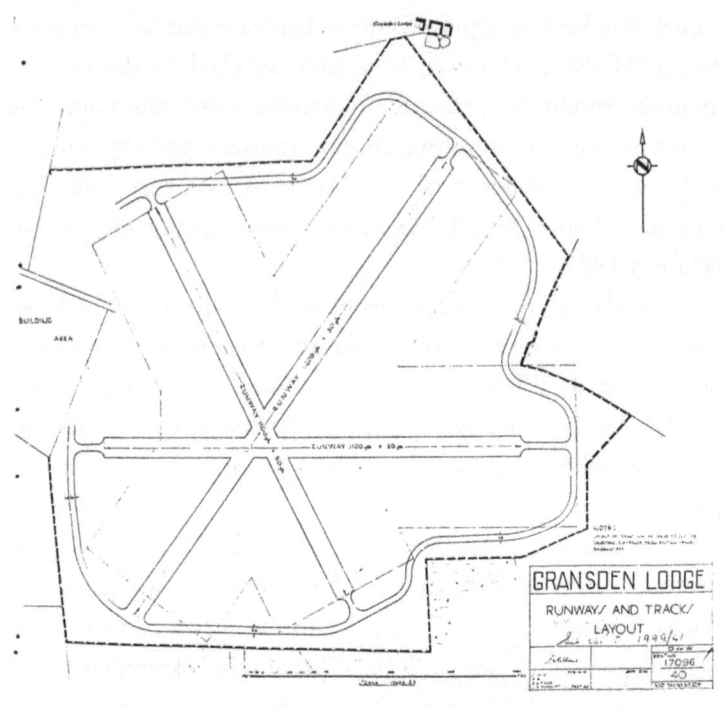

Runway and perimeter track layout as planned in 1940
(Cambridge Gliding Centre)

all) of the living and other communal areas at Gransden Lodge were dispersed into sites some distance to the west and north-west of the airfield proper. Derek Daniels, then a boy living in the Gransdens, remembers the building of the airfield, and recalls that around 1940 his family provided lodgings for two of the workers, coincidentally both named Michael, who were engaged in building these living quarters. We must presume that many other families in the area were also called upon to house those building the airfield.

Gransden Lodge was probably not alone in this, but the very dispersed nature of the facilities for the men and women living and working on the station was, as we will find, a continuing

LAYING FOUNDATIONS

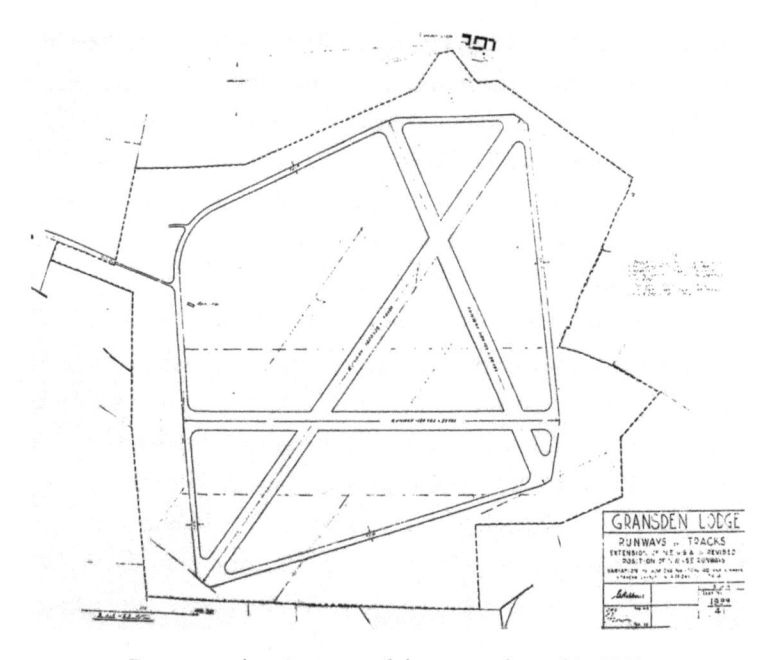

Runway and perimeter track layout as planned in 1941
(Cambridge Gliding Centre)

cause of discontent. By the time construction was eventually complete, accommodation had been provided for almost 2,000 male and over 200 female personnel.

Evidence that work was under way at Gransden Lodge to meet the schedule of having runways available by February 1941 can be found in the fact in January 1941 it was recorded that there was a requirement for 830 men and 88 lorries to be at the site. The workmen beavering away to meet their deadlines would not have been helped when a revised set of plans for the airfield, shown above, were produced.

As can easily be seen, the most radical changes were the complete repositioning of the NW-SE runway further east and the replacement of the rather pleasingly sinuous perimeter track with a more utilitarian one comprised mainly of straight sections (an intermediate drawing shows the original runway layout - but with slightly lengthened runways - and straightened perimeter tracks). What is not quite so obvious is that it was now planned that the main runway should be increased in length to 1,600 yards (1,463 m). Although there would still be many changes to the design, this layout is becoming recognisable as the airfield that eventually evolved.

The planners at the Air Ministry had formulated a requirement for Bomber Command's airfields that would necessitate the next re-working of the layout at Gransden Lodge, when in April 1941 they decreed that from now on, every bomber airfield should have a main runway 2,000 yards (1,828 m) long, and a further two subsidiary runways each of 1,400 yards (1,280 m) in length.

The reasoning behind this ruling was that in future all Bomber Command squadrons would be equipped with heavy, four-engined bombers, and the runways then available would be too short to allow safe operation of these aircraft, especially at night. This specification of the number and length of runways formed the basis of the 'Class A' standard for R.A.F. airfields, though that standard also specified the optimum alignment and maximum gradients of the runways, clear space alongside them, and other parameters.

Even though the airfield must have been far from complete, thought was already being given to the question of which units might take up residence at the new base. In an amendment to a plan of June 1941 for Bomber Command's expansion, it was noted that the intention was that No. 218 Squadron would re-equip with the Short Stirling bomber and move to Gransden Lodge. In the end, this was not to be.

The world's politics also touched the Cambridgeshire countryside in a different way in June 1941, when the young King Peter II of Yugoslavia arrived to take up residence, albeit temporarily, in Great Gransden. His mother, Queen Marie, and

LAYING FOUNDATIONS

his two younger brothers, the Princes Tomislav and Andrej, were living in the Mill House adjacent to Gransden windmill when King Peter joined them after being exiled from his native country.

King Peter's autobiography contains a photograph taken at the time showing the King, his mother and members of the Yugoslav government-in-exile in the garden of Mill House, looking rather uncomfortable and self-conscious. Living in a foreign land, surrounded by the noise and upheaval caused by the building of a new airfield, must have been a strange experience for these displaced royals, especially for the young princes. Some of the youngsters from the Gransden villages befriended them; the fact that the princes possessed a rudimentary motorised go-kart on which to ride was a great attraction for the local lads.

The King, a great-grandchild of Queen Victoria – he referred to King George VI, his godfather, as 'Uncle Bertie' - was keen to fly in combat, but the political realities of his position precluded this. Shortly after his arrival he began studies at Cambridge University before eventually moving to Cairo and then, on his return to the U.K., taking up residence in the south of England. His mother and brothers also moved away from the Gransdens, but they did visit the units eventually to be based at Gransden Lodge in an official capacity on occasion, as we shall see. Having completed pilot training King Peter, entirely unofficially, flew at least one operational mission in a North American Mustang fighter over France. Following his death in 1970 he became the only European monarch to be buried in America, though his remains were returned to Serbia in 2013 and re-interred there.

A rather confusing map was produced, dated July 1941, outlining another scheme for allocating airfields to groups. The legend for this map informs us that some stations were classified as 'constructed', and some are marked as 'under or awaiting construction'. Gransden Lodge was shown as neither, implying that building was not under way at this date, but this should probably be treated as an oversight, as we have already seen that construction had started some time before this. Bassingbourn is also shown as 'under construction', but flying units had been based there since May 1938. Perhaps this indicates the beginnings of the building of hard runways on that previously all-grass airfield.

As an aside, the annotation for Tempsford indicates that it was thought 'not suitable for bomber operations' even before it was operational. One reason for this was the rising ground to the east of the airfield, which would make takeoff and landing in that direction, especially in a heavily loaded aircraft, tricky. Of course, we now know that Tempsford's future role would mean that bomb-laden aircraft would not be using the airfield to any great extent anyway.

The organisation of Bomber Command's units was still in flux, but what is certain, however, is that the assertion made in November 1940 that Gransden Lodge would have 'two runways ready by February 1941' was proving rather optimistic.

The first definite mention of a specific R.A.F. unit serving at the new station can be found in late 1941, when:

> On the 2nd. of December the undernoted personnel of 816 Defence Squadron, TEMPSFORD, took over temporary occupation of No. 4 Site at R.A.F. Station, GRANSDEN LODGE. (Satellite Station to R.A.F. Station, TEMPSFORD.) One Officer, one senior N.C.O., one hundred and ten other ranks. Arms and equipment consisted of the following:- Three Vickers Air Cooled Guns, Five Vickers Water Cooled Guns. Eight Lewis Machine Guns. Five S.M.L.E. Rifles. Seventy Two Ross Rifles. Twenty Five Thompson Sub Machine Guns.
>
> [AIR 28/820]

LAYING FOUNDATIONS

It is not completely clear for how long this defence squadron, later to become No. 2816 Squadron of the R.A.F. Regiment (R.A.F.R.), remained at Gransden Lodge, but it was probably for not more than a few months at most, as the squadron converted to a field role in April 1942. The construction of the airfield was clearly sufficiently advanced by this date, though, to warrant a defence and security force of some size being put into place. The administration of the new station was obviously being organised at this time, too, as in January 1942 one Flying Officer Brant was posted to Gransden Lodge for duties as one of the station's administrative officers.

By early 1942 discussions were going on to try to allocate units to the new and existing stations in No. 3 Group. On 20th January 1942 Air Vice-Marshal J.E.A. Baldwin, C.B., C.B.E., D.S.O. wrote to Air Vice-Marshal Charles Medhurst, Assistant Chief of the Air Staff (Intelligence), on the subject. In this letter he reiterated that the intention was to segregate the special duties squadrons from the other operational units, and put them under the command of the Station Commander at Tempsford. He also noted that the plan was for No. 109 Squadron to be based at Gransden Lodge when the airfield was available, and expressed his concern at the hold-ups in getting the new airfields completed.

Baldwin, the Air Officer Commanding of No. 3 Group, was a well-liked commander who flouted the rules by occasionally flying on operations, and at this date he was briefly acting as caretaker Air Officer Commanding-in-Chief of Bomber Command as well.

Medhurst replied a few days later, concurring with Baldwin's suggestions for the disposition of his units and offering reassurance that things were moving to provide bases for them, and that, in light of the fact that a base for No. 109 Squadron was required, a

TRIALS AND TRIBULATION

higher priority would be needed for the works at Gransden Lodge.

On 25th January 1942 Baldwin wrote to Medhurst again, outlining the current construction situation with regard to the provision of runways, perimeter tracks etc. at Graveley, Tempsford and Gransden Lodge, where it was noted that there were now runways of 1,600 and 1,100 yards in place, but that the program to extend these to 2,000 and 1,400 yards had not yet started. The perimeter track was 90% complete, but only 15% of the planned dispersal areas had been built.

From this, we can be sure that by the first month of 1942 all three runways at Gransden Lodge were complete at their originally intended lengths, although to comply with the Class A requirements they would have to be extended.

Looking ahead some years to the final airfield layout, we can see that neither of the original plans for the runway layout were followed precisely, but rather a modified amalgam of the two. The result was a far cry from the very basic satellite station originally planned. Precisely why the runways were not built to meet the Class A standard from the outset is not obvious, given that the recommendation to build all bomber airfields to this standard had been made in April 1941. As we will soon see, Gransden Lodge would be in use within three months, so it seems certain that work on the runway extensions, perimeter track, dispersals etc. would still have been in progress when operational flying had begun. It also seems that at this point Gransden Lodge was still intended eventually to become a satellite of Bassingbourn, but this never came about during the war, no doubt due to the fact that Bassingbourn was transferred to the American forces in October 1942.

There was obviously a pressing need to bring the new airfields into use as quickly as possible, in order to consolidate the widely

LAYING FOUNDATIONS

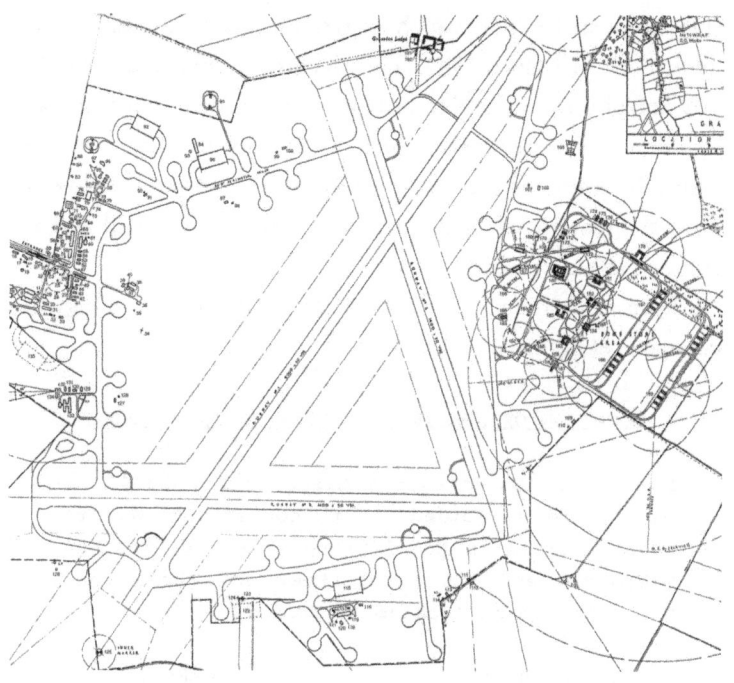

Runway and perimeter track layout, October 1944
(R.A.F. Museum)

scattered elements of the units earmarked to occupy them. In mid-February 1942 we find that discussions were still under way on the subject of where various squadrons should be based when Tempsford became available following the departure the next month of the Operational Training Unit that was based there. These imply that the thinking was that No. 161 Squadron was now intended to be based at Gransden Lodge, which was forecast to be ready for occupation by May or June of 1942, and that the 'necessary arrangements' for moving the squadrons would be made.

By the end of February 1942 an (apparently) definitive decision had been made as to where these squadrons should be located, and numbered among these was one that was named as No. 1418

TRIALS AND TRIBULATION

(Development) Flight, which, it was proposed, should move to Tempsford in March 1942. This document confirmed that No. 109 Squadron was slated to be based at Gransden Lodge, and also mentioned that the date by which it was estimated that the airfield would be ready for use was still June 1942. However, unlike the normal situation when builders are involved, it would actually come in ahead of schedule.

Even given the above decisions, by 1st April 1942 things had changed yet again:

LOCATION OF SPECIALIST UNITS IN NO. 3 GROUP

Further to Organisation Circular No. 30/42, it has now been decided not to concentrate all the special Units in No. 3 Group at R.A.F. Station, TEMPSFORD and its satellites, and these units will instead be located as follows:-

No. 138 Squadron	) TEMPSFORD
No. 161 "	)
No.1418 Flight	MILDENHALL
No.109 Squadron (Sqdn. H.Q., Wireless Development Flight and Wireless Investigation Flight)	STRADISHALL

[AIR 14/1121]

Thus No. 109 Squadron ended up at Stradishall in Suffolk, not at Gransden Lodge, but No. 1418 Flight would also, as will soon become clear, finish up with a different home to that planned.

The security of the airfield was either enhanced or put into new hands on 7th April 1942, when the Tempsford O.R.B. records that:

LAYING FOUNDATIONS

> On this date a transfer took place of 71 Airmen from R.A.F. Station, WEST MALLING, to R.A.F. Satellite GRANSDEN for Defence Duties.
>
> [AIR 28/820]

They would soon have something worthwhile to defend - Gransden Lodge was about to come to life.

SPECIAL DUTIES

At the beginning of April 1942, the plan had been for No. 1418 Flight to take up residence at Mildenhall in Suffolk, but within days this was changed, and on 8th April 1942 No. 1418 Flight and its Vickers Wellingtons arrived from Tempsford to become the first flying unit to be based at Gransden Lodge.

No. 1418 Flight had been formed at Marham in Norfolk in December 1941, and was known at its formation as the TR1335 Development Unit, before being renamed as No. 1418 Flight in January 1942. The rather odd name that the flight originally carried indicates the reason for its formation, as TR1335 was the R.A.F. type number for the *Gee* radio navigation aid, and the flight, whose role was to develop operational techniques for the use of various radar aids, was involved in service trials of this new equipment.

Experience early in the war had shown that the standard of navigation of bomber crews was far below that needed to allow accurate bombing of targets far into occupied Europe. The *Gee* system, the fundamentals of which were proposed by R.J. Dippy of the Telecommunications Research Establishment (T.R.E.) as early as 1937, was designed to provide Bomber Command navigators with a precise and easy-to-use aid to improving their accuracy, ideally to such a level that *Gee* could be used for bomb aiming. The system worked by the transmission of coordinated

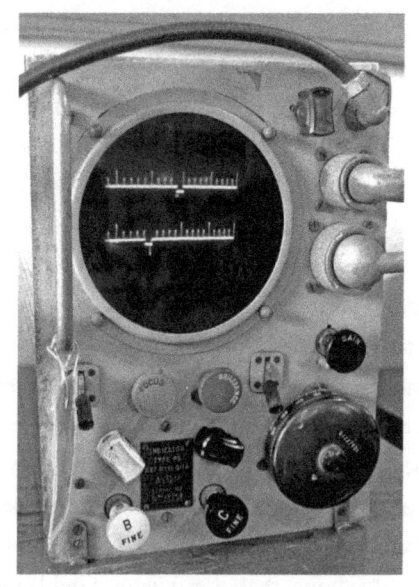

Gee set (Author)

radio pulses from ground-based stations, a 'Master' and two or more 'Slaves'. The pulses were picked up by a receiver in the aircraft and displayed as traces on a screen, and by measuring the distance between the peaks in these traces, the differences in arrival time between the pulses from the different transmitters could be calculated. When plotted on special charts, this enabled the aircraft's position to be established to an accuracy of around a few miles or less at a distance of 350 miles (560 km).

The first operational trials of *Gee* had been carried out somewhat clandestinely (as they did not have Air Ministry approval) by three aircraft from No. 115 Squadron in mid-1941. In August 1941 one of these aircraft was shot down over Germany, and it then became only a matter of time before the secrets of *Gee* were discovered and countermeasures were put in place. At this point, the large scale adoption of *Gee* by Bomber Command was at least seven months away, so Dr. R.V. Jones, Assistant Director of Intelligence (Science) at the Air Ministry, set in train a scheme to conceal the true nature of the *Gee* system.

It was vital to mislead the German intelligence authorities over any information that might be extracted from aircrew who had been shot down since *Gee* testing had begun, and who thus knew of its existence. The first of these rearguard actions was to change the type number of the *Gee* receivers from the R3000 series to TR1335 (hence the flight's name), as this was a number that would be associated with radio transmitter-receiver equipment, not a navigation system. The use of the term *Gee* was also banned, but in its place Jones, an inveterate practical joker, invented an imaginary piece of navigation equipment called *Jay*, professing that it worked on completely different (but feasible) principles to *Gee*. Through various means, including deliberate indiscretions close to listening ears, details of this *Jay* system were leaked, in the hope that the enemy would assume that any mentions of *Gee* picked up during questioning were in fact misheard references to *Jay*. The ruse worked, and *Gee* was still un-jammed when it came into operational use in March 1942, so the development work to be done by No. 1418 Flight would not be in vain.

Within days of No. 1418 Flight's arrival at Gransden Lodge, the 'brass' came calling to view the newly-operational station, when the Air Officer Commanding, Air Vice-Marshal Baldwin, paid a visit, and No. 1418 Flight got straight back into the swing of test flying after its move with the first flights, which were investigating the use of *Gee* to carry out a blind approach to an airfield (Shawbury in Shropshire in this case), being carried out on 12th April 1942. Unfortunately, the Wellington carrying out the tests crashed after landing. It is not completely clear from the documents where this crash happened, but if it was at Gransden Lodge, this trial also caused the airfield's first flying accident.

The next day, the flight carried out two test flights, during one of which it was noted that bombing had been carried out over

SPECIAL DUTIES

Scarborough in Yorkshire. This seems a little hard on Scarborough, but it is safe to assume that these were test bombing runs. Many of the tests being carried out were described as 'bombing' or 'photographic checks'; these were in fact testing the suitability of *Gee* as a blind bombing aid and checking the accuracy of *Gee* by photographic means, respectively. Over the next days and weeks, these tests continued, with a good number of the flights involving photography of the Menai Bridge and Sea Gull Isle (off the south coast of the Lleyn Peninsula in North Wales), and cities such as Leeds, Winchester, Lincoln and Doncaster were also used.

As would be expected with new and important technology, part of the job of No. 1418 Flight was to demonstrate *Gee* to interested parties, and, to some extent, to act as salesmen for it. Over two consecutive days in mid-April 1942, for instance, nine R.A.F. officers, none of lower rank than Squadron Leader, were taken for demonstration flights, and a few days later representatives of the U.S. and Australian forces also received the same treatment. While these demonstrations were taking place the testing was interspersed with more lowly, but still important, activities when local defence exercises were carried out on the station, and on 8th May 1942 the airfield's defensive positions were inspected by the local army sub-area commander.

From that day's entry in the O.R.B. we can find a clue as to what other new equipment was being tested by No. 1418 Flight. The entry notes 'Check on A.P.I.', which is a reference to a device known as the Air Position Indicator. This was essentially a mechanical analogue computer that, once it had been fed a set of known coordinates, used an aircraft's airspeed and heading information to calculate its latitude and longitude at any given time in flight.

Some members of the flight decamped from Gransden Lodge for Fairwood Common (an airfield on the Gower Peninsula in South Wales, and now Swansea Airport) in the middle of May

TRIALS AND TRIBULATION

1942, initially taking with them one Wellington, and for the next three or four weeks the testing effort would be split between the two sites. One of the party detached to Fairwood Common, Pilot Officer Killip, will appear again later in our story. Four of the tests made while the detached section was based in Wales involved acquiring information on using *Gee* 'with evasive action'. For *Gee* to be of use under operational conditions, it would obviously be vital that it could be used when the aircraft carrying it was manoeuvring to evade nightfighters and searchlights; very different to benign 'straight and level' test flying.

For the bulk of the flight back at base testing also carried on, included flights that were being made to examine the possibility of using the Southern and Eastern *Gee* chains. A *Gee* chain consisted of the Master station, its Slave stations, and sometimes a Monitor

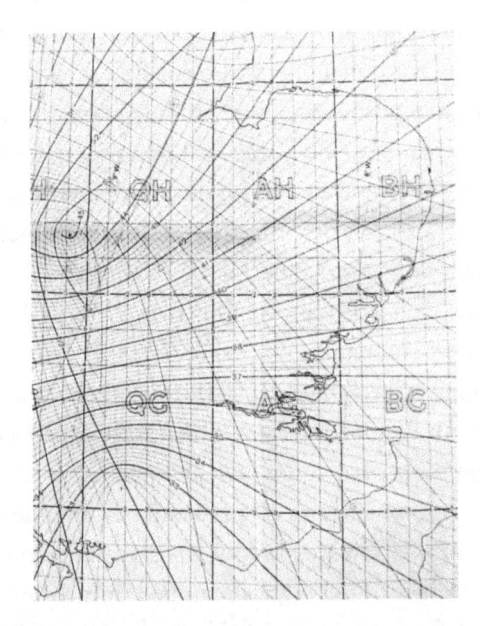

Gee chart showing the lattice for the Eastern chain over the south-eastern corner of England (Author)

station. There would eventually be a number of these *Gee* chains, including the Eastern chain, whose coverage extended into Germany, the Southern chain covering the English Channel and northern France, the South Western chain and the Northern chain. Coincidentally, the Monitor station for the Eastern chain was at R.A.F. Barkway, just 15 miles (24 km) south-east of Gransden Lodge.

The flow of visitors to No. 1418 Flight for demonstrations and other consultations also continued, including representatives of the School of Navigation in the last week of May 1942, and during this period the flight had also arranged for a demonstration to take place at Hendon near London.

On 1st June 1942 authority was received to increase the size of No. 1418 Flight. From now on the flight would have nine officers and 97 N.C.O.s and other ranks, making a total establishment of 106. Part of the reason for this increase was that the flight now had two Handley Page Halifax four-engined bombers on strength as well as its Wellingtons.

A few days later the detachment returned from Wales, and another important visitor to Gransden Lodge was given a demonstration of *Gee* and the A.P.I. The guest was Sir Henry Tizard, a member of the Air Council and advisor to the Ministry of Aircraft Production.

Tizard was a long-standing advocate of the applications of radar, and a committee under his chairmanship had been instrumental in ensuring that the U.K. had its early-warning radar system in place in time to play its pivotal role in the Battle of Britain. He had also led the British 'Tizard Mission' to the U.S.A. in 1940, which would pave the way for exchanges of technology between the two countries. His influence would soon be felt at Gransden Lodge, as we shall see.

In the meantime, testing of the operation value of the A.P.I. took a more prominent role, and these trials continued all through

TRIALS AND TRIBULATION

June 1942. The aircraft of No. 1418 Flight flew the length of England on these tests, using locations as far apart as Land's End in Cornwall and Hexham in Northumberland. On 12th June 1942 the flight received a visit from Wing Commander Saye, who, as Bomber Command's Chief Navigation Officer, headed a team that, within a few months, would introduce a major new testing program to Gransden Lodge.

Transatlantic interest in the progress of the flight's testing was also evidenced on the last day of June 1942, when Wing Commander E.E. Vielle of the British Air Commission in Washington was given a demonstration flight, as was another representative from the U.S. Army Air Corps on, appropriately enough, 4th July 1942. In a letter dated that day, or thereabouts, in which wrangling over the availability of labour to carry out building works on airfields was taking place, it was clear that the decision to fit *Gee* throughout Bomber Command had been made, and that 'Huts, T.R. 1335' would be needed at all airfields to support it, following Gransden Lodge's lead.

The Royal Navy was obviously also interested in *Gee*, since on 10th July 1942 two visitors from the Admiralty received a demonstration of the device, though there was, it was noted, 'No flying'. That day also marked the end of No. 1418 Flight's sole tenancy at Gransden Lodge.

During July 1942, No. 109 Squadron at Stradishall had been undergoing some reorganisation, as part of which Bomber Command had given authority for two flights of the squadron to be split off into independent units, to be known as No. 1473 Flight and No. 1474 Flight respectively. As a result of this, on 10th July 1942 the newly-formed No. 1474 Flight - not the whole of No. 109 Squadron, as had been briefly planned the previous February - arrived at Gransden Lodge, along with its nine Wellingtons.

Due to the high level of security surrounding the operations

SPECIAL DUTIES

carried out by the units at Gransden Lodge, official records can be tantalisingly terse. For instance, the O.R.B. entries for No. 1474 Flight, whose role was radar intelligence gathering, generally (but with one notable exception) just give details of the aircraft, the crew, the fact that they had carried out a Special Duty Flight, and the general geographical area in which they had been operating. Because of this, it can be difficult to work out the exact nature of the operations being undertaken. This need for secrecy soon became evident to newly-arrived crews, and those already serving were reluctant to talk about what operations entailed, telling them that they'd find out soon enough. In an article entitled *'March of Technology: Closing the Radar Gap'*, Bill Barry, a navigator with No. 1474 Flight, recalled a time when his pilot's brother, also a pilot, came to visit Gransden Lodge and expressed an interest in inspecting the flight's aircraft, and was told in no uncertain terms that this was impossible, and that he'd probably be shot if he tried.

Despite this secrecy, we can get a general idea of how operations were carried out on No. 1474 Flight from a letter written in 1971 by Flight Lieutenant (later Wing Commander) E.P.M. Fernbank, one of the founding members of the flight:

> *"The information we had to pick up included enemy radar frequencies, signal strengths, pulse repetition frequencies, type of scan equipment (in so far as it could be judged from variations in signal strength over short periods), all to be timed so as to tie in with the navigator's log and so enable the back-room boys at home to assess what the Hun had and what it was capable of. Monitoring was done by the Special Duty Operator using special receivers coupled up to an oscilloscope which was in addition to the standard radio equipment of Bomber Command. An operator was usually given a special band of frequencies to monitor: thus to cover a wide spectrum in any detail, more than one aircraft would often be*

allotted to a given route. Routes were devised to ensure that our aircraft were present in areas of greatest likely radar activity, which of course meant wherever Bomber Command were going on any particular night. Bomber Command's plans for the night were phoned or teleprinted direct to our Squadron Operations Officers, usually at about ten in the morning; and then we made our own plans. When Command were using several different targets on the same night we would sometimes plan to go in with one stream, jump across to a neighbouring target area and return with that stream. Alternatively we would put up a Mosquito to fly independently of the streams and cover several target (and non-target) areas in one sweep....

In the early days of flying over enemy territory we did carry bombs when joining a Bomber Command stream, but stopped doing so when the Boffins protested that they could not afford the risk (any more than absolutely necessary) of losing their special receivers. When you consider that we were searching the spectrum up as high as the unheard of frequency of 5000 megacycles this was understandable."

Flight Lieutenant Fernbank and his crew made the first successful operational flight from Gransden Lodge on 14th July 1942, an attempt the previous day having been thwarted by the weather. This flight, over south-west England, north-west France and the English Channel, was the sole operational sortie made by No. 1474 Flight in July 1942.

After the departure of No. 1474 Flight for Gransden Lodge, the remainder of No. 109 Squadron moved to Wyton, about 2 miles (3 km) to the east of Huntingdon (then in Huntingdonshire, now in Cambridgeshire) in August 1942, and became the unit that pioneered the use of the *Oboe* precision bombing system.

As we know, the hope had originally been that *Gee* could be used for bomb aiming as well as for navigation, but it was found to be insufficiently accurate and, eventually, too easily jammed. *Oboe* was, by contrast, extremely accurate and, at least initially, unjammed.

The way in which *Oboe* worked was in theory simple: two coordinated ground stations in the U.K. (known as '*Cat*' and '*Mouse*') transmitted pulsed radar signals that were received by the *Oboe* aircraft and transmitted back to the ground stations. The transit time of the pulses allowed the distance from the ground stations to the aircraft to be calculated. The route of the *Oboe* aircraft was planned so that it flew along a circular track that passed through the target, centred on the '*Cat*' ground station; this station transmitted a signal that guided the pilot to fly along the circular track. The '*Mouse*' station measured the aircraft's distance until it reached a pre-calculated position at which, if the aircraft was flying at the correct speed on the circular track, it should drop its load to hit the target. At this point the '*Mouse*' station transmitted a signal directing the crew to release their bombs. Using *Oboe* required great flying accuracy, and it was limited in the number of aircraft that could be handled and the distance from the U.K. at which it could be used, but it allowed bombs, and more importantly target markers, to be placed with then unheard-of accuracy.

The arrival of new neighbours was not the only upheaval that No. 1418 Flight had to endure. On 23rd June 1942 the 30th meeting of the Air Ministry Bombing Committee had been held, the subject under discussion being 'The re-establishment of the Bomber Development Unit'. As the introduction in the minutes of the meeting records, there had been a previous meeting between committee members and Sir Henry Tizard to discuss methods by which new scientific developments could be introduced into Bomber Command. One potential pitfall was the realisation that the scientists might not appreciate the difficulties faced by the crews on night bombing missions, and so might come up with operationally impracticable schemes. The document then went on to note the fact that No. 1418 Flight and No. 109 Squadron were carrying out similar testing work, and that the two units might form a nucleus around which to build a more comprehensive organisation.

Those present at the meeting included many of the great and good of the Air Ministry, Bomber Command and the Admiralty, and after some deliberation, their conclusions were published on 28th June 1942 as follows:

> (i) That the Committee agrees as to the necessity for some organisation which will act as a link between the scientists engaged in the development of equipment affecting bombing and the operational users of that equipment.
>
> (ii) That the re-establishment of a unit on the lines of the old Bomber Development Unit, the main purpose of which would be the formulation of approved principals on the technique of using equipment affecting bombing, is the best way of meeting this requirement.
>
> (iii) That the <u>terms of reference</u> of the unit should be as follows:-
> (i) to <u>develop the technique of using new equipment affecting bombing</u>, and to determine its tactical application.
> (ii) to <u>try out equipment affecting bombing</u> under simulated or actual operational conditions.
> (iii) to <u>compile draft operational and training instructions</u> for the use of new equipment connected with bombing.
> (iv) to <u>maintain close liaison</u> with similar development units in other Commands, with the

SPECIAL DUTIES

```
    various experimental establishments and the
    controlling authorities of the relevant
    departments concerned.
(iv) That the Unit should be called the Bombing
    Development Unit (B.D.U.)
```
                                              [AIR 14/683]

This decision formed the background to the announcement on 20th July 1942 that No. 1418 Flight was to be disbanded on that date, in order to be absorbed by the 'Bomber Command Development Unit'. This shows that even in its formative stages there was some confusion over the correct name for the unit, which seems to have persisted for the whole of the B.D.U.'s life (Bombing Development Unit appears to be the correct title). It is safe, though, to refer to the new organisation as the B.D.U.

There is also a suggestion that, even before the new unit was established, the unfinished state of the airfield at Gransden Lodge might mean that it would only be a temporary base, since in a conference to discuss the June meeting, it was agreed that while Gransden Lodge would be the best place at which to locate the new unit, the lack of hangars at the airfield might mean that an alternative site would have to be found. In the end, the B.D.U. remained at Gransden Lodge until circumstances other than the availability of buildings necessitated a move.

Some other new arrivals at Gransden Lodge noticed that the airfield was not yet finished, as well as feeling disappointed with it as their new base. Bill Barry recalls that his crew, after leaving their Operational Training Unit (O.T.U.), had expected to be operating four-engined bombers, but that, as he put it, their hopes were shattered when they arrived at Gransden Lodge only to find that they would be flying the Wellington, and that the airfield did not even appear to be graced with a bomb dump.

Given that the airfield was being used for special duties

missions, the lack of a bomb dump would be understandable, but aerial photographs of the airfield taken during June 1942 by an aircraft of No. 8 O.T.U. clearly show that there was, in fact, a bomb dump at the airfield, albeit small and possibly still under construction.

Some of the aircraft of the B.D.U. and/or No. 1474 Flight are visible on the same aerial photographs. No. 1474 Flight was flying the Wellington, and at its formation the B.D.U. operated two Halifaxes, one Stirling, one Avro Lancaster heavy bomber, six Wellingtons and a Percival Proctor communications aircraft. The photographs also bear out the assertion that there were no hangars on the airfield at this point. Indeed, many of the other buildings that would later appear on the station had not yet been built – the airfield had a definite look of 'work in progress'. The runways were in place, but one section of perimeter track appears not to have been built, and work on the runway extensions seems, as expected, still to have been underway.

Before its transformation into the B.D.U., No. 1418 Flight's O.R.B., while not exactly overflowing with information, had at least given an indication as to what duties were being carried out. For some reason, for the first few months of its existence the B.D.U.'s new O.R.B. became rather uninformative, but later quite full weekly progress reports were included, and those from November 1942 onwards that survive make it possible to piece together in some detail (sometimes retrospectively) the tests being carried out. Through these reports we can find the first indications of the de Havilland Mosquito being based at Gransden Lodge, when on 28th July 1942 the B.D.U. carried out tests using one of these superb twin-engined, largely wooden, light bombers. The Mosquito and the Lancaster would eventually become the principal aircraft types flying from the airfield.

As well as carrying out trials of new equipment, the B.D.U.

was also responsible for the initial training of operational crews in its use. We can see evidence of this on the first day of August 1942, when ten members of the Royal Navy arrived at Gransden Lodge for a course – though on exactly which piece of equipment is not clear. An intelligent guess can be made that it was to be trained on *Gee*, given that the Senior Service had received a demonstration a few weeks earlier. Next day a further two naval officers joined the course, and a week later a mixed bag of five U.S. and Canadian officers also arrived for training. These courses seem to have been of seven days' duration and to have been run fairly much back-to-back.

On 10th August 1942 the moment came that had been expected, but feared – crews on the previous night's raid on Osnabrück had confirmed that *Gee* was being jammed. Since there was, as yet, nothing that could replace *Gee* as a navigational aid, it was decided that an attempt should be made to come up with an anti-jamming device. As a first step, the exact nature of the jamming had to be determined, and quickly. So it was that the next night a Wellington from the B.D.U. took off from Gransden Lodge to follow the bomber stream's route on that night's raid on Mainz, with its crew carefully briefed to watch their *Gee* screen for signs of interference. Their efforts were successful, and yielded detailed information on the jamming being carried out. Following an inspired piece of work by a radar sergeant on No. 97 Squadron and round-the-clock labours at Bomber Command, within days a potential modification had been designed to mitigate the jamming. A few days later the B.D.U. carried out a test of a modified *Gee* set that proved that the modification worked, and, in a Herculean effort, 600 modified *Gee* receivers were built by 21st August 1942, not two weeks after the jamming was first detected.

While these struggles had been going on, No. 1474 Flight had begun operations again after a layoff of a month or so. The flight on 15th August 1942, over the North Sea and the Dutch coast, was successful, but the next day another in the same area had a more dramatic ending when the aircraft caught fire as it landed and was burned out. All the crew were safe, though one suffered burns.

For the rest of the month No. 1474 Flight's operations were confined to an air-sea rescue search on 20th August 1942, and special duties flights on 24th August 1942 (over France to Mons and Frankfurt in Germany) and on 28th August 1942 over France as far as the Rhine. Two further special duties flights were carried out on the first two days of September 1942, and it is recorded that on 2nd September 1942 Aircraftsman Jasper was killed while on active service. It does not seem as though this occurred on that day's operation but it is the first confirmed death in service at Gransden Lodge.

The continuing modernisation of Bomber Command's fleet was inevitably making some older aircraft, such as the twin-engined Armstrong-Whitworth Whitley, surplus to front-line requirements, and some newer machines that were not proving a success (the Avro Manchester, for example) were also becoming available for second-line duties. An attempt was made to palm some of these off onto No. 1474 Flight, but No. 3 Group successfully convinced H.Q. Bomber Command that the Whitley was far too vulnerable to be used on the special duties operations that it would be required to undertake, and that it was too small to house all the equipment that would be needed anyway. With regard to the Manchester, the low serviceability rate of this unloved aircraft was given as the reason that the flight would not find it acceptable.

These arguments having been taken to heart, No. 1474 Flight continued operating the Wellington, and apart from another air-sea rescue operation on 14th September 1942, the flight's O.R.B. reports that no further flying was carried out during the month. This is, however, at odds with the log book entries of members of the flight, which record, for example, fighter affiliation flights and instrument landing practice. It seems likely, then, that when the O.R.B. asserts that 'No flying took place' that this is referring just to operational flying.

In early September a new aircraft type had appeared in the list of those taking part in trials with the B.D.U., when an Armstrong-Whitworth Albemarle was used for the first time. This aircraft, a twin-engined bomber designed to be built without the use of strategically-important materials such as light alloys, was never a great success and was already obsolescent on its introduction to service. Unfortunately, we have no record of what use was being made of the Albemarle, but whatever its function, the Albemarle would appear regularly on the Gransden Lodge runways during the coming months.

Over the next few weeks the B.D.U.'s tests continued, including some formal trials of the A.P.I. Another new aircraft type also made a fleeting appearance at Gransden Lodge in September 1942 when a single test flight was carried out in a Bristol Bisley. This aircraft was the singularly inelegant ground-attack variant of the Bristol Blenheim twin-engined light bomber, and was soon to be renamed the Blenheim Mk. V.

In the last days of September 1942 there was a flurry of visitors to the B.D.U. Several were from the T.R.E. in Malvern, and one was from the electronics company E.M.I. The reason for the unusual popularity of Gransden Lodge was that the B.D.U. was about to begin service trials of a new radar device that would, it was hoped, transform the effectiveness of Bomber Command. The code name for this new device was *H2S*, and the leader of the R.A.F.'s team liaising with T.R.E. was the aforementioned Wing Commander Saye.

A group at T.R.E. under Bernard Lovell, who would become famous in post-war years as a pioneering radio astronomer and director of the University of Manchester Jodrell Bank radio telescope, had been working on *H2S* since early 1942. Their aim was to produce a ground-mapping radar system that would show surface features in sufficient detail to allow aircrew to use it for navigation and bomb aiming. There had been numerous political and technical difficulties, not the least of which was producing a radar signal of sufficient power at a short enough wavelength to make *H2S* feasible. The cavity magnetron, invented by John Randall and Harry Boot at the University of Birmingham, offered a solution, but there was still disagreement about whether this most secret device or a transmitter built using the lower power (but well known) klystron technology should be used.

The plan had been to test both systems side by side, but the crash of the Halifax equipped with a magnetron-powered *H2S* on 7th June 1942, resulting in the loss of both the equipment and the vital personnel, had caused a rethink. The decision was made to go ahead with just the magnetron *H2S*, and, on Prime Minister Winston Churchill's instructions, to have two squadrons of Bomber Command equipped with it by October 1942. This was clearly impossible, and this demand was scaled back to having 24 Halifaxes and 24 Stirlings ready by the end of the year. Even this was an extremely tall order, and it was only on 30th September 1942 that the first *H2S*-equipped Halifax arrived at Gransden Lodge, accompanied by its begetters from T.R.E. and manufacturers from E.M.I., to begin its testing for introduction to service. The trials began immediately, and as Lovell recalled in his book *'Echoes of War'*, the navigators on the B.D.U. were enthusiastic about the potential of *H2S*, but found the equipment's serviceability 'hopelessly bad'.

The B.D.U. weekly progress reports show that at around this time the unit had also been involved in trials recorded under the heading 'Napier air compressor'. It is not clear exactly what it was

SPECIAL DUTIES

that these trials were testing; there are number of possibilities, but we will probably never know for sure. They were carried out using a borrowed Lancaster that was duly returned to its rightful owners.

By mid-October 1942 trials were in progress on a development of the A.P.I.: the Ground Position Indicator, or G.P.I. This instrument took the aircraft's position in the air, as calculated by the A.P.I., and applied to it the effects of a wind vector set by the navigator. The device used this to calculate the aircraft's position on the ground, which was ingeniously displayed by projecting a lighted arrow onto the navigator's chart, showing the aircraft's location in real time – an early moving map system, in fact.

October was proving to be a busy month for the B.D.U., as it also began general trials on a new aircraft, the Wellington Mk. X. The Mk. X was the last and most numerous variant of the Wellington, which had first flown in 1936. In this final incarnation

Reconstruction of the navigator's position in a Lancaster showing *Gee* (upper left), A.P.I. (lower left) and *H2S* (right) installations (Author)

TRIALS AND TRIBULATION

the Wellington was fitted with more powerful engines, and had fuselage components manufactured from light alloy rather than steel, in order to improve its performance. During the month or so that the tests were carried out, the B.D.U. would no doubt have commented upon the success of these modifications in the context of operational use.

14th October 1942 saw a visit from Lovell and his colleagues to check on the progress of the *H2S* trials. He recorded in his diary that the work at the B.D.U. was going well, and that the unit was pleased with the progress being made. The month was rounded off with some *Gee* related trials, which including testing the repositioning of its aerial, and trials of a 'Modified T.R. 1335' – which we can safely assume was *Gee* Mk. II, the trials of which would start in anger in the following weeks.

October 1942 also saw a marked increase in the number of operations carried out by No. 1474 Flight. On the 10th, 11th and 13th October 1942 its operational area was the North Sea and Dutch coast (with Denmark also receiving a visit on the 13th), whilst on 15th October 1942 three aircraft shadowed that night's raid on Köln (Cologne). On the 18th, 22nd and 29th October it returned to the North Sea and Dutch coast, but the remaining operations for the month, on the 22nd, 23rd, 24th and 28th October 1942 were to carry out investigations along the north and west coasts of France and the English Channel. For some of these flights the Wellingtons operated from St. Eval airfield on the north coast of Cornwall.

At some point around this time – the exact date is not certain – a weary series of entries in the B.D.U.'s O.R.B. began, regarding a device called the Marconator. For many years radio transmissions had been used as a means of direction finding, but to make use of these an operator had to rotate a loop aerial while listening to the received signal to detect the direction in which the transmissions

SPECIAL DUTIES

were strongest, and so calculate the bearing of the transmitter relative to the aircraft. The German authorities, incidentally, were obviously aware of this, and often shut down radio stations in cities when raids were expected, so that they could not be used by the bombers to home onto the target.

As its name suggests, the Marconator was an invention of the Marconi company, and was designed to make it easier to use radio beacons for direction finding by automating much of the process and giving the pilot a simple visual indication of the direction of the transmitter. This would have been an obvious candidate for trials by the B.D.U., but over the coming weeks there was a sequence of O.R.B. entries detailing the delays and problems in getting this equipment installed. It would be the following April before testing could actually take place.

A much more focussed and clearly defined set of trials commenced in November 1942, in which the Mk. VIII autopilot was put through its paces. These tests would run for some months, and would also involve the use of another device that the B.D.U. was investigating, a new form of sextant for astro-navigation. Further investigations were also being made to ascertain the performance of the autopilot at low temperatures.

As hinted at previously, in late November 1942 trials began on Mk. II *Gee*. The jamming that had been circumvented by sheer effort in August had long been expected, and the Mk. II version of *Gee* offered a more elegant solution to the problem. This new development allowed more than one frequency to be used for receiving the *Gee* signals, so that if one frequency was jammed, another could be used. Up to four interchangeable tuning units, which could be changed in flight, could be used with Mk. II *Gee*. The Eastern *Gee* chain would be equipped to support this new variant, which was to become operational in early 1943.

During November 1942 No. 1474 Flight increased its tally of

operations by continuing with the increased tempo of flying begun the previous month. Special duties flights were carried out on the 6th, 7th, 11th, 14th, 16th, 17th, 20th, 22nd, 26th, 28th, 29th and 30th November 1942, but electrical and equipment failures seem to have been a common problem, curtailing a number of flights. Once again some of the flight's aircraft were based away from Gransden Lodge, with one operating from Lossiemouth in northern Scotland to patrol off the south-west coast of Norway, and others were again in Cornwall at St. Eval and Predannack. The usual locations for the investigations were the North Sea and Dutch and French coasts, with some missions venturing quite a long way inland over France.

New aircraft for No. 1474 Flight also began arriving during November and December 1942, including three Mosquitoes. The fact that these three aircraft were delivered by female pilots of the Air Transport Auxiliary service is reported to have been a cause of some amazement to the flight's pilots. A little conversion flying in these new arrivals began immediately, but fitting them out with special equipment and training the crews meant that their use on operations was still some way in the future. The trusty Wellington, with its ability to carry large quantities of radio monitoring equipment and a sizeable crew, would still be the Flight's workhorse for some time to come, and one of them was about to embark upon an epic flight.

THE SNOOPERS

Up until now, our story of the operations at Gransden Lodge has mainly concentrated on the work of the B.D.U. This is not because the tasks being carried out by No. 1474 Flight were insignificant, but rather because, as was previously stated, it is difficult to work out with any certainty what the flight was actually doing on any given date. As was also stated earlier, there was one major exception to the paucity of information in No. 1474 Flight's O.R.B., and the events leading to that exceptional entry occurred in early December 1942.

By this point in the war, the R.A.F. was becoming increasingly convinced that the Luftwaffe had introduced a new device into its nightfighters to direct them to the attacking British bombers. Many radio transmissions between the nightfighter pilots and their controllers included the code phrase *Emil-Emil*, which, from its context, was believed to refer to a radar system. This *Emil-Emil* was subsequently found to be the *Lichtenstein* airborne interception radar, and in order to be in a position to develop countermeasures to this, it was vital that the British determined its operating frequency and other properties.

Investigators from the Air Ministry, led by the same Dr. R.V. Jones, father of *Jay*, had already, based on knowledge of German ground-based radars, successfully detected *Lichtenstein* transmissions from listening posts on the Suffolk coast. What was not clear, however, was whether the frequency of these intercepted transmissions was the only one at which *Lichtenstein* operated, and whether it was, in fact, an airborne interception radar system at all. It was eventually decided that the only sure way to get all the information required on *Lichtenstein* was to send a monitoring aircraft along with the bomber stream, in the hope that it would be attacked by a *Lichtenstein*-equipped nightfighter and be able to measure the characteristics of the radar.

This would patently be a dangerous occupation, so in late September 1942 Jones had visited Air Vice-Marshal R.H.M. Saundby at Bomber Command headquarters to petition for the use of two suitably-equipped Mosquitoes as the monitoring aircraft, hoping that the blistering performance of these aircraft would allow them to escape from the attacking nightfighter after the required information had been gathered. Jones successfully persuaded Saundby of his case, in part by displaying an intelligent interest when shown Saundby's model railway engines and the track layout that ran around his bedroom. Two months later the promised Mosquitoes were still not forthcoming, but the need for the information was so great that the decision was made that the mission would have to be attempted using the much more vulnerable Wellington. Jones's recollection in his book *'Most Secret War'* was that that the operation was launched on the morning of 3rd December 1942 by No. 1473 Flight from an airfield near Huntingdon. However, he was incorrect in his assertion that the mission was undertaken by No. 1473 Flight. No. 1474 Flight's O.R.B. shows that *it* was the unit that carried it out, and that the 'airfield near Huntingdon' was Gransden Lodge.

The mission went according to plan, but the O.R.B. entry for the operation, which is the flight's most detailed for this period and runs to almost five pages, makes hair-raising reading. The Wellington was intercepted by a nightfighter, the radar transmissions were measured and the precious information about their frequency relayed back to base. Almost immediately the attacking Ju. 88 let fly with its cannons, inflicting serious damage on both the Wellington and its crew, several of whom were wounded and one, the special wireless operator Pilot Officer Jordan, temporarily almost blinded. The nightfighter was eventually shaken off and the crew limped their way back towards the U.K., but the damage to their aircraft was so severe that the pilot decided to ditch in the sea off the town of Deal, once it was light enough to do so. The battered crew were then picked up by a small rowing boat and taken to shore. What is also apparent from the entry is that this was the eighteenth time that such an operation had been attempted.

After the operation the crew, captained by Pilot Officer Ted Paulton and including Bill Barry as navigator, received immediate congratulations from the Chief of the Air Staff, Air Chief Marshal Sir Charles Portal; within weeks three crew members had been decorated, with another two being awarded medals early the following year.

Postscript: on 9th May 1943 the crew of a *Lichtenstein*-equipped Junkers Ju. 88 nightfighter defected and landed at Dyce airfield, near Aberdeen. With an operational *Lichtenstein* set at their disposal, investigators were soon able to confirm the findings of No. 1474 Flight. This aircraft still exists, and can be seen today in the R.A.F. Museum.

It is worth mentioning that this was not the first time that the flight, or its predecessors, had rendered assistance to Jones, the most well-known occasion being the part that they had played earlier in the war in the 'The Battle of the Beams'. This was the campaign to counter the *Knickebein* radio beam bombing aid

TRIALS AND TRIBULATION

The Ju. 88 that landed at Dyce, showing the
Lichtenstein radar aerial array on the nose (Author)

being used by the Luftwaffe in its attacks on the U.K. The Blind Approach Training Development Unit/Wireless Intelligence Development Unit (from which No. 109 Squadron - and thus No. 1474 Flight – had been formed) had used their specialised radio equipment to follow and characterise the *Knickebein* signals. In fact, the *Jay* system invented by Jones to hide the existence of *Gee* was a thinly disguised version of *Knickebein* – and to make that deception (or 'spoof') more convincing, some functioning *Jay* stations were actually set up, and Bomber Command crews were encouraged to use them. Evidence of the success of the deception was that the Germans detected the *Jay* beams, but once they became convinced that they had been put in place as a hoax to hide *Gee* they ignored them, and *Jay* continued to give valuable navigation assistance to the R.A.F. throughout most of the war.

We believe that No. 816 Defence Squadron R.A.F.R., which had been providing protection to the airfield from air attack, departed for pastures new some time before April 1942. Its replacement appears to have been No. 4265 Flight R.A.F.R.; it is equally unclear when that unit arrived to take over, but it must have been before 1st December 1942, as the Tempsford O.R.B. records that a Pilot Officer Cairns was posted to No. 4265 Flight R.A.F.R. at Gransden Lodge on that date.

While No. 1474 Flight was undertaking its heroic flight of discovery, the B.D.U. was pressing ahead with its testing program, including trials of the new sextant that began in the first week of December 1942. A week later the unit was visited by Air Commodore Vasse, the R.A.F.'s Director of Air Tactics – clearly, the trials work being carried out by the B.D.U. on new equipment would be of great interest to his department. One such investigation began two days after his visit, when, in order to carry out tests of 'Bombing of moving targets with Mark XIV bomb sight', two Halifaxes of the B.D.U. were detached to R.A.F. Catfoss in Yorkshire, and would remain there until early the following January.

No. 1474 Flight's *raison d'être* was signals monitoring, but as we have seen it was also, on occasion, called upon to embark on air-sea rescue missions attempting to locate downed aircraft. As would be expected, these were normally carried out to search for crews lost from other units, but a series of rather poignant O.R.B. entries from late December 1942 show that sometimes they were searching for their own. On 18th December 1942 a Wellington captained by Flight Sergeant Couper took off from Gransden Lodge on a test flight, but disappeared after having been seen off the Norfolk coast. For the next two days crews from the flight searched for their lost comrades, but on 20th December 1942 the body of Pilot Officer Pickles, who was one of those on board the missing aircraft, was found in the North Sea off Lowestoft. So in the end their efforts had come to nought, and it was sorrowfully accepted that the crew of the Wellington had perished.

TRIALS AND TRIBULATION

During the time that the members of No. 1474 Flight had been engaged in their ultimately fruitless search, the B.D.U. had played host to some important foreign guests when two American scientists, Dr. Van Dyke and Dr. Seeley, visited. These two visitors from the U.S. were at Gransden Lodge to discuss their own work on navigational systems with the staff at the B.D.U. Their system, known as SHORAN (for Short Range Navigation) had been born almost by accident as a result of Seeley's work in attempting to remove ghost images from T.V. pictures caused by radio echoes. He realised that timing these echoes could give an accurate measure of the distance that the signal had travelled, which led to the development of a system somewhat akin to *Oboe*.

The big difference between *Oboe* and SHORAN was that in the latter system the *aircraft* transmitted the signal and the *ground stations* responded, and equipment in the aircraft used this information to calculate its position. Because of this, it was more flexible than *Oboe*, in that a pair of ground stations could handle many aircraft simultaneously, rather than just one. Whether it was a coincidence or not, the British developed a system called *Gee-H* (sometimes known as *G-H*) that was very similar to SHORAN and could handle up to 80 aircraft at a time, but since it was designed to use the existing *Gee* transmitters, which operated at a lower frequency, the positional accuracy of *Gee-H* was lower than that of SHORAN, but of the same order as *Oboe*. One advantage of using the *Gee* transmitters was that the *Gee-H* system could also function as a standard *Gee* receiver. Another development of the principles of *Gee*, but using longer wavelength signals to increase its range, became the LORAN (Long Range Navigation) system.

In a letter written at this time we can find a reference to both the flying units then based at Gransden Lodge. It relates to another piece of radar equipment, code named *Monica*, which was being tested for service:

> In October there was an urgent operational requirement for "Monica" in 3 special Wellingtons of 1474 Flight, and a signal was therefore sent ... to arrange for 4 sets to be delivered to Marham from the 10 remaining sets at Defford.... A few weeks ago P.C.E. (Mr. Bennett) was asked to arrange for the 11 sets (i.e. 6 + 5 repaired by R.A.E.) to go to Wyton for fitting to the Halifax aircraft there. I understand however that these sets have now been diverted for other purposes with the exception of one in the "Monica" T.I. Halifax at B.D.U. ...
>
> [AIR 2/5443]

This device, which on first consideration seems most useful, was a radar system designed to be fitted into the tail of bomber aircraft to warn of the approach of enemy nightfighters. Given that we know that in October 1942, the date mentioned in the letter, R.V. Jones was requesting aircraft to go in search of *Lichtenstein*, it seems plausible to suppose that this was the reason for the 'urgent operational requirement' that No. 1474 Flight's aircraft should be fitted with *Monica* systems: that is, in order to offer some extra defence while carrying out their dangerous mission.

Like any active radar system, *Monica*'s weakness was that the nightfighters against which it was supposed to be offering a defence could actually track its emissions to locate their target. In fact, the Germans very quickly discovered *Monica* sets in crashed R.A.F. aircraft, and produced the *Flensburg* system to home onto the *Monica* transmissions. It would be August 1944 before the British authorities captured and tested a *Flensburg* set, but once its capabilities were known, *Monica* was immediately removed from Bomber Command aircraft.

TRIALS AND TRIBULATION

In the final weeks of December 1942 No. 1474 Flight was kept busy receiving nine new Wellingtons onto strength, and the first Christmas of operations at Gransden Lodge brought a day's stand down for the B.D.U. on Christmas Day 1942, followed by three further days with no flying due to bad weather. Work resumed for the B.D.U.'s crews on 29th December 1942 though, and it must have been in their minds that the deadline of the year's end was fast approaching, by which time 48 aircraft should have been equipped with *H2S*, as had been promised before testing had begun.

From the beginning, the major complaint levelled at *H2S* by the B.D.U. was not its usefulness but its serviceability - it was difficult to keep the thing working. However, modifications and experience had eased this problem and by the last day of 1942 there were 24 *H2S* equipped aircraft available, if not the 48 that had been requested: twelve Halifaxes of No. 35 Squadron at Graveley, and twelve Stirlings of No. 7 Squadron at Oakington, which lies about 5 miles (8 km) north-west of Cambridge. Permission was given for them to be used on operations, starting in January 1943.

No. 1474 Flight, apart from the gallant *Lichtenstein* mission and its abortive air-sea rescue attempts, also carried out special duties flights to France and the Belgian and Dutch coasts on the 6th, 8th, 9th, 11th and 13th December 1942. Having seen out 1942 with a month of mixed fortunes, the first few days of the new year would bring an increase in its status and strength. A flight of Halifaxes was to be added to the existing flights of Wellingtons and Mosquitoes, and so on 4th January 1943 the Air Ministry gave its authority for No. 1474 Flight to be re-formed as a squadron in its own right: No. 192 Squadron. This was, in fact, the second appearance of No. 192 Squadron, as it had first been formed in 1917 and had trained pilots for night bomber and home defence squadrons until its disbandment at the end of 1918.

THE SNOOPERS

Because of its clandestine activities, the re-formed No. 192 Squadron was sometimes known by the nickname 'The Snoopers', and the squadron seems to have revelled in the title. The official squadron badge showed an owl's head before a bolt of lightning and carried the motto 'Dare to Discover', but squadron wags soon came up with another. This unofficial version depicted a handlebar-moustached R.A.F. officer peering lasciviously through a bathroom keyhole, above the motto 'We Snoop to Conquer'.

At its re-formation the squadron was equipped with seventeen Wellingtons, three Mosquitoes and a Tiger Moth 'hack' aircraft, and within days two more Wellingtons and two Halifaxes were added. It seems that the Halifaxes and Mosquitoes were not being flown operationally at this stage of the war, and the squadron's Wellingtons of various marks were used exclusively. This expansion in the number of aircraft operated by the new squadron meant that, for a while at least, operations had to cease, since the new aircraft had to be fitted out with the radio equipment, aerials etc. required for their eavesdropping role.

Though the weather was typically poor at the beginning of January 1943, the B.D.U. continued with its test flying whenever possible, and on 2nd January 1943 it began trials on a rotatable astrodome. Since an astrodome is a completely transparent hemispherical blister through which stellar observations for navigational purposes can be made, it is hard to understand why a rotatable one would be required. Apparently someone on the B.D.U. agreed with this sentiment, as at some later point the plaintive question *"What's this for?"* was pencilled into the O.R.B. by an unknown hand.

Probably due to the bad weather of early January 1943 the highly-skilled personnel of the B.D.U. were put to unusual employment, as there was no flying but all the aircrew were sent wood cutting. Perhaps an attempt to keep the home fires burning?

TRIALS AND TRIBULATION

After this distraction, testing soon continued, with trials of the Stabilised Automatic Bomb Sight fitted with a Pilot's Direction Indicator commencing in mid-January 1943. The indicator (which helped the pilot position the aircraft during the run-up to the target) was found to be a useful addition, and the sight itself would eventually achieve very accurate results. One inherent problem with the S.A.B.S. was the requirement for a long, straight, run-in to a target that rendered the bomber using it vulnerable to attack. The Mk. XIV bombsight, which was to be fitted to the majority of Bomber Command's aircraft, could achieve an acceptable level of accuracy in good hands, and was much more tolerant of the aircraft's behaviour before bomb release.

There was a change in command on the B.D.U. on 19th January 1943, when Wing Commander P.H. Cribb took over the reins from Wing Commander P.F. Webster. Two days later, while the refitting of No. 192 Squadron's new aircraft was in progress, and the B.D.U.'s new C.O. was settling in, there was official recognition of an occasion the previous month when the Gransden Lodge emergency crews had proved their worth. The incident in question involved the station's fire crews, and the swiftness with which they had responded to the crash of a Stirling that had been on a test flight. Indeed, their behaviour was thought sufficiently praiseworthy for the Commander in Chief to request that it was brought to the notice of all ranks.

This was not a run-of-the mill flying accident, and in fact it was investigated by the Accident Investigation Branch of the Air Ministry. The aircraft, which was from No. 149 Squadron at Lakenheath in Suffolk, was on an air test, and the first indication that it was in difficulties was when it suddenly appeared below cloud at low altitude, at which point the Stirling's tailplane broke off and the aircraft, disintegrating the while, dived into the ground with the loss of all the crew. The subsequent investigation concluded that the cause of the accident was structural failure caused by overstressing the Stirling in the pull-out from a dive, after loss of control in or above cloud. The pilot's inexperience was cited as a contributory factor.

By 25th January 1943 enough work had been done on No. 192 Squadron's aircraft to enable test flying to be re-started using the modified machines. Unfortunately, this was to lead to another test flight with a fatal outcome, when the Wellington of Pilot Officer Wilson and his crew crashed near Papworth, only some 5 miles (8 km) from base. Four members of the crew were killed and one seriously burned, so this was not a promising start for the new squadron. In spite of this, operations commenced again next day on a limited scale, as by now five of the new Wellingtons had been fully kitted-out with the essential electronics.

Even though it only had a few newly-equipped aircraft available, by the end of its first month in existence No. 192 Squadron had managed three successful operational flights. These were on the 26th, 27th and 30th January 1943, over the Belgian and Dutch coasts and into Germany to Düsseldorf and Hamburg. The flight on 30th January 1943 would have been shadowing that night's raid on Hamburg, during which *H2S* was used operationally for the first time, after having been proven fit for service by the B.D.U. One of the crews from No. 35 Squadron using *H2S* (though their set failed and they aborted the mission) was commanded by Squadron Leader R.J. Lane; this officer would later play a leading role in Gransden Lodge's story.

On 30th January 1943 Gransden Lodge was also inspected by No. 3 Group's new A.O.C., who had taken over command from Baldwin during the previous September:

```
The Air Officer Commanding No. 3 Group, Hon. R.
A. Cochrane, C.B.E., A.F.C., carried out an
inspection of R.A.F. Station, Tempsford and
```

TRIALS AND TRIBULATION

```
Satellite, Gransden between 09.00 hours and
15.00 hours approximately on 30th January, 1943.
After his visit the following signal was
received:- "Please inform all ranks at Tempsford
and the Gransden Lodge that I appreciate the
hard work that has gone into organising these
two stations for their duties. What I saw on
Saturday satisfies me that they will meet the
important tasks which they will be given this
year. These tasks will include Station Defence
which is now the responsibility of all ranks on
the Station".
```

[AIR 28/820]

Unfortunately, on the same day on No. 192 Squadron we find that:

```
TIGER MOTH T.6862 was extensively damaged by a
very severe gale. The aircraft was double
picketed down and sand bagged and fully chocked
at the time of the accident.
```

[AIR 27/1156]

The wording of this entry has the definite feel of people covering themselves against any possible future repercussions, but an O.R.B. entry for the B.D.U. confirms the severity of the weather, since it notes, with a little hyperbole, that there was a 'hurricane' with wind speeds of 70-80 miles per hour (over 100 km/h).

In February 1943 the B.D.U. began a series of tests on the American Martin B-26 Marauder bomber, in order to determine its operational performance. This twin-engined aircraft had gained a reputation as a handful to fly, and especially to land, as its performance came at the cost of a high wing loading and concomitant high approach speed. Some pilots who were unused to landing such a 'hot ship' tended to approach too slowly, stall and crash. Later marks of the Marauder were an improvement, but it had already earned its (probably unwarranted) reputation as a killer. The R.A.F. did put the Marauder to limited use operationally in North Africa, but it was successfully used much more extensively by the U.S. air forces.

Bomber Command mounted an operation against Köln on 2nd February 1943, and this raid was only the second time that *H2S* had been used operationally. As bad luck would have it, an *H2S* set was recovered from a crashed aircraft, presenting an unexpected gift to the German scientists. It allowed them to examine the new device in detail and eventually to develop the *Naxos* receiver that homed onto the *H2S* transmissions in a similar way to that in which the *Flensburg* system homed onto *Monica*.

Following a slow month for operations, February 1943 was much busier for No. 192 Squadron. Special duties flights to its usual haunts (around the coasts of France, Belgium and Holland, with the occasional foray inland and to Germany) were attempted on every day except the 1st, 6th to 10th, 13th, 15th, 20th to 24th and 27th, though some were aborted due to equipment problems. We have seen that it was not unusual for aircraft to be detached away from Gransden Lodge for short periods, but in February 1943 one Wellington from No. 192 Squadron was sent abroad on a more permanent basis when Ted Paulton (who had been the pilot on the *Lichtenstein* mission) and a new crew set off for warmer shores, as they were to carry out radio surveillance operations in the Mediterranean area.

Although he had declared himself satisfied with what he had seen on his inspection some two weeks before, it appears that Cochrane, the A.O.C., actually believed that there were some underlying problems at Gransden Lodge. On 12th February 1943 he wrote:

```
                    GRANSDEN LODGE.

    I  recently  carried  out  a  full  administrative
```

TRIALS AND TRIBULATION

> inspection of Gransden Lodge, including B.D.U. and No. 192 Squadron. As a result I have reached the conclusion that in several respects the efficiency of the station is below a desirable level. The appointment of a Station Commander will do much to improve matters, for it is clear that the Officer Commanding, Tempsford, who has important operational responsibilities of his own, cannot give sufficient time to the many difficult problems which arise at Gransden Lodge....
>
> My impression of the two units as a result of my visits, is that much enthusiastic work has been put in by comparatively junior officers, but that there is urgent need for a more senior officer to control and co-ordinate the various activities on the Station. I believe that this will lead to an all round improvement in efficiency.
>
> [AIR 14/1121]

Steps were quickly taken to implement his recommendation, but in the meantime the station's life carried on as before, and the B.D.U. began tests on 'Flash Flares for Bomber Defence', a device that sounds equally alarming for both the bomber crew and the attacking fighter against which it would be deployed:

> The intention of the trials is to experiment with a blinding flash which is released on the approach of an enemy fighter.... It is also desired to ascertain the effect of the flash on the crew of the bomber.
>
> [AIR 29/769]

Slightly more conventional tests also commenced, on the Mark III Angular Velocity Sight, a bombsight designed to be accurate when used from low level and intended for use against ships and submarines. The aircraft used for this was another new type for Gransden Lodge – the Douglas Boston twin-engined light bomber. It would later be joined by a Mosquito in the trials.

The A.O.C. was becoming a regular visitor to Gransden Lodge, as on 19th February 1943 he visited the station again, and was this time accompanied by the real top brass in the person of Air Chief Marshal Ludlow-Hewitt, the Inspector General of the R.A.F., who had previously been Air Officer Commanding-in-Chief of Bomber Command.

Action on Cochrane's recommendations after his previous visit had been swift, as two days earlier Tempsford had been notified that the appointment of an officer of the rank of Group Captain to act as Station Commander at Gransden Lodge had been approved, but actually assigning someone to fill the newly-created position would not be quite so speedy.

The Cambridgeshire winter weather then came into play, when for several days there was no flying due to fog. This did not prevent ground-based activities such as official inspections, parades and visits taking place, including another by Cochrane and his soon-to-be replacement as A.O.C. of No. 3 Group, Air Vice-Marshal R. Harrison. Cochrane was bound for No. 5 Group to become A.O.C. there.

Once the weather had improved, flying recommenced, and 25th February 1943 saw almost the whole menagerie of the B.D.U. being put through its paces, as on that single day tests were carried out using the Marauder, Halifax, Lancaster, Boston, Wellington and Mosquito. Amongst the testing programs being carried out was an investigation into the temperature in aircraft fuel tanks. One reason for the presence of a *Monica*-equipped Halifax on the strength of the B.D.U. can be found when:

> A report on the comparison between Monica and Booser was forwarded 26th February, 1943

[AIR 29/769]

TRIALS AND TRIBULATION

This refers to another radar warning system, the correct name of which was actually *Boozer*. Unlike *Monica*, *Boozer* was a passive system, in that it just detected the emissions of both airborne and ground-based radars to give a warning when the aircraft carrying *Boozer* was being tracked, and, since it emitted no signals itself, it could not be detected in use. It would be introduced into service that spring. The B.D.U.'s involvement with the development and use of *Gee* also continued as the end of the month approached, when one aircraft was dispatched to the even colder climes of R.A.F. Tealing, near Dundee in Scotland, to use Mk. II *Gee* to test the accuracy of the Northern *Gee* chain.

The month-end summary figures for February 1943 give us an indication of the expansion taking place at Gransden Lodge, as by that time the B.D.U. had 281 personnel based there, and No. 192 Squadron had 269. If we add to this 550 those involved in the running and defence of the station, we can see that the numbers were beginning to become fairly substantial.

Those stationed at the airfield would have had a disruption to their normal routine when, for several days in March 1943, Gransden Lodge became an operating base for forces taking part in Exercise SPARTAN, which has been described as 'the greatest offensive exercise ever staged in the military history of these islands'. In this exercise, which was used as a testing ground for tactics eventually to be employed in the liberation of Europe, England was to be divided into three imaginary European countries: Westland, which was assumed to be neutral; Eastland, which was occupied by German forces; and Southland, which was unoccupied. Gransden Lodge lay firmly in Eastland. The two squadrons that would briefly be based there during the exercise, No. 169 Squadron and No. 421 (Red Indian) Squadron R.C.A.F., were masquerading as Luftwaffe fighter squadrons, and as such they were painted with special markings to show that they were 'the enemy'.

THE SNOOPERS

On 5th March 1943, the Mustangs of No. 169 Squadron arrived from Barford St. John, and the Supermarine Spitfires of No. 421 Squadron landed from Croughton, both north of Oxford. As an indication that all participants were getting into the spirit of the exercise, No. 169 Squadron's O.R.B. for the day of their transfer notes that the squadron's ground party met with many difficulties during their trip from Barford St. John to Gransden Lodge, including, it was stated, many bridges being blown up. We can only hope that this was just enthusiastic simulation on the part of the defenders, and that bridges were not really being blown up. For the next few days the squadrons played their part in the exercise, flying escort missions, engaging in dogfights, strafing ground columns and 'enemy' airfields and generally supporting their ground forces. They did not get it all their own way though, as soon there was retaliation against No. 169 Squadron when two members of the squadron, after a visit to their army headquarters, were 'attacked' by a small detachment of British special forces troops at Tempsford. Several of No. 421 Squadron's Spitfires were also 'lost' in air combat.

On 10th March 1943 the progress of the exercise called for both squadrons to move, No. 169 Squadron to Bottisham, just east of Cambridge, and No. 421 Squadron to Fowlmere, south of Gransden Lodge, so by the end of that day the fleeting visit by the fighters was over. It all sounds as if it had been great fun, for the aircrew anyway…

Fortuitously, further aerial photographs of the airfield were taken whilst this exercise was in progress – possibly by the opposing forces? – and they show a very busy scene indeed, with not only fourteen or so of the resident aircraft visible (including one taxying on the runway), but also nine or more of the visiting fighters, which were apparently camped out in the vicinity of the bomb dump. They also show that considerable progress had been made in the provision of facilities on the airfield, with one Type T2 hangar now in place and a second (Type B1) under construction. Many of the offices and other administrative buildings on the airfield were seemingly complete by this time, as was the full complement of flying control and associated buildings, but the improved and enlarged station headquarters and briefing room complex had barely been begun, and workshops and the station sick quarters were still being built.

No. 192 Squadron had been having its own excitements whilst all this was going on, as one of its Wellingtons had landed short of the runway after a special duties flight and broken in two, though the crew were unharmed (but probably embarrassed). This was part of the continuing increased level of activity by No. 192 Squadron. Special duties flights, sometimes several per day and some taking place from Cornwall, were attempted every day from the 1st to 15th (apart from the 2nd, 6th, 10th, 12th, and 13th), with another from St. Eval on 19th March 1943. These flights had mainly been to its customary locations, although some went as far over Germany as Berlin.

Following the departure of the fighters, the pace of life had returned to normal at Gransden Lodge, and two more sets of tests related to *Monica* commenced on the B.D.U. One of these, entitled '*Monica* and Flame Damping' is a little obscure, as flame damping refers to the reduction of the flames emitted from the exhausts of an aircraft's engines, but the objective of the other is crystal clear: 'Effect of "*Window*" on "*Monica*"'.

Window was the code name for bundles of seemingly-innocuous aluminium foil strips. These, because of their carefully calculated dimensions, acted as very efficient radar reflectors, and when dropped literally in their millions were designed to swamp the German early warning and nightfighter attack radars with echoes, effectively blinding the radar operators. So effective was

THE SNOOPERS

Strips of *Window*. Each strip is around 25 cm long and 2 cm wide (Author)

Window found to be that its operational use was delayed for some months, until agreement could be reached that the likelihood of its secrets being discovered and used against the U.K. radar defences (such as *Monica*) was outweighed by its operational advantages. In fact, the Germans had already developed a similar system called *Düppel*, but had also refrained from using it for the same reason.

The B.D.U.'s exiles in Scotland returned to Gransden Lodge from Tealing in March 1943, and preparations also began for testing a combination of two of the navigational aids currently under investigation, G.P.I. and *H2S*. These trials were designed to determine whether the use of G.P.I. in conjunction with *H2S* would help in the identification of a target when an aircraft was taking evasive action. As was noted once the tests had been completed, this was indeed the case.

These tests coincided with another set of new trials that were planned to begin about then, on the use of ultra-violet light for instrument panel illumination, but these were being hampered as 'the weather has not been fit for night flying recently'. A few days later, on 20th March 1943, No. 192 Squadron's commanding officer, Squadron Leader Willis, was promoted to Wing Commander, and Flight Lieutenant Fernbank was also promoted, to Squadron Leader.

The slow trickle of new aircraft onto the squadron continued, with another Mosquito arriving on 21st March 1943, and on that day three flights were carried out from Lossiemouth to patrol the southern coast of Norway. As it would turn out, these operations would not only be the final ones carried out in March 1943 by No. 192 Squadron, but also its last while based at Gransden Lodge.

However, the B.D.U. was still working away at its trials, and soon yet another new aircraft type was seen on the airfield when a Bristol Beaufighter twin-engined fighter arrived. This temporary visitor was involved in the testing of *Monica* and flame damping. Another fighter, this time a Spitfire, was also involved in trials, and though it is not documented, it seems probable that it, too, was involved in testing *Monica*.

In late March 1943 the B.D.U. recorded, in relation to *H2S*, that:

> Training of American Navigators still in progress. Three Navigators have been detached to 8 Group to assist in instruction, Flight Lieutenant Killip to 35 Squadron, Flying Officer Grant to 156 Squadron and Flying Officer Glasspool to 83 Squadron.
>
> [AIR 29/769]

For one of these officers at least, this was probably not their first training attachment. Glasspool had left Gransden Lodge on attachment to Headquarters Bomber Command in November 1942, but had returned to the B.D.U. in February 1943, promoted to Flying Officer, from No. 35 Squadron. This squadron, it will be remembered, was one of the first two to be equipped with *H2S*, so given the dates it seems highly probable that Glasspool had trained the navigators of No. 35 Squadron for their first operation. Flight Lieutenant Killip would go on to join Bernard Lovell's development team in August 1943, and we will hear of him again in relation to the successor to *H2S*.

In the meantime, as hinted at above, changes were in the air at Gransden Lodge. Beginning on 3rd April 1943, No. 192 Squadron moved out of Gransden Lodge for its new base at Feltwell in Norfolk, and its relocation was complete by 7th April 1943. At the same time, the B.D.U. moved to the same new location, with its move being completed a day earlier.

And so it was that after almost exactly a year of use as a location for secret trials and investigations, the squadrons that had been carrying out this important work had left Gransden Lodge. Within days the airfield would become the base for operations of an altogether different kind, as we will see in the next chapter.

PATHFINDERS

The urgency of the need for an improvement in the effectiveness of the British night bombing campaign was brought into sharp focus in a report, published in August 1941, by David Bensusan-Butt. The findings of this Butt Report, which analysed the actual accuracy of bombing raids (as determined by aiming-point photographs) when compared to the results claimed by crews, were bleak. Of the crews that claimed to have bombed successfully, only one in three had actually dropped their bombs within a radius of five miles (8 km) of the target; that is, within an area of 75 square miles (195 square km) centred on the aiming point. When we take into account the fact that only a proportion of the crews dispatched on a raid actually *claimed* to have attacked the target, then the number drops to one in five of those who set off. On difficult targets or when weather conditions were poor, performance was worse.

What could be done to rectify this unsatisfactory and expensive situation? One answer, which made a dubious virtue of a necessity, was to switch away from attempting to make precision attacks on targets to a policy of area bombing, attacking large areas of German cities in the hope of destroying the manufacturing facilities located there and also lowering the morale of the citizens by rendering them homeless. In his official account of the bomber offensive, written after the war, Air Chief Marshal Arthur Harris (later Marshal of the Royal Air Force Sir Arthur Harris G.C.B., O.B.E., A.F.C.), the wartime Air Officer Commanding in Chief of Bomber Command, stated that the way in which Bomber Command would achieve the objective that had been set for it would be by destroying up to eighteen large industrial cities in the Ruhr and elsewhere in Germany.

Another answer to the problem of accurate bombing, and a more palatable one given the presumption that bombing was inevitable, was to improve the precision of the bombers. As we have seen, *Gee* was meant to be one solution, but the reduction in its accuracy with distance, and the fact that it could be jammed, meant that it did not live up to its early promise. That said, when used outside jamming range and closer to home, *Gee* was crucial to allowing accurate position fixes to be made on the way out to the target, and, just as importantly, on the way back to base. Other technological advances such as *H2S* and *Oboe* were likely to prove invaluable, but they were a long way from being available in numbers to Bomber Command's squadrons, and because of its nature *Oboe* could only be used by small numbers of aircraft at a time anyway.

Perhaps, then, the way to solve the problem would be to bring together a group of highly skilled and experienced crews, give them the best navigation equipment, tactics and training available, and use them as 'target finders' that would mark targets in order to provide clear aiming points for Main Force squadrons to attack. This, in essence, was the role of the R.A.F.'s Pathfinder Force (P.F.F.).

The birth of the P.F.F. was not easy. Although the 'target finder' concept was supported in many quarters, there was also vehement disagreement about how the object should be achieved. Arthur Harris in particular, while supportive of the idea, was very much against the foundation of a specialist corps comprised of the best squadrons, transferred from each R.A.F. Group; he would have preferred the creation of an expert squadron *within* each Group, which would carry out the target marking missions for the remainder of the Group's squadrons. Argument raged to and fro, but eventually, in early 1942, the Air Staff decided the matter and directed Harris to form the new force. Once faced with the inevitable, he set to and chose Wing Commander D.C.T. (Don) Bennett, an Australian, as commander of the new Pathfinder Force, which officially came into being on 15th August 1942. Much has been written about Bennett, but suffice it to say that he was acknowledged to be an outstanding flyer who had pioneered long-distance aviation between the wars, and had also served with distinction as a bomber pilot and squadron commander prior to his appointment to head the new force.

The conditions under which the P.F.F. operated when it was first formed were anything but normal, and in fact verged on the chaotic, as Gordon Musgrove discusses in his book *'Pathfinder Force: A History of 8 Group'*. Bennett was not of a sufficiently high rank officially to be placed in charge of a number of squadrons, so the P.F.F. was nominally under the direct command of Harris. In addition, the force's squadrons were accommodated at their new home stations only under sufferance and their orders actually came through No. 3 Group, and all their replacement personnel and equipment had to be obtained with the blessing - which was naturally enough in short supply - of the Groups from which they had been seconded.

Despite this, and in the face of varied initial results, the P.F.F. began to flourish and become more organised. On 8th January 1943 its position was formalised and it became No. 8 (P.F.F.) Group, and Bennett, now promoted to Air Vice-Marshal, became the new Group's A.O.C. After considering the region's weather

PATHFINDERS

history and communication facilities, Bennett chose to base his force in the area around Huntingdon, with the airfield at Wyton as his headquarters, and so this area naturally became the location for the stations under his control. By April 1943 No. 8 Group's improving performance was leading to more demands for its services, and expansion was called for.

This is why, on 5th April 1943, the Tempsford O.R.B. recorded that Gransden Lodge was reassigned to become a satellite of R.A.F. Oakington, and ten days later Oakington noted that its own airfield and those at Bourn and Gransden Lodge had been transferred to No. 8 Group. Oakington was actually one of the original stations assigned to the P.F.F. at its formation, along with Graveley, Wyton and Warboys (located about 5 miles - 8 km - north-east of Huntingdon), but it had still operated as part of No. 3 Group until this date.

One of the first changes to be made when Gransden Lodge was transferred to the P.F.F. took place almost immediately, as on 10th April 1943 the Path Finder Force Navigation Training Unit (P.F.F.N.T.U., sometimes shortened to N.T.U.) was formed at the station.

The role of this new unit was to carry out the final navigation training of entire crews that were destined to join P.F.F. squadrons. In the light of the Butt Report, the provision of navigation training to the crews whose mission was to mark targets for other, less experienced and skilful crews, seems self-evidently necessary. The P.F.F. Navigation Training Unit immediately began accumulating personnel and aircraft from around No. 8 Group.

There was a hierarchy of roles for which the crews in the P.F.F. had to be trained, and each had a specific job to carry out when marking a target for the Main Force aircraft that followed. These roles included:

Illuminator:	Illuminators would arrive early at the target area, correctly identify it and drop flares to illuminate the aiming point
Supporter:	Crews new to the P.F.F. would act as Supporters, and carry only bombs. They would arrive at the target and bomb at the same time as the Illuminators
Primary Marker:	Using the light from the flares dropped by the Illuminators, the Primary Markers would identify the aiming point and accurately mark it with Target Indicator (T.I.) pyrotechnics
Backer Up:	Since the Target Indicators would burn out rather quickly, the crews operating in the Backer Up role would put down further Target Indicators to keep the aiming point marked for the duration of the raid. These crews were sometimes also known as Visual Centerers

Depending on the weather conditions, the target marking could be done visually or using *H2S*. If *H2S* was being used, then this was termed 'blind' marking, and the various roles could be prefixed accordingly, for example '*Blind Backer Up*'.

At Leeming in Yorkshire, events were taking place that would provide the P.F.F.N.T.U. with its first customers. No. 405 Squadron of the Royal Canadian Air Force, which was based at Leeming, had been formed in April 1941 at Driffield in Yorkshire, and was the first Canadian bomber squadron to be formed overseas. Flying the Wellington, it went into action for the first time in June 1941, this being the R.C.A.F.'s, as well as the squadron's, first operation. Shortly after this the unit moved to a new base at Pocklington, also in Yorkshire, and continued operating there until October 1942. During this period the squadron took full part in the escalating air war, with its targets, initially coastal and maritime, giving way to those in Germany, include Köln on 30th May 1942 - Operation MILLENIUM, the first 1,000 bomber raid. By this time the squadron had re-equipped with the four-engined Halifax, a more capable machine than the twin-engined Wellington. This new aircraft was put to use in a very different role when No. 405 Squadron was transferred to Coastal Command in October 1942, based at Beaulieu near the New Forest in Hampshire. While here the squadron took part in anti-submarine patrols, convoy escort and shipping strikes. This task, demanding in its own way, came to an end in March 1943 when No. 405 Squadron was transferred back to Bomber Command to become part of the recently-formed No. 6 (Royal Canadian Air Force) Group at Leeming.

The sojourn at Leeming was to be brief, as within a month No. 405 Squadron was selected to be No. 6 Group's contribution to the P.F.F., and it was soon on the move again. In the middle of April 1943, the personnel of No. 405 Squadron were hard at work packing ready to move, and loading their effects and equipment onto lorries and trains ready for the journey south.

By 20th April 1943 the squadron was established at Gransden Lodge, and had a new commanding officer:

> SQUADRON MOVE:- The rear party, consisting of one Officer and 19 O.R.s under the command of 49161 P/O J. Durling, left Leeming Bar Station, at 0818 hours, and arrived at Gamlingay Station at 1842 hours, proceeding to R.A.F. Station, Gransden Lodge by transport. Personnel devoted the day to unloading the second equipment train and arranging working accommodation at the new station.

TRIALS AND TRIBULATION

```
CHANGE IN COMMAND:- Wing Commander J.E. Fauquier,
DFC, who resumed command of the Squadron,
addressed aircrew personnel at 0930 hours,
outlining the training programme to be undertaken
for P.F.F. work. W/C Fauquier previously
commanded the Squadron during the period of 20th
September, 1941, to 8th August, 1942, and many
of the personnel of the Squadron renewed
acquaintances, having served under him during
this period.
```
[AIR 27/1788]

The logistics of this move are impressive. In the space of five days, over 700 people were relocated a distance of around 160 miles (260 km), along with their equipment, in a move that involved eighteen aircraft, a road convoy and two special trains, in addition to regular rail services. At the end of those five days, the squadron was in place at its new home, and ready to begin training for its new role in the Pathfinder Force.

Probably because it was based on the same airfield as the P.F.F. Navigation Training Unit, and possibly because it had aircraft available – the P.F.F.N.T.U. had scraped together only one Stirling, one Halifax and two Lancasters by this point - eight of No. 405 Squadron's crews made up the first course through the P.F.F.N.T.U., which began on 21st April 1943 and was complete five days later. In fact, the P.F.F.N.T.U. would train crews exclusively from No. 405 Squadron for a month or so, after which time the unit began running courses made up from crews from other Pathfinder Force squadrons.

At this time Bomber Command was in the thick of a campaign against the industrial heartland of Germany known as the Battle of the Ruhr. The Ruhr valley, 'Happy Valley' as it became known to the crews, was a centre of heavy industry and contained such important targets as armament, rubber, synthetic fuel and steel works. In addition to being well defended, the many factories created an industrial haze that made accurate visual bomb aiming difficult. Bomber Command's big advantage in this battle was that the Ruhr lay within the range of *Oboe*, and this very accurate navigational aid allowed targets to be marked with precision even when few – or indeed no – ground features were visible. Even with the help of *Oboe*, raids were not always as successful as they might have been, since it was a relatively new and slightly temperamental system, and equipment failures or the shooting down of the aircraft carrying out the marking could have a serious effect on the outcome of an attack.

The newly-arrived squadron carried out its first operation from Gransden Lodge on 26th April 1943, when it sent eleven Halifaxes to take part in a raid on the inland port city of Duisburg in the Ruhr. The night's operations also gave rise to the squadron's first casualties when operating from their new base, as the crew of Sergeant Crockett failed to return. After this it was back into the regime of training again, until on 30th April 1943 the call came for No. 405 Squadron to supply six aircraft for a raid on Essen, again in the Ruhr; and again, one crew was lost, that of Flight Lieutenant Atkinson. So far, things did not bode well.

As May 1943 began, there were no operations for a few days, but training continued apace. On one day the crews had got as far as their aircraft before the planned operation was cancelled. Instead:

> As most crews had been detailed for operations, the training was restricted. Navigators took their logs to the Navigational Leader of N.T.U. for criticism.
>
> [AIR 27/1788]

Given the reputation of the Canadians for speaking their mind, this criticism may not have been all one way. The late cancellation of the operation was probably a nerve-jangling affair, but there was

TRIALS AND TRIBULATION

no such reprieve when, on 4th May 1943, the target was Dortmund for ten aircraft. One of these crashed at Graveley on its return, and one more did not return at all, the aircraft of Pilot Officer Lennox. The score at Gransden Lodge was now three 'ops', three crews lost.

Training was again the order of the day now, though several times over the next week or so operations were cancelled after the crews had been briefed. In early May 1943 the British spring weather was doing its worst with strong to gale force winds and heavy showers, so, as no flying training could be done, parachute and dinghy drills were carried out on the ground, and the squadron's wireless operators were given three hours of *Tinsel* practice.

Tinsel, in this context, was not a Christmas decoration but a potentially life-saving countermeasure against enemy nightfighters. Simply put, it consisted of a microphone mounted inside one of a bomber's engine cowlings, which, when the radio operator detected a fighter controller directing a nightfighter into the attack, would be used to transmit engine noise on the same frequency so as to render the controller's instructions unintelligible. This system's name had caused some domestic friction for the A.O.C., since Don Bennett (as he relates in his autobiography *'Pathfinder'*) had had to forbid his wife from naming a new puppy 'Tinsel' - without being able to give a reason - lest this should give some clue that a new device with that code name was being developed.

The next operation for No. 405 Squadron was not until 12th May 1943, and on that day, while preparations for the raid were being made, 'the drain man cometh', as Oakington's O.R.B. notes:

```
Eight (P.F.F.) Group Sanitary Assistant arrived
at Oakington on a Sanitary Inspection, which was
completed on 10.5.43. On 11.5.43, he inspected
Bourn, and 12.5.43 Gransden. Reports on all
three Stations have been received.
```

[AIR 28/607]

This might sound like a trivial thing to record, but in the early days at Graveley there had been some quite serious problems with the sewerage systems, which gave rise to many gastric illnesses in the personnel based there. These in turn led to some unfortunate intestinal consequences for crews while on operations.

Later that day the five Halifaxes that had been requested set out on the raid, which was again on Duisburg, and all returned, one of them early as the aircraft's bomb aimer was unconscious. Five aircraft were again in action the next night, 13th May 1943, against Bochum. This time luck was against Flying Officer Beattie and his crew, who failed to return. After this, No. 405 Squadron had a rest from operations for a few days, and the continuing training program included converting newly-arrived crews onto the Halifax.

On 16th May 1943 there was only one squadron operating from the whole of Bomber Command. This was No. 617 Squadron of No. 5 Group, which was carrying out Operation CHASTISE against the dams in the Ruhr – the Dambusters raid, probably the best-known bombing raid ever. Although there has latterly been much discussion about the ultimate effectiveness of this operation, it was without doubt a morale booster for the country, and the bravery of the crews taking part is attested to by the fact that this specially-formed squadron suffered almost 40% losses in a single raid. The 'Master of Ceremonies' method of controlling the attacks of the aircraft taking part by radio, pioneered by Wing Commander Guy Gibson on this operation, was later adopted by the P.F.F. as the 'Master Bomber' technique. The almost charmed status that this raid endowed on the whole of No. 5 Group was to lead to rivalry, and some animosity, between No. 5 and No. 8 Groups, and particularly between the group commanders Cochrane and Bennett, in the future. It was rumoured at the time that Bennett and Cochrane had challenged one another to a bombing match, each using the other's headquarters as the target. Cochrane, it will be remembered, was the officer who, while commander of No. 3 Group, decided that Gransden Lodge's efficiency required the appointment of a station commander.

The feeling that No. 5 Group occupied a privileged position was not limited to the higher echelons. During crew-room gossip regarding whom the young Princess Elizabeth, later Queen Elizabeth II, might one day marry, one voice is reported by Spencer Dunmore to have declared wearily that whoever it was, it was bound to be someone from No. 5 Group...

No. 405 Squadron went to war once more on 23rd May 1943 with fourteen aircraft, the target being in the Ruhr again, this time Dortmund. The raid was a large one, and the squadron suffered one more loss, the crew of Sergeant Martin, and other aircraft were attacked and damaged by nightfighters but returned safely. The next target was Düsseldorf, on 25th May 1943; no crews were lost on this operation, but one had a narrow escape when their Halifax crashed on takeoff when an engine cut before leaving the ground.

There was no operation for them on 26th May 1943, and instead some members of No. 405 Squadron had a more enjoyable task to carry out when the C.O. Johnny Fauquier, Pilot Officer Gowan and 25 representatives of the squadron's air and ground crews, accompanied by a Halifax, visited Wyton to be presented King George VI and the Queen.

After that visit, the crew that had escaped an untimely end when crashing on takeoff was in action again the next night when theirs was among the six aircraft from the squadron that set out for Essen. For one crew, Sergeant Lebihan's, it was to be their last 'op', as they did not return. To bring the month's operations to a close, fourteen crews from Gransden Lodge attacked the Ruhr city of Wuppertal on 29th May 1943.

Ed Miller (far right) and his ground crew colleagues pose with
a Halifax of No. 405 Squadron
(Ed Stanley Miller, The Memory Project, Historica Canada)

There would be no operations for Bomber Command for ten days as it was the full moon period, which made for easier hunting for the German nightfighters, but Gransden Lodge was not inactive, as both No. 405 Squadron and the P.F.F.N.T.U. were still hard at work with training. However, all was not well at the latter unit. By the end of May 1943 the shortage of accommodation at Gransden Lodge in which to feed and house those being trained was causing the P.F.F.N.T.U. enough difficulty for the unit to complain to No. 8 Group that it needed more space, and it was suggested that perhaps a move to Upwood and Warboys would be required. These representations were obviously well received, for on 1st June 1943 'Group' indicated that such a move would indeed take place.

Members of No. 405 Squadron found time during this lull in operations to relax a little by indulging in some sports – the squadron headquarters team played a softball match against R.A.F.

TRIALS AND TRIBULATION

Tempsford and won 5-1, while the Maintenance Flight beat a team from R.A.F. Wyton by a score of 6-4. This break also saw the arrival, on 5th June 1943 or thereabouts, of Group Captain S.W.B. Menaul D.F.C., A.F.C. to take up the position of Station Commander. It had taken almost four months from the establishment of the post to the appointee's arrival, but Gransden Lodge at last had a 'Station Master'.

Operations began again after the full moon period on 11th June 1943, when the Battle of the Ruhr was re-joined with another raid on Düsseldorf. Twelve aircraft from No. 405 Squadron took part, and again one of them failed to return. Pilot Officer Harty, the captain of the lost Halifax, was an American serving in the R.C.A.F. alongside his Canadian crewmates, and there was another U.S. flyer in his crew. On the following day the target was Bochum, and the six crews from the Gransden Lodge squadron that took part all returned safely. Another Halifax was lost on 16th June 1943, but not this time on operations. The aircraft in question, piloted by Flight Lieutenant Lawson, crashed close to King's Lynn in Norfolk, and the accident was apparently caused by the Halifax being struck by lightning.

The uncomfortable situation at the P.F.F.N.T.U. was resolved by its planned move, and between the 11th and 19th June 1943 the unit relocated, as expected, to Upwood and Warboys. The airfield must have been getting crowded, too, as the P.F.F.N.T.U. had accumulated fourteen aircraft by this time, only just over half of the planned establishment, and No. 405 Squadron had 21 Halifaxes on charge at the end of June 1943. There was a sting in the tail for some who had commenced their course just before the P.F.F.N.T.U. left Gransden Lodge, as an entry from the unit's O.R.B. shows that five navigators on the course were returned to P.F.F. headquarters, all, it was said, 'poor material'. This gives an indication of the high standards required of the crews forming the

P.F.F. As it turned out, the P.F.F.N.T.U. was just exchanging bases with another unit, since its place at Gransden Lodge was taken by No. 1507 B.A.T. Flight, which began moving in from Warboys with its seven Airspeed Oxford twin-engined trainers as the P.F.F.N.T.U. started moving out. The new unit, commanded by Squadron Leader J.N.S. Cumming, had a strength of four pilots and around 40 ground personnel when it arrived on 17th June 1943.

The initials 'B.A.T.' in No. 1507 B.A.T. Flight's title stand for Beam Approach Training, indicating that the flight's role was to train pilots in the dark (literally) art of making instrument approaches and landings. B.A.T. originally stood for Blind Approach Training, but this was later altered, possibly to remove any negative connotations of 'blind approaches'. The flight had been formed as No. 7 B.A.T. Flight at Finningley in Yorkshire in January 1941, and had operated there until March 1943, at which time it had moved to Warboys.

The 'beam' referred to was the product of the Standard Beam Approach (S.B.A.) blind landing system, a development of the pre-war German *Lorenz* system. Gransden Lodge's S.B.A. installation, which would be crucial in assisting crews returning from operations in bad weather, had only just been completed at around this time, so the move of the flight to the airfield took early advantage of the new equipment and allowed the move of the P.F.F.N.T.U. to Upwood.

S.B.A. operated by transmitting narrow, overlapping radio beams that were aligned along the runway on which the aircraft was to land. A pilot flying 'on the beam' would hear a pattern of 'dot' signals over the radio if he was to one side of the runway centreline, and 'dashes' if he was to the other. When he heard a continuous tone, he was centred on the beam and correctly lined up on the runway. In addition, there were two vertically-oriented marker beams that intersected the main beam at known distances from the touchdown point. By listening for the signals from these markers, the pilot was able to judge and maintain the correct descent path. Ironically, the S.B.A./*Lorenz* system was essentially the same as that employed in the Luftwaffe's *Knickebein* bombing aid, which the ancestors of No. 192 Squadron had gone to great pains to neutralise.

The Ruhr was given some relief on 19th June 1943 when the target was shifted to Le Creusot in France and the armament factory there. The eleven aircraft from No. 405 Squadron that took part in that raid all returned safely, but two days later another was lost, that of Flight Lieutenant Murrell, from the fourteen who were sent back to the Ruhr to attack Krefeld. Murrell was another American serving in the R.C.A.F. The squadron was luckier the next night when it successfully joined an attack on Mülheim and all the five participating crews returned to base.

A series of entries in the squadron's O.R.B. for this period give

An Oxford of No. 1536 B.A.T. Flight in the R.A.F. Museum. Those of No. 1507 B.A.T. Flight would have carried similar markings (Author)

a clue that the work previously done by the B.D.U. was coming to fruition, back on the station where it had been carried out. It appears that No. 405 Squadron began training using *H2S*, or '*Y*' equipment as it was usually called, at about this time, as we can see:

> Three crews underwent training flights with new secret equipment.
>
> Three flights detailed for H2S training and two air to sea firing.
>
> Bomb aimers were given lecture on "Y" equipment.
>
> [AIR 27/1788]

From this point onwards the records show an increasing effort being made on *H2S* training. Following these training days, operations resumed once more on 24th June 1943, when Elberfeld was the target for eleven aircraft, but only ten made it back to Gransden Lodge, as Sergeant Andrews and his crew were shot down.

The A.O.C. of No. 6 Group, Air Vice-Marshal Brookes O.B.E. was at the airfield on 27th June 1943, to visit his countrymen – it should be remembered that, even though it was part of the P.F.F., No. 405 Squadron was still affiliated to its former Group. The next day Bomber Command launched a series of raids against Köln, and No. 405 Squadron contributed twelve crews to the first of these. There was then a few days' break, during which the squadron's softball team played a match against the Americans at Bassingbourn, and, no doubt to their satisfaction, beat the 'Yanks' 4-0. In fact, playing softball against all-comers from the local airfields was becoming a regular pastime for the squadron.

Its next operation was a return trip to Köln, on 3rd July 1943. Eleven of the squadron's aircraft took part, and one of these, that captained by Pilot Officer Smith, failed to return. It was only by dint of excellent flying and teamwork that another made it back to Gransden Lodge, after the Halifax of Welshman Sergeant John 'Pee Wee' Phillips suffered major damage in an attack by a nightfighter. In an interview recorded for the Imperial War Museum, he recalled that:

> "… the only way I could keep the thing on an even keel was to tie a big rope round - I couldn't hold it - round the column, the pilot's column - joystick column - and two of my crew to pull the rope when I wanted to ease the tension on the joystick. And we came back like this to Gransden Lodge, and I had to call for an emergency landing procedure, and I managed to land this aircraft with three lads pulling when I said, 'Pull, ease off, pull, ease off' to try and land this aircraft. We eventually did get down on the ground, and when we inspected the aircraft there was half the tail gone and all the elevators at the back were all blown off; we were very fortunate indeed to get away with it."

Sergeant Phillips was awarded the D.F.M. for his efforts in bringing his aircraft safely home, but in an often-expressed sentiment, he said:

> "I felt very upset, really, when I got the D.F.M. because I felt my crew deserved it as well, to be quite frank about it. It wasn't a one-man effort, it was a seven man effort…"

The defence of this grateful crew's airfield against both air and ground attack was, as has been noted before, in the hands of the R.A.F. Regiment. No. 4265 Flight R.A.F.R. had apparently been carrying out this vital function since sometime in early to mid-

1942 (though other units may well have replaced it at some point and the transitions not recorded), but on 7th July 1943 we know that a party from No. 2708 Squadron R.A.F.R. arrived to take over, and 55 members of the squadron started their duties at the airfield that day. This squadron had arrived at Oakington from Greencastle in Northern Ireland three days before, and was providing defensive cover at a number of local airfields.

It was to be almost a week after its last operation before No. 405 Squadron flew on 'ops' again, though it had stood by for operations that were later 'scrubbed' (cancelled) several times. Good use was made of this break, with the seemingly never-ending training program taking in *H2S* and *Gee* practice for navigators, pilots flying with the local B.A.T. flight and air-to-sea and air-to-air firing for the gunners. On 9th July 1943 it was back to the fray, when four Halifaxes were sent to Gelsenkirchen. Although the Battle of the Ruhr was not yet completely done, that embattled industrial area was to get some relief from raids for a while as other cities were attacked by the R.A.F. For the Gransden Lodge squadron, this meant a raid on Aachen, close to the Dutch and Belgian borders, on 13th July 1943, but it was to prove equally hazardous, as the crew of Squadron Leader Wolfe, one of the twelve that set out, found to their cost – they did not return. On the next raid, two days later, the target was further afield, at Montbeliard in France, and once more twelve aircraft took part. This attack was not particularly successful as the markers were inaccurate and a neighbouring town was hit. A worrying development for the already hard-pressed crews was also recorded when one Halifax:

> ... was attacked by an enemy aircraft which was identified by both gunners as a Dornier 217. Both gunners also recognised British camouflage and roundels on the attacking aircraft.
>
> [AIR 27/1788]

TRIALS AND TRIBULATION

The crew survived to relay this piece of intelligence, but Flight Lieutenant Foy's was not so lucky, and failed to return.

Unbeknownst to the squadrons out in the field, the top brass at Bomber Command were planning a raid that would later become infamous. To enable preparations to be made for this, there were no operations for some days towards the end of July 1943, and for part of this time the weather was, as is to be expected in July in the U.K., poor, with low cloud, rain and drizzle. This did not prevent training continuing, with replacement crews for those who had been lost being brought up to speed on aircraft systems, and, in a new departure, clay pigeon shooting for the gunners was introduced. The drains were also inspected again, as was the night vision of the aircrew, who went to Oakington for testing. No. 405 Squadron's training efforts did not meet with universal approval at No. 8 Group headquarters, though, as was made clear in the Group's monthly reports, relating to practice bombing:

> 29. No. 405 get the wooden spoon this month, with only 47 bombs dropped during July. An increase during August is expected.
>
> [AIR 14/539]

It appears that the bomb aimers of No. 405 Squadron were not the only ones to be on the receiving end of some ribbing about the standard of their practice bombing, as in the same report we can find that:

> 41. It is rumoured that the Group Armament Officer went practice bombing and fell for the old gag of the reciprocal wind, narrowly missing a farmhouse with his first bomb! He improved a little, however, when this initial trouble had been overcome.

> 42. Gransden's suggestion that he be detailed to carry out a practice on the East Hatley range for Bassingbourn's benefit, and return the "compliments" showered on their W.A.A.F. quarters, has **not** been approved.
>
> [AIR 14/539]

If only we knew what embarrassments had been caused to the innocent ladies of the W.A.A.F. at Gransden Lodge by the Americans at Bassingbourn...

Finally, on 24th July 1943, the planning was complete, and an unsuspecting German city was about to suffer ordeal by fire. Two technological advances came together in time for the attacks on Hamburg in late July and early August 1943. The first of these, *H2S*, we know was already being used, but Hamburg, which was out of range of *Oboe*, was an ideal target for it, as the lakes and waterways in and around the city would contrast with the built-up areas and show up well on the *H2S* screens. The second innovation, which was to be used for the first time on the Hamburg raids, was *Window*, in the testing of which the B.D.U. had been involved the previous March.

The scene was thus set for the first raid of the ominously named Operation GOMORRAH. Fifteen Halifaxes set out from Gransden Lodge, and the disruptive effect of *Window* was such that only twelve aircraft from the entire force of 791 taking part were lost, and none were from Gransden Lodge. So confused were the defences that one crew from No. 405 Squadron, after bombing and flying some 50 miles (80 km) back towards home, discovered that three of their bombs had 'hung up', so they returned to the target, dropped their remaining munitions and then turned safely for home again. There was severe damage to Hamburg, compounded by the raids carried out by the American bomber forces in daylight after the night bombers had left, but the next night, to take advantage of the newly-found superiority given to the bombers by *Window*, the R.A.F. attacked Essen in the Ruhr, and in particularly the Krupps engineering complex. Eleven aircraft from No. 405 Squadron took part in that raid on 25th July 1943, but *Window* had not rendered them invulnerable, and Flying Officer Tomczak and his crew did not return. But it was, as the Oakington O.R.B. entry for that day recorded:

```
A bad night for the Axis - Mussolini resigned
miserably - Essen revisited successfully.
```
[AIR 28/607]

It is also said that when Dr. Gustav Krupp saw the destruction that had been wreaked on his factories, he immediately fell into a fit.

Following this the Americans carried out another daylight raid on Hamburg, but the night attack that came later was not successful, due to the strong winds and thunderstorms that disrupted the bombing to the point where almost no bombs fell on the target. However, the next night, 27th July 1943, was to be devastating in the extreme, and Operation GOMORRAH lived up to its name. The previous days and nights of bombing had caused extensive damage to buildings, leaving much combustible material exposed, and had also weakened the city's infrastructure and fire-fighting abilities. This, coupled with the dry weather, left Hamburg primed to become an inferno, and the bombing, to which No. 405 Squadron contributed fourteen crews, lit the fuse. So intense were the fires that night that they caused immensely powerful convection currents that sucked in, with huge force, further air to feed the flames, causing a classic firestorm. The devastation was massive, and over 42,000 deaths are estimated to have been caused in that single night. Joseph Göbbels, the Nazi propaganda minister, called it "the greatest crisis of the war" for

Germany, and Don Bennett felt the same way, believing that the consequences of the raids could have hastened the end of the conflict if political action had been taken that would have allowed the German side to begin moves towards a negotiated peace.

Hamburg's ordeal was not yet over, as on 29th July 1943 it was attacked again, with fourteen of No. 405 Squadron's crews taking part. The squadron did not operate again in July, but on 2nd August 1943 it took part in the final raid of Operation GOMORRAH, and it was to prove its most expensive, as three of the sixteen Gransden Lodge crews taking part were lost. Two were those of Sergeant Gregory and Flight Lieutenant Dare, and the third was that of Sergeant Phillips, who, with his crew, had struggled valiantly to get his aircraft home only weeks before. His Halifax was struck by lightning on the run up to the target, and with two engines out of action, he turned north to get clear of Hamburg. All the crew baled out and landed in neutral Sweden, where they were interned, eventually to return to the U.K. He later described what it was like after a raid when comrades had been lost:

> *"Empty beds and people taking all their kit away in kit bags the next morning was a sight which was a normal sight on a squadron - not a happy sight - and you just hoped that they were prisoners of war, and unfortunately most were not. The squadron lost a lot of men."*

Happily, he was one who returned to tell the tale.

LANCASTERS AND V-WEAPONS

As the summer of 1943 continued into August, No. 405 Squadron was rested after the raids on Hamburg, but this did not mean that its crews were idle, since the unremitting training program continued. We can also see the first signs that the squadron was soon to be re-equipped with new aircraft, as the flight engineers were being prepared to operate their new machines by receiving lectures on the intricacies of the Lancaster Mk. III.

The Lancaster was a development of the fairly disastrous twin-engined Manchester, which was underpowered and cursed with unreliable Rolls-Royce Vulture engines. In an attempt to rectify these problems, the manufacturer retained the successful features of the Manchester – its huge bomb-bay, for instance – but replaced the wing with one of larger span, and, crucially, substituted four Rolls-Royce Merlin engines for the two Vultures. After some further development the Lancaster entered service with Bomber Command and was thought by many to be one of the finest bombers to emerge during the war. The Lancaster Mk. III, which No. 405 Squadron was about to begin operating, was essentially the same as the original Mk. I, except that the Mk. III used a version of the Merlin built under license in the U.S.

The operations planned for 8th August 1943 were cancelled, and the weather was so poor that even training was difficult, but in the evening the personnel of Gransden Lodge took the opportunity to let their hair down:

> The 405 R.C.A.F. Squadron Dance given by the Aircrew in honour of the Ground Crew was at first postponed due to operations, but when operations were scrubbed, arrangements were proceeded with. The R.C.A.F. Overseas Dance Orchestra provided excellent music which contributed greatly to the success of the dance. Due to the original postponement, a full attendance of invited guests was not possible. The Squadron was honoured by the presence of Air Commodore F.G. Wait, from R.C.A.F. Overseas Headquarters. There was a large attendance of personnel from Station Headquarters, B.A.T. Flight and R.A.F. Regiment, who had been cordially invited to attend as guests.
>
> [AIR 27/1788]

Possibly with a slight hangover, operations resumed again the following day, when nine Halifaxes were dispatched against Mannheim, but Flight Lieutenant Gray and his crew did not make it back to base that night. Their aircraft was shot down and crashed close to the village of Awenne in Belgium, and their sacrifice is marked by a memorial, which was dedicated in September 2012.

On 10th August 1943 the target was Nürnberg (Nuremburg) for fourteen aircraft, and all returned safely – at least as far as the airfield. For one crew the operation had one last surprise in store, when their pilot managed to taxi into a ditch after landing. Even more embarrassing was the fact that the aircraft in question was that piloted by the 'boss', Johnny Fauquier. We can be sure that this cost him a few beers, and a certain amount of leg-pulling from his subordinates. There was a chance to investigate and put the damage right next day, as this was a day off for No. 405

TRIALS AND TRIBULATION

Squadron, and its members took the opportunity to spend the afternoon engaged in various sports.

In Italy, things were not going well for the Axis - as we have seen, Mussolini had resigned the previous month - and the Italian forces had been offered the chance to capitulate, with the threat of heavy aerial bombardment if they chose not to do so. On 12th August 1943 No. 405 Squadron joined the effort to persuade the Italians to sue for peace when it participated in a raid on Turin, sending fourteen aircraft.

Following this raid, the pilots of the squadron joined the rest of their crewmates in preparing to become operational on their new aircraft, when conversion training from the Halifax to the Lancaster commenced, with dual instruction being given by Johnny Fauquier. It is interesting to note that this training was being done 'on the job', as it were, with the squadron commander instructing his crews.

The squadron went back to work in the Halifax on 16th August 1943, when Turin was attacked again – fifteen of the bombers set out, but sadly only fourteen returned, the crew of Pilot Officer Manning being posted missing. Of the remainder, only six returned directly to Gransden Lodge, the others, presumably due to fuel shortage, landing at various airfields around the south of England, including Dunsfold, Hartford Bridge (now known as Blackbushe) and Church Stanton.

For some time, British Intelligence had been using a number of sources to track the development of new German secret weapons. By late June 1943 they had amassed a sufficient body of evidence to convince them that prompt action was required to prevent the deployment of one of these, the V-2 rocket:

```
The evidence shows, beyond doubt of "planting",
that the Germans have for some time been
developing a long range rocket at Peenemünde. In
```

its present form this rocket is about 38 feet long by 6-7 feet diameter, with probably three tail fins, and a weight of 40-80 tons; it has been photographed. It is uncertain how much of the development and constructional work is done at Peenemünde, but it would be consistent with the large majority of the reports if Peenemünde were the sole site.

The principal trouble experienced has been that of controlling the rocket in flight, and it is doubtful whether this trouble has yet been entirely overcome. The technical authorities would therefore probably prefer to delay using the rocket until next year at least, but the Führer is said to be demanding its operation as soon as conceivably possible, within the next few months. In this case the rocket is likely to be erratic, and London would be the only worthwhile target. The present production of rockets is probably small, so that the rate of bombardment would not be high. The only immediate counter measure readily apparent is to bomb the establishment at Peenemünde.

[DEFE 40/12]

The decision was made to attack the Baltic coast site of Peenemünde, as recommended, on 17th August 1943, and the raid marked a number of firsts. It was the first time that a Master Bomber was used to direct a full-scale Bomber Command raid (following the example set on the Dambusters attack), and it was the first operation on which No. 6 Group flew the Lancaster. On the German side, it was the first time that the Luftwaffe used its new *Schräge Musik* (literally 'Slanting Music', but more colloquially, 'Jazz Music') weapon. This was particularly deadly, comprising as it did two upward-firing cannon that allowed a nightfighter to approach a bomber in its blind spot beneath the fuselage and then fire upwards into the belly of the aircraft, but since its target could fall upon them, it was not without risk for the attackers.

No. 405 Squadron had dispatched twelve bombers on this raid, but in addition to a number of firsts, it also was the last operation for Flying Officer McIntyre and his crew, who were posted missing. Despite the losses, and the fact that many bombs had hit residential blocks and not the technical site for which they were intended, the operation was considered a success, as it was estimated that raid had set back the development program of the V-2 by over two months.

After this important operation, No. 405 Squadron was stood down for some days, but air and ground instruction continued, including more training to prepare the aircrew to go to war in the Lancaster. The crews may also have found time to visit their favourite local watering-hole. As Angus Robb recalled in his memoir *'RAF Days'*:

> *"There are two villages, Great and Little Gransden, and in the village of Great Gransden stands the 'Crown and Cushion' - a village pub. It was to this establishment that most of the Air Crew of the Squadron gave their custom.*
>
> *It was run by a wonderful couple, who, while obviously in the business to make money, did not see it as a way to make a profit above all else. For example, each morning the landlady made coffee available at the bar for those who thought it too early for 'the hair of the dog'; no charge was made for this, only a donation to the Red Cross. Needless to say the Red Cross box on the bar always needed emptying. Another peculiarity was the fact that they would not sell spirits, only beer. The only spirits available were in the form of a mixture of Rum and Orange Juice known as a 'Blockbuster' and that*

was for the pleasure of females only. One other aspect of the house stands out in my memory. The normal crew of a Lancaster numbered seven men. Attached to the wall behind the bar was a fixture of seven shelves which held seven pint glasses on each shelf. The glasses on each shelf were similar but there were different types of glasses on each of the other shelves. The longest serving crews, of those who were regulars, had their own shelf, and when you went into the 'pub you did not have to ask for your favourite 'tipple', it was put in front of you in a glass from your crews shelf. Ronnie and I were fortunate to be part of Bill Weicker's crew and had our own glasses. When Bill went back to Canada, our new crew took over the 'shelf' and we continued to have the privilege. I know all the foregoing may sound childish now, but believe me, at the time it was considered of great importance. The only way a vacancy occurred was if a crew were posted away or were killed. It was not often that crews were posted away."

It was to be 23rd August 1943 before the squadron was called upon to take part in operations again, and, in a foretaste of what was to become all too familiar to the crews the following winter, the target was Berlin – in fact, this operation could be considered to be the opening shot in what later came to be known as the Battle of Berlin. Johnny Fauquier was the Master Bomber on this raid (the first time that a Master Bomber had been used in a raid on a German city target), and was accompanied by fourteen other aircraft from Gransden Lodge. Of these, four returned early due to mechanical problems, but two more, with the crews of Flying Officer Harman and Warrant Officer Smith, failed to return at all, though the latter had ended up in Sweden and were interned there. For the remainder of the squadron it was then back to training, which included taking part in a 'Bullseye' exercise. It was common for crews to take part in these 'Bullseyes', which were combined navigation and simulated bombing exercises. Another frequently undertaken exercise was 'fighter affiliation', in which fighters would make simulated attacks on the bombers. The bomber crews would, in turn, practice evasion techniques and the gunners would use camera guns to record their attempts to down the fighters. However, on 27th August 1943, it was 'ops' again for real, when twelve aircraft were sent against Nürnberg.

Two days later No. 97 Squadron at Bourn found that it would need to relocate for a while, when it was told that its airfield would be unserviceable for about four or five days while the runways were reconditioned. To allow this work to be carried out, the three flights of No. 97 Squadron were detached, one each to Graveley and Oakington and one to Gransden Lodge, this flight being under the command of Wing Commander Burns D.F.C.

The next operations for both squadrons were on 30th August 1943. No. 405 Squadron provided aircraft for two raids; seven for an attack on Mönchengladbach, and three for a raid on a location enigmatically recorded as 'Forest' – apparently an ammunition dump in a forest near St. Omer in France – which was partly to give Main Force crews experience in the bombing of markers. No. 97 Squadron's crews also took part in the Mönchengladbach raid.

Another, similar, 'Forest' target was attacked on 31st August 1943, again by three crews from No. 405 Squadron, but nine other of its aircraft had a sterner task, as their target was Berlin. Two abandoned the mission with mechanical and instrument failures, and a third, the unfortunate crew of Pilot Officer Maddock, did not return. In *'The Berlin Raids'*, Martin Middlebrook's exhaustive study of the air campaign against the German capital, he records the thoughts of Harry Gowan (who in happier times the previous May had met with the King and Queen) about this raid. Gowan described well the feelings of extreme vulnerability caused by the German tactic of laying a line of parachute flares above the bomber stream so that fighters could attack using only visual means to find their targets. The crews, flying towards the target while brightly illuminated, felt that the enemy knew exactly where they were all of the time, and that every second could easily be their last.

For No. 97 Squadron the story was similar, as it was also detailed for the Berlin attack. The squadron had several aircraft return early due to crew sickness and equipment problems, and, more seriously, lost the crew of the commander of the flight operating from Gransden Lodge, Wing Commander Burns.

It is interesting to note the constitution of No. 405 Squadron at the end of August 1943. This shows that, whilst this was nominally a Canadian squadron, other nationalities made up a sizable minority:

R.C.A.F.	117 aircrew and 351 ground crew
R.A.F.	57 aircrew and 119 ground crew
R.A.A.F.	1 aircrew and 1 ground crew
R.N.Z.A.F.	1 aircrew

So at this point the squadron still had around 650 'bodies' on strength at Gransden Lodge, of whom over 450 were Canadian, and it was equipped with ten Halifax II and nine Lancaster Mk. III aircraft. Whether Don Bennett was aware of the percentages of the various nationalities is not known, but he claimed that he would not allow the crews of No. 405 Squadron to be 'more than 50 per cent Canadian'. He had rejected requests for there to be an Australian Pathfinder squadron on the basis that he wanted no segregation, as he termed it, within the P.F.F., but, since No. 405 Squadron represented a Canadian Group, he supported their presence with the aforementioned proviso – and he agreed that the squadron's C.O. should always be a Canadian. At this time, the balance in the squadron at 117 Canadian aircrew to 59 of other nationalities was far from 50-50.

As the autumn drew near and September 1943 dawned, good news came through to No. 405 Squadron when a message was received announcing that the immediate award of the Distinguish Service Order to Johnny Fauquier had been approved. The citation for the decoration explicitly mentioned Fauquier's conduct on the night of the Peenemünde raid, and also his general energy, drive and courage.

Perhaps fortuitously, given the likely celebrations, there were no operations for the squadron until 3rd September 1943. The target was once again Berlin, and six Lancasters were detailed for the raid. All returned to base, although one had bombed Brandenburg in error. This operation marked the temporary end of the bombing campaign against the German capital, which would be taken up again with a vengeance later in the year.

It was also on that day that the raids on Italy paid the hoped-for dividend, when the government of that country signed an armistice with the Allies. The war in Italy was far from over, though, as German forces occupied the parts of the country not already under Allied control. The visiting aircraft from No. 97 Squadron also made the short trip back to Bourn as planned.

On the 5th and 6th September 1943 raids were mounted on Mannheim and München (Munich), respectively. No. 405 Squadron took part in both, sending fourteen aircraft on the former and seven on the latter, but unfortunately, Sergeant Brunton and his crew did not return from the raid on Mannheim. The sporting instincts of the Canadians were also to the fore with the changing of the season, as both air and ground crew members participated in the first Canadian touch rugby practice sessions after work was done, and the squadron's field hockey team was victorious over a team from Station

LANCASTERS AND V-WEAPONS

Headquarters, who came second by a score of 4-1.

Although the actual invasion of continental Europe was still months away, in mid-1943 a plan was hatched to attempt to convince the German forces that an invasion, centred on the Boulogne area, was to take place in the autumn. The code name given to this subterfuge was Operation STARKEY. It was originally conceived as a large-scale air, sea, and land operation, but it was progressively scaled back. Despite his misgivings, Harris made at least a token effort to comply with the requests made to Bomber Command, and No. 405 Squadron contributed three Halifaxes to the proceedings on the night of 8th September 1943. Daybreak the next morning saw a motley flotilla of 355 varied craft heading out into the English Channel, which, in response to a pre-arranged code word, smartly turned around at 09:00 hours and sailed back to the U.K. This 'invasion that never was' was largely ignored by the enemy forces, but many French citizens had been needlessly killed in the bombing raids that had preceded it. Unusually, the R.A.F. had been joined in these night-time attacks by five American B-17 crews, who normally operated in daylight.

Following this raid of dubious utility, there was a lull in operations, though some were planned and scrubbed before taking place, but, of course, training continued. This training was not just for the primary tasks that aircrew were expected to carry out, but sometimes also for any secondary roles that they might have, or in the duties of other members of their crew. For example, on some occasions we find wireless operators being lectured on *Gee* and astro navigation, and bomb aimers on *H2S*. The sportsmen of No. 405 Squadron, and it appears that there were many, also managed some action, when on 14th September 1943:

```
The Squadron played against S.H.Q. Gransden in
field hockey and the teams tied 3-3. Members of
```

TRIALS AND TRIBULATION

```
the Squadron also participated in another
Canadian Touch Rugby practice. The boys are
really keen on this game and a large number have
turned out to practice.
```

[AIR 27/1788]

The target for most of Bomber Command on 15th September 1943 was again in France, but this time it was the rubber factory at Montluçon. No. 405 Squadron's involvement was the dispatch of twelve aircraft, and all these returned safely – in fact, the losses on this raid were very light, with only three aircraft in total being lost. However, for another unit its operations that night were extremely expensive, with over 60% losses, as No. 617 Squadron raided the Dortmund-Ems canal at low level. This level of losses confirmed that such low-level attacks could not be considered viable, and the squadron switched to become a high-altitude bombing unit. This new role for No. 617 Squadron would eventually lead to it developing its own marking techniques, which would further add to the tensions between No. 5 and No. 8 Groups.

The following day, 16th September 1943, it was the turn of the railway yards at Modane, in the French Alps close to the Italian border, to receive the bombers' attentions. The bombing was not considered to be accurate, and the three Halifaxes that took part from No. 405 Squadron returned safely to Gransden Lodge. This was to be the last time that the squadron operated the Halifax – from now on, only Lancasters would be flown. Despite the lukewarm assessment of the raid, it obviously made a lasting impression on the town of Modane, where today there is a 'Place du 17 septembre 1943', which, ironically, houses an exhibition centre dedicated to the Lyon-Turin railway.

During the pause before the next operations, the anti-aircraft gunners on No. 2708 Squadron R.A.F.R. got a new 'boss' on 19th September 1943 when Pilot Officer W.H. Brain took over as flight commander from Flying Officer G.W. Simpson, and No. 405 Squadron then had another excuse for a party in order to celebrate the promotion of Johnny Fauquier to the rank of Group Captain. This brought No. 405 Squadron into line with normal P.F.F. practice, where the holder of a post tended to be of one higher rank than in Main Force squadrons, in recognition of the increased dangers and longer tour of duty that the P.F.F. crews faced.

After a day to recover, the attacks switched back to Germany on 22nd September 1943, when No. 405 Squadron sent nine aircraft to Hannover to join the main attack, and a further four to the spoof attack on Oldenburg, designed to divert defences away from the main raid. Next night it was the turn of Mannheim, and all of the fourteen crews from Gransden Lodge that took part returned safely.

There were to be two more operations before the end of the month, when on 27th September 1943 nine aircraft joined a raid on Hannover and two the accompanying spoof on Brunswick. One crew from No. 405 Squadron was lost from each of these raids, those of Flying Officer St. Louis and Squadron Leader Logan. The second of these officers was especially unlucky, as this was the second time that Squadron Leader Logan, the 'A' Flight commander, had been shot down. The first occasion had been the previous March, when he had evaded the enemy and, after repatriation, had re-joined his squadron. Ironically, earlier on that day crews had been shown films on the interrogation of prisoners of war.

The remaining members of the squadron saw out the month with the usual round of training and sports, and although the event is only loosely related to Gransden Lodge, in that it happened to an aircraft based at its parent airfield Oakington, an entry in that station's O.R.B. for the time shows that a wartime sense of humour survived:

TRIALS AND TRIBULATION

> The only sortie of the day for 1409 Met flight was to Eckenforde and Amrum. Whilst taking photographs the Mosquito was intercepted by a F.W.190, but by a steep and rapid dive to the nearest cloud cover, the Hun was shaken off. This dive cost the observer his cap and his composure, and the aircraft returned without the top hatch and minus a considerable quantity of fabric.
>
> [AIR 28/607]

Incidentally, an earlier entry in Oakington's O.R.B. shows that Don Bennett, even though he was A.O.C. of the Pathfinder Force, was keeping his hand in by flying on operations occasionally. On 1st October 1943 Gransden Lodge began recording its history independently, when the first entry was made into its new O.R.B.:

> Gransden became self administered.
>
> [AIR 28/317]

Short and to the point. Other information relating to the station, particularly associated with medical matters, was still recorded in the Oakington O.R.B. for a while, though. In truth, until the beginning of December 1943 the Gransden Lodge O.R.B. was effectively just documenting the work of No. 405 Squadron - some pages were even mistakenly titled as being part of the squadron's O.R.B., until these titles were crossed out and corrected by hand.

The station's new status made no difference to the work being carried out, and after its break five of No. 405 Squadron's aircraft were sent to attack Hagen in the Ruhr that day. This was the first of a busy few days of operations, since on 2nd October 1943 fourteen aircraft went south on a raid on München, then next day twelve took part in an attack on Kassel. On 4th October 1943 only five of the squadron's aircraft were required, to join the operation against Frankfurt.

Also on that day the Station Commander, Group Captain Menaul, was posted to take over command at Graveley, and Johnny Fauquier assumed temporary command of Gransden Lodge. Strangely, the Gransden Lodge O.R.B. does not record when Johnny Fauquier was succeeded by the new permanent Station Commander, but it must have been before the end of October 1943 since the O.R.B. entries for the month are signed by the new incumbent, Group Captain G.P. Dunlop A.F.C. Group Captain Dunlop was destined to be the longest serving station commander that Gransden Lodge would have.

No. 405 Squadron then had a breather for a few days, during which some of the sportier members enjoyed more touch rugby practice, but on 7th October 1943 the run of operations resumed, with eleven Lancasters being sent to Stuttgart and three on a spoof raid on Friedrichshafen. Next day a further fourteen bombed Hannover, at the cost of the loss of Squadron Leader Schneider and his crew, and it is also recorded that on 8th October 1943:

```
Flight Lieutenant M. Sattler, D.F.C., flew the
1st Canadian Built Lancaster, 'Ruhr Express'
from base to Linton-On-Ouse, today.
```
[AIR 27/1788]

This entry, while short, is testimony to the successful culmination of a political and engineering partnership spanning two continents.

By late 1941 the need to produce aircraft in ever-increasing numbers, ideally in safety away from the risk of bombing, had led to a decision to build Lancasters in Canada. In August 1942 a Lancaster had been flown to Canada to act a pattern for the Canadian-built examples, which were to be known as the Lancaster Mk. X. This mark, based on the Mk. III, differed from the

TRIALS AND TRIBULATION

The roll-out of the first Canadian-built Lancaster Mk. X, KB700 'Ruhr Express', on 1st August 1943 (Bomber Command Museum of Canada)

British-built Lancasters in having North American radios and instruments, among other detailed differences.

On 1st August 1943 the first Lancaster Mk. X, numbered KB700 and christened the 'Ruhr Express', was rolled out of the hangar of Victory Aircraft at Malton, Ontario, near Toronto. There had been a big press build-up to this event, and in Canada there was understandable national pride in their country's new contribution to the war effort.

The pilot chosen to fly KB700 across the Atlantic was Squadron Leader Reg Lane D.S.O., D.F.C. Lane had completed two tours of operations with Bomber Command, the second at Graveley with No. 35 Squadron (during which we previously heard of him in relation to the first use of *H2S*. At the time of his selection he was being rested at the P.F.F.N.T.U., so he travelled back to Canada, enjoyed some leave back home and made ready for KB700's maiden flight.

Unfortunately, when he and his crew were preparing for the flight, they found that there were major problems with the engine instrumentation - in fact, the aircraft's wiring had been installed incorrectly - and it would be impossible to fly the aircraft across the Atlantic in that condition.

As Lane later recalled, in view of the amount of media interest that the event had generated, and with all the factory workers and officials present, it would have been a public relations disaster not to have taken off as scheduled. The crew therefore decided that they could not refuse to make the flight, so having weighed up the risks and agreed that they were acceptable, they departed as planned, but only to fly to Dorval, near Montréal. Here KB700 was, with no publicity, extensively worked upon for another month - more leave! - before Lane and his crew ferried the aircraft to the U.K., where they arrived on 15th September 1943.

The crew of KB700 after their arrival in the U.K. Squadron Leader Reg Lane is on the far left (Imperial War Museum)

TRIALS AND TRIBULATION

One of the first jobs after arrival was to offload the unofficial cargo, marked 'spare parts', which had been secreted in the bomb bay by the Rolls-Royce representative who had made the trip alongside the crew. These 'spare parts' consisted largely of hard-to-get foodstuffs, such as hams. Another supernumerary member of the crew was 'Bambi', a small dog brought along by one of its human companions, and the crew also had the assistance of a very experienced ferry pilot on the trans-Atlantic leg of the trip.

After its acceptance into service, KB700 was assigned to the foremost Canadian squadron of the time - No. 405 Squadron, at Gransden Lodge.

Following early October's brief but intense spell of operations, the Gransden Lodge squadron was stood down for a while. During this period the training continued as normal, and included an opportunity for the aircrew to see and understand how their ground crews worked, as a four-hour exercise involving bombing-up the squadron's aircraft was carried out, with the squadron's bomb aimers in attendance.

There were some new arrivals on the station on 13th October 1943 when No. 2955 Squadron R.A.F.R. moved in, for what would initially be a brief visit. It may have caused dismay to a number of the newly-arrived squadron's members when they found out next day that the majority of them were not required to man the guns, since:

> 20 of the squadron personnel are necessary to co-operate with P/O BRAIN whose detached flight from 2708 Squadron are manning Hispano guns. Remainder of squadron were moved to GRANSDEN to primarily do the tasks allotted to Works Flight personnel and ACH/GD's i.e. construction of a concrete path.

[AIR 29/136]

LANCASTERS AND V-WEAPONS

The hard labour was under way by the following day, and:

> Roadmaking continued and no opportunity availed itself for training of any description.... Roadmaking continued on October 16, 17, 18, 19 and 20
>
> [AIR 29/136]

The navigators of No. 405 Squadron, like the bomb aimers, were, however, able to get some training done by learning new techniques with *H2S*, and other crew members continued to be taught the basics of the skills of their comrades in their aircraft.

This breather from operations came to end on 18th October 1943, when Hannover was again the target for fifteen aircraft from Gransden Lodge. The next attack was on 20th October 1943, target Leipzig, and one of the fourteen pilots on the raid, Arthur Bonikowsky, recalled the operation many years later. As usual, the bombers departed and began climbing up through the dense overcast to their cruising altitude. When his Lancaster suddenly broke clear of cloud, Bonikowsky remembered that he was presented with a picture that, as he put it, "staggered the senses". Around him were hundreds of aircraft emerging from the clouds, all on course for the Dutch coast, determined to rain down destruction upon the enemy. The destruction that night was not solely inflicted by the Allies, though, as one of the other crews taking part from No. 405 Squadron, that captained by Pilot Officer Wood, did not return from Leipzig.

Two attacks were planned for 22nd October 1943 – the main raid on Kassel, and a diversionary attack on Frankfurt. No. 405 Squadron participated in both, with seven and five aircraft respectively. None of the crews taking part were lost, although icing, that bane of high-flying, heavily-laden aircraft, was experienced by many, and was sufficiently serious for one crew to return early. With a note of resignation, No. 2955 Squadron R.A.F.R. recorded that day that 'roadmaking continues apace'.

It is not mentioned by name until the following month, but it seems probable that in late October 1943 the wireless operators of No. 405 Squadron were being introduced to the *Fishpond* radar system, which they would soon be expected to operate. *Fishpond* was an early warning radar that used a signal derived from the *H2S* system to show aircraft attacking the bomber from below.

Over on the P.F.F.N.T.U. at Upwood, to which Squadron Leader Reg Lane had returned after his delivery flight of KB700, the routine of life had begun to pall and Lane was looking for a new role. His plan was to enrol at the R.A.F. Staff College with the intention of remaining in the air force when the conflict was over,

Reconstruction of the wireless operator's position in a Lancaster, showing the *Fishpond* display in the centre (Author)

but instead he was offered the chance by Don Bennett to return to operations with No. 405 Squadron, which he accepted. Thus it was that, also on 25th October 1943, the 'Ruhr Express' was reunited with its delivery pilot, when Reg Lane arrived at Gransden Lodge to join No. 405 Squadron and take command of 'A' Flight. On joining the squadron Lane had 51 operations to his credit, and he was promoted to Wing Commander.

Other changes of a more substantial nature, from the station's point of view anyway, were also being planned. On the day that Reg Lane arrived on No. 405 Squadron, those in charge of the purse-strings in London were considering how money should be spent on 'works and bricks' at various airfields. The expenditure envisaged at this point for Gransden Lodge was £8,000 in 1944 (equivalent to about £280,000 today), to fund additions to the perimeter track. By December of 1943 this had risen to £16,800 (about £590,000 today), this being the estimate of the sum needed to provide, among other facilities, extra perimeter track, a gunnery trainer and a second radar workshop. The reason for this requirement for extra radar workshops, not just at Gransden Lodge but also at other airfields, was that:

> **These are for H2S purposes and are projected for those Stations being upgraded to a 2 squadron basis. A Workshop is essential for each Squadron.**
> [AIR 20/298]

So from this we can see that it was planned that No. 405 Squadron should be joined by another operational squadron at some time in the next year or so – and this would indeed come to pass. We must not forget, though, that there was another unit flying from the airfield even in October 1943. Although the main focus of our attention has been on the activities of the bomber squadrons, for

TRIALS AND TRIBULATION

the whole time that they had been carrying the offensive to the enemy the little Oxfords of No. 1507 B.A.T. Flight had been busily and without fuss engaged in their training task, generally recording between 200 and 300 flying hours per month – unless the weather or other circumstances intervened. From the 26th to 28th October 1943 was one such period, as the flight's O.R.B. for those days records that the runways were unserviceable, that the airfield was fog-bound, and that the total flying for the days was 'nil'.

The flight had by now been expanded to cope with an increased demand for its services, having a strength of nine pilots at the end of October 1943, including one U.S.A.A.F. instructor. The commanding officer of the unit had also changed on 22nd October 1943 when Squadron Leader Cumming was posted to No. 109 Squadron, his place being taken by Flight Lieutenant J.A. Robertson, who was already serving with the flight.

The poor weather also prevented any further operational flying for the rest of October, though the 'Ruhr Express' was being shown off around the local airfields, and on one day, as some light relief from their training, all the crews were stood down and buses were provided to take them for an afternoon off in Cambridge.

This inclement weather was no bar to operations on the ground, of course, so, in a no doubt welcome break from their exertions on the road-building chain gang, No. 2955 Squadron R.A.F.R. took part in Exercise UMBRELLA. It was tasked with guarding No. 8 Group H.Q. in Huntingdon, and, in shades of *'Dad's Army'*:

> Close liaison was maintained with Home Guard Company defending and at app. 11.00 part of the attacking force was contacted and repelled. No umpires were available to award "casualties" and "enemy" never reached the precincts of G.H.Q.
>
> [AIR 29/136]

LANCASTERS AND V-WEAPONS

The weather improved sufficiently in early November for No. 405 Squadron to be detailed for operations again, and on 3rd November 1943 twelve aircraft were dispatched to Köln along with two on a spoof on Düsseldorf, and all returned safely. The same could not be said of Flying Officer Pringle, who was killed in a local flying accident on 5th November 1943.

No. 2955 Squadron R.A.F.R. had completed its work on road construction by the first week in November 1943, and in recognition of this the:

> Group Defence Officer arrived and personally thanked the Squadron for their roadmaking efforts, weather forbade a squadron parade
>
> Squadron Farewell Dance in Concert Hall a great success – a large gathering of Canadian personnel had a very enjoyable evening

[AIR 29/136]

The squadron also supplied some personnel to help out the locals when one flight from the squadron took part in a village British Legion parade.

This was to be its last contribution for a while, however, as on 8th November 1943 at 05:30 the whole squadron departed for R.A.F. Davidstow Moor in Cornwall, although, as it turned out, it would soon be back. It rather sounds as if living conditions in Cornwall were little better than at Gransden Lodge, as once the squadron had arrived, its O.R.B. noted glumly:

> Camp app 1000 feet above sea level annual rainfall believed to be 84 inches. Personnel had 25 minutes march to dining hall

[AIR 29/136]

TRIALS AND TRIBULATION

On the flying side of things, there had been a break from operations for a week or so until 10th November 1943, despite many 'ops' being planned then scrubbed. The little town of Modane in France is unfortunately positioned, in that it straddles the main railway line from France into Italy, and because of this it became the target for attack again on that day. Fourteen bombers from No. 405 Squadron took part, and as the Gransden Lodge O.R.B. notes:

> The defences were negligible, and the whole operation was looked on by the crews as a practice raid with an interesting moonlight view of the glaciers of the Alps.

[AIR 28/317]

A further week's stand down followed, but the next target was altogether tougher as No. 405 Squadron was detailed to supply aircraft to join the raid on Mannheim on 17th November 1943. This small raid, carried out just by No. 8 Group crews, was to use *H2S* alone to identify the target - possibly to see how well the Main Force squadrons could be expected to cope when they were equipped with *H2S* – so the request went out for as many crews as possible, even those still under training, who could bomb 'blind' using *H2S*. Ten such crews were found, and of these ten, two returned early with problems with their gun turrets, but the aircraft of Flight Sergeant Larson was shot down, its crew being the only one lost on the raid.

Nightfighters and flak were not the only dangers faced by the bomber crews; as we have seen, the weather was also a constant hazard. In addition to such dangers as icing and thunderstorms when airborne, bad visibility and fog when they returned to their bases was another potential killer. The beam approach system, which No. 1507 B.A.T. Flight was training pilots to use, was an important but partial answer – in thick fog, the pilot still could not see the runway in the last few vital seconds of the landing. A solution to this problem was proposed by Arthur Hartley of the Petroleum Warfare Department, and received the enthusiastic backing of Don Bennett. The system was known by the acronym F.I.D.O., standing for 'Fog Investigation and Dispersal Operation', though other words were often later fitted to those initial letters (for instance Fog, Intense, Dispersal Of). Whatever the official name of F.I.D.O., it was an intrinsically simple idea, as it used the extreme heat generated by lines of petrol burners on each side of a runway to disperse fog, giving a clear slot in which pilots could see to land. Bennett's impression, when he carried out the first test of F.I.D.O. in February 1943, had apparently been that it put him in mind of lions at a circus jumping through flaming hoops, but despite this he considered the system to be usable.

The first installation of F.I.D.O. at an operational airfield was at Graveley, and it was used in anger for the first time on the night of 19th/20th November 1943. The availability of this new aid was to prove vital, since on almost the same day that F.I.D.O. was first used, Bomber Command began a new campaign against the German capital in the winter weather of 1943/1944.

THE BATTLE OF BERLIN

"... and we got into the winter and of course, the winters and living in Nissen huts and the conditions ... come back from a raid and we climb into a wet bed - literally you climb in - the beds were damp as could be - no way, no heat - so that it was dreadful to get out of your flying gear and then crawl into a sticky bed. Everything! The food was bad, you couldn't get beer; if we wanted to have a party we literally had to go round the countryside and visit every brewery we could to see if we could steal a barrel of beer. Hard liquor was just not available - there may have been an allocation from N.A.A.F.I. of perhaps a bottle a week, or something like that, for the whole mess; scotch or gin. Things were dreadful, clothing coupons had just about dried up – it was rough. It was in that ground environment, atmosphere, that we launched ourselves into the Battle of Berlin."

When he recorded a series of taped interviews for the University of Victoria some thirty years after the event, that is how Reg Lane remembered the conditions at Gransden Lodge in early November 1943, when one of the costliest, and, it could be argued, least successful of Bomber Command's campaigns was about to commence.

The Battle of Berlin is generally reckoned to have begun with

THE BATTLE OF BERLIN

a raid on 18th November 1943, although, as we have seen, earlier skirmishes had taken place in August and September. Arthur Harris's thinking regarding the battle was clear, as he confidently told Churchill in November 1943 that he expected that the campaign against Berlin might cost the R.A.F. 400 to 500 aircraft, but that it would cost Germany the war.

On that opening day of the battle, 18th November 1943, No. 405 Squadron joined the fray by participating in raids on two targets. Nine aircraft were detailed for an attack on the German capital, while another five were sent again to Mannheim, as they had been the previous night, possibly as a diversionary raid. All the participants returned, but two aircraft landed at other airfields due to lack of fuel, one having a particularly undignified arrival at Friston on the Sussex coast, as after making four approaches to the airfield the pilot bounced his Lancaster off a Nissen hut and damaged its undercarriage.

Over the next few days the weather settled into its common East Anglian winter pattern of fog and frost, but it was not bad enough to prevent another raid on Berlin being mounted on 22nd November 1943. Fourteen aircraft took part, and amongst them was KB700, marked 'LQ-Q' and better known as the 'Ruhr Express', on the first mission of a Canadian-built Lancaster. Disappointingly, it returned early when it suffered an engine failure and did not reach Berlin, as the station's O.R.B. records:

> One aircraft 405/Q turned back with port outer engine u/s from 52.36 N. 1110 E a few miles from Berlin, this was particularly unfortunate, as this aircraft was the first Canadian built Lancaster on its first trip, and the news and camera men were particularly interested for publication purposes.
>
> [AIR 28/317]

TRIALS AND TRIBULATION

The German capital was again the target for thirteen Lancasters from No. 405 Squadron on 23rd November 1943. Once more there were losses, as two of these aircraft, captained by Flight Lieutenant Lefroy and Flying Office Clark, did not return. Berlin was beginning to take its toll. There then followed a few days off operations, but training continued unabated, and the numbers on No. 2708 Squadron R.A.F.R. were also beefed-up when more gunners were posted in from No. 2884 A.A. Squadron R.A.F.R.

The short break ended on 26th November 1943 when fourteen aircraft from No. 405 Squadron travelled once more to the 'Big City'. For one crew it was a particularly trying 'op', as they were coned by searchlights for over ten minutes, and their aircraft was out of control for a time while diving steeply to escape. Once out of danger, the crew found that two of their number had decided that discretion was the better part of valour, and had abandoned ship by baling out against orders. The impression formed by the remainder of the participants from Gransden Lodge was that this had been the most successful attack on Berlin yet. In fact, although the bombing on this occasion was indeed very concentrated, it was established after the war that the raid four days earlier had actually been the most effective against Berlin.

There were no further operations for No. 405 Squadron in November 1943, and it began Christmas celebrations early, on 30th November 1943 - that day's mission against München was cancelled. The mention of the filming of the event shows that propaganda value was being extracted from it for use back home closer to Christmas, and may explain why it took place so early:

> A very successful Squadron Christmas Party was held in the British Legion Club, Great Gransden, commencing at 1930 hours. This party was attended by the Station Commander, Squadron Commander and Aircrew and Ground Crews personnel who have been with the Squadron almost since its inception.

THE BATTLE OF BERLIN

```
The menu for dinner included, soup, roast turkey,
dressing, greens, and plum pudding. Press
Relations Officers from R.C.A.F. Overseas
Headquarters were there to 'shoot' pictures of
the general gathering for future showing in
Canadian theatres. This was a 'bang on' party
and all personnel participating in 'ops' returned
safely to base.
```
[AIR 27/1788]

The increasing independence of Gransden Lodge was marked on 1st December 1943, but the entry recording this event in the O.R.B. is also tempered slightly by the inevitable bureaucracy:

```
R.A.F. Station, Gransden Lodge, became self-
accounting. It is now self supporting for the
whole range of equipment.

Mr. Hampton, Air Ministry Auditor, visited the
station for a short inspection of Equipment
Accounts Section.
```
[AIR 28/317]

From this date onwards, day-to-day life at Gransden Lodge was also documented much more fully in the O.R.B. The departure of its satellite stations (Bourn became independent, too) was also recorded at Oakington, but the apron-strings were apparently not yet completely cut, since Oakington still had to house the sick from its former satellites and they had, as yet, no sick quarters of their own.

The first operation of the final month of 1943 took place on 2nd December 1943, with twelve aircraft from No. 405 Squadron marking for yet another attack on Berlin. The next night the squadron was in action again, this time against Leipzig. Fourteen crews set out but only thirteen returned, that of Flying Officer Bowring being posted missing.

TRIALS AND TRIBULATION

After this operation, No. 405 Squadron was stood down for some days. One contributory factor, apart from the winter weather, may have been:

> A mild epidemic of Corzya (Influenza) started a week ago. Number at Sick Parade increased to 60 per day. Temperatures in a number of cases rose to 103 and dropped to normal in most cases within 48 hours. Immediate steps were taken to isolate these cases and two huts were taken over, one for W.A.A.F. and one for airmen. The epidemic was under control in less than a week.
>
> [AIR 28/317]

In the first week of December 1943, to make the most of the propaganda opportunities afforded by the entry into service of KB700, the publicity machine began, possibly somewhat belatedly, to swing into action, when a number of R.C.A.F. officers and technicians from the Canadian Public Relations Department came to visit Gransden Lodge in order to photograph the first Canadian-built Lancaster and its crew and to make a recording of its first operational sortie. But on the same day that they came calling, showing the common combination of the noteworthy with the mundane, we find that there was a:

> Medical inspection of all N.C.O. aircrew for head louse. No infection found.
>
> [AIR 28/317]

We must assume that officer aircrew were not thought susceptible to such infestations.

Those unsung but vital guardians of Gransden Lodge, No. 2708 Squadron R.A.F.R., whose guns provided anti-aircraft cover for the airfield, left on 8th December 1943 to take part in a course

THE BATTLE OF BERLIN

on Browning and Hispano guns at Filey in Yorkshire, and No. 2955 Squadron R.A.F.R. returned from Davidstow Moor to take over its duties on the same date. It is not clear whether No. 2708 Squadron R.A.F.R. ever returned to the station after this course, but it seems likely that it did not.

A few days later there was an entry in the station's O.R.B. that today, with our knowledge of the effects of radiation on the human skin, has an odd ring to it, since it notes that two hours a day of ultra-violet light treatment was being given to those who required it. Why this treatment with ultra-violet radiation? It seems that a number of stations were equipped with ultra-violet light apparatus, and personnel were treated with it in the hope that they would catch colds (especially a problem for aircrew) less often. There is no evidence that this treatment actually worked, though it was thought to be of great psychological benefit to those receiving it - and possibly it also gave them a winter suntan.

The bad weather or head colds did not prevent No. 1507 B.A.T. Flight continuing with its instrument training, as the flight's aircraft were airborne almost every day during December 1943, with over 18 hours instructional flying being recorded on a single day.

No. 405 Squadron's break from operations came to an end at 09:55 on Thursday, 16th December 1943, when orders were received for another attack on Berlin. This was the first of a sequence of events that culminated in a terrible day for the squadron, and Bomber Command as a whole, to be known thereafter as 'Black Thursday'.

Things began normally enough, with details of the aircraft required, bomb loads, routes, timings etc. being received during the day. The squadron's thirteen aircraft took off and successfully carried out the raid, but the weather report for the day shows that their problems were far from over:

TRIALS AND TRIBULATION

WEATHER
10/10 cloud all day base 1,000' – 2,000' lowering to 100' at midnight. Vis. 3 – 4 miles at first then gradually going down all day becoming 1,800 yards by 24,00. Winds light SE'ly.

[AIR 28/317]

When the crews from the squadrons taking part in the raid returned at around midnight, weary and low on fuel, they found their airfields covered with low cloud and fog. Reg Lane took part in this raid, and though his recollections differ from the recorded facts in some details, it is obvious that the unfolding disaster made a deep impression on him. With the weather closing in fast, his was the last of the five Lancasters to make a successful landing at Gransden Lodge, using the beam, but even taxying was difficult because the visibility was so poor. He groped his way around the airfield until he knew that he was in the vicinity of the control tower, then shut his aircraft down and:

> *"I ran up into the control tower and I was furious, screaming into the control tower and I said 'For Christ's sake, why haven't you diverted everybody – what's wrong with you? For crying out loud, we shouldn't be landing here, we're going to have crashes all over the place!' And I said, 'I only just made it' - I was furious! The controller and the base commander were there, and both ... just almost white, and the controller said 'I'm sorry, sir, but there isn't a base open in England, this is right across the country.' And I said 'Oh, my God, my God!' Well, I didn't know what the hell to do; there was nothing I could do..."*

Of the many remaining aircraft still airborne, those that could attempted to land at their bases, and others were eventually

THE BATTLE OF BERLIN

diverted to airfields where the weather was marginally better, or to Graveley, newly equipped with F.I.D.O., in the hope that they could land there. Sadly, many of them could not. Some simply ran out of fuel and crashed, their crews in some cases having first baled out, and others crashed while trying to land in the appalling visibility.

The Gransden Lodge squadron, like those from the neighbouring airfields, did not escape unscathed. The description of the raid from the station's O.R.B., after giving details of the attack, tells of what happened on the crews' return:

> All aircraft returned over base on E.T.A. and the cloud was then down to 500 feet and lowering steadily.
>
> V, Z, K, G and T managed to land at Gransden, but 5 aircraft were sent to Graveley, where it was thought that the fog dispersal flares would aid them; and two aircraft were sent to Marham where the cloud base was slightly higher. 3 aircraft successfully landed at Marham and one at Bourn and one at Warboys but 'R'/405 was reported at 02.25 crashed near Marham and four of the crew killed and the Pilot, Flying Officer Drew seriously injured. D/405 crashed near Graveley at 00.50 hours, and all the crew were killed except Warrant Officer Nutting, who was only slightly injured. O/405 also crashed near Graveley at 23.58 hours, 3 of the crew were killed and the rest of the crew injured. A disastrous ending to a successfully executed attack.
>
> [AIR 28/317]

As the description records, the three aircraft lost from No. 405 Squadron that night were piloted by Flight Lieutenant Allen and Flying Officers McLennan and Drew.

TRIALS AND TRIBULATION

No. 97 Squadron at Bourn lost five aircraft in weather-related crashes that night, and personnel from Gransden Lodge were involved in attempts, futile as it turned out, to aid the crew of one of them that had crashed somewhere near the railway station close to Longstowe. The search went on throughout the night, but when the aircraft was located all the crew members were found to be dead.

For the next three days, the whole of Bomber Command was stood down from operations, but on 20th December 1943 No. 405 Squadron was requested to supply three aircraft to take part in a spoof attack on Mannheim, and another eleven to mark a raid on Frankfurt. Despite some mechanical and equipment failures, both operations were carried out without loss. In an attempt to reduce the travelling to and fro for crews after their post-operation debriefings, after this raid a combined 'operational breakfast' was

The funeral procession at Cambridge Cemetery for those members of No. 405 Squadron killed on the night of 'Black Thursday'
(Jane Pilling-Cormick, Bill Bessent and Jennie Gray)

THE BATTLE OF BERLIN

served to both officer and N.C.O. aircrew together for the first time. Until this innovation was put into place the officers had had a round trip of several miles after their debriefing to get their breakfast and then to their beds.

On 22nd December 1943 the station bade farewell to those whose lives had been claimed by the weather the previous week, when a mass funeral was held at the Borough Cemetery, Cambridge, for eleven of the fourteen men who had been killed on 'Black Thursday'. As the eleven were all members of the R.C.A.F., the Canadian Padre from Gransen Lodge performed the funeral service, which was also attended by the Station Commander.

Despite the shock over the deaths, there was 'a war on' - to use the stock phrase of the day - and life had to continue. On 23rd December 1943, thirteen Lancasters of No. 405 Squadron returned to Berlin, this time with better weather, and all landed back at base.

Christmas was approaching, and on Christmas Eve 1943 preparations for the season were in hand, but before festivities could commence Gransden Lodge had some unexpected visitors who, like Santa Claus, arrived from above:

> Five U.S.A.A.F. personnel baled out of their Liberator aircraft. They were picked up by S.S.Q. staff … and these airmen were transferred by U.S.A.A.F. ambulance to an American base hospital.
>
> [AIR 28/317]

With the American crew safely dispatched, celebrations could get under way, but it must have been with mixed feelings of relief at his survival and regret for the loss of his crew on 'Black Thursday' that Warrant Officer Nutting took part:

> A concert party, "Slipstream", from R.A.F. Oakington staged a show in the Concert Hall

TRIALS AND TRIBULATION

```
commencing at 2000 hours. Like all shows made up
of local R.A.F. and W.A.A.F. talent, it was
greeted with a great deal of applause which it
well deserved.

S/Ldr. Michaud from R.C.A.F. H.Q. Peterborough
visited the station and celebrated Midnight Mass
in the Concert Hall.

W/O Nutting, rear gunner, discharged from R.A.F.
Hospital, Ely.
```
[AIR 28/317]

Events on Christmas Day 1943 began early, for those so inclined:

```
A Communion Service was held in the village at
0700 and 0800 hrs. Later at 0900 hrs. a service
was held by F/Lt. Ferguson for R.C.A.F. personnel
and any R.A.F. and W.A.A.F. personnel who wished
to attend.
```
[AIR 28/317]

Later, a further raid on Berlin having been cancelled, the normal service tradition of 'other ranks' being served Christmas dinner by their officers and N.C.O.s was observed:

```
Lunch was served to the airmen and airwomen at
1300 hrs. by 40 officers and 40 N.C.Os in the two
dining halls on No.1 Communal Site which had
been decorated by the Physical Fitness Officer,
F/O Armstrong, for the occasion with bunting,
and leaves and branches gathered from the
surrounding countryside. Cigarettes and beer
were distributed and the lunch consisted of
Soup, Fish, Chicken and Christmas Pudding.
```
[AIR 28/317]

THE BATTLE OF BERLIN

That done, the remainder of the day was then taken up with general jollification:

> There was a film show in the afternoon. Tea consisted of cold ham, mince pies and cake. The cake, which seemed to consist mainly of fruit, was sent to 405 Squadron from Canada by the Vancouver Women's Canadian Club and was shared by all at the request of 405 Squadron. The new Sergeants' Anteroom was taken over for the evening in order that a Station Dance could be held, there being no other room available. This, once again, was decorated by F/O Armstrong. The music was provided by the Station's voluntary dance band. The dance finished shortly after midnight.
>
> [AIR 28/317]

No. 405 Squadron had been adopted by the city of Vancouver, British Columbia, and the gift from the local Women's Canadian Club would surely have been very welcome. This was not the end of the Christmas celebrations, though there was a hitch on 26th December 1943:

> A Church Parade was held and the service began at 0900 hrs. The film show that had been arranged for the evening unfortunately had to be cancelled owing to the non arrival of the film.
>
> [AIR 28/317]

However, there was another event for the staff of the station to enjoy next day, when:

> The W.A.A.F. held a special invitation dance on the W.A.A.F. Site. Many prizes were given, some of which were Savings Certificates.
>
> [AIR 28/317]

TRIALS AND TRIBULATION

And on 28th December 1943 the hard work of those who had enabled the festivities to take place was recognised, as:

> A party was organised by the Catering Officer, S/O Cheales, for the Staff of all the messes at the Village Hall. Members of the Station's Voluntary Dance Band offered their services and gave up another engagement to do this. The Station Commander, Group Captain G.P. Dunlop, A.F.C., accompanied by the W.A.A.F. Admin. Officer, S/O Harrison, looked in during the evening. The Station Commander expressed his appreciation of the work done by the staff of all the messes, particularly at Christmas. The Padre, F/Lt. Ferguson, came later in the evening.
>
> [AIR 28/317]

There was an interruption to No. 405 Squadron's Christmas break when, on 30th December 1943, Berlin was again the target for fourteen of its aircraft. All made it back to the U.K., but one was sufficiently badly damaged by flak that it could not reach Gransden Lodge and landed at the emergency airfield at Woodbridge in Suffolk.

Next day, an operation to Frankfurt was cancelled in the afternoon, so in the evening, New Year's Eve 1943 could be celebrated by all:

> A W.A.A.F. invitation dance was held on the W.A.A.F. Site. During the course of the evening, three of the W.A.A.F. sang with the band. Two other airwomen tap danced together. Their efforts were very much appreciated. As it was New Year's Eve the dance was allowed to continue until 0015 hours in order that the New Year could be celebrated in the usual jolly way.
>
> [AIR 28/317]

It is perhaps unsurprising that so many parties and dances were organised. It must have been a welcome relief from the pressures of more than four years of war, and the mounting losses, to be able to relax and celebrate in this way. It is also clear that, despite food rationing, service personnel were able to enjoy at least an approximation of the usual Christmas fare; and they were no doubt thankful for it, given the usual standard of food and drink. The British civilian population were not so lucky. The Ministry of Food reckoned that only one family in ten would get turkey or goose for their Christmas dinner, and getting hold of any special foodstuffs, even a Christmas pudding (let alone meat), could be difficult. They would have had to do their best to make merry on the meagre weekly food ration, which in 1943 was, per person:

4oz (100 g) bacon or ham	3oz (75 g) cheese
2oz (50 g) cooking fat	2oz (50 g) butter
8oz (225 g) sugar	2oz (50 g) tea
1 egg	Approx. 1lb (0.5 kg) meat
3 pints (1.7 l) milk	

Even for the families of No. 405 Squadron's members back home in Canada - where rationing was nothing like as severe as in the U.K. - butter, sugar, coffee, tea and meat were rationed. This did not prevent visitors from the U.K. marvelling at the apparent abundance of the food there, or prevent No. 405 Squadron's supporters assembling sufficient ingredients for the Christmas cake that they supplied.

The end of 1943 also saw the departure of most of No. 1507 B.A.T. Flight. By early December the decision had been made to disband the flight, and the flight's aircraft were to be distributed, one (with an instructor and ground crew) to each of the No. 8 Group stations, in order to maintain the ability to carry out beam

TRIALS AND TRIBULATION

approach training in the future. By the beginning of 1944 all of the flight's Oxfords, except for the one that was to remain at Gransden Lodge, had departed to Oakington, Bourn, Wyton, Graveley, Upwood and Marham.

January 1944 brought with it no great change in tactics, and the relentless grind of operations against Berlin continued from the outset. On the first day of the New Year, fourteen of No. 405 Squadron's crews were detailed for a raid on Berlin, but in the event only twelve set out, as, rather embarrassingly, one of the Lancasters taxied into another before departure. Two other crews were much less fortunate, as those of Flying Officer Campbell and Flying Officer Donnelly took off but did not return.

Berlin was to receive no relief from the air attacks as it was the target again on 2nd January 1944, with the crews from Gransden Lodge beginning their participation in the mission a few minutes before midnight. It may have been that the continuing pressure of these long and dangerous missions was, understandably, taking its toll on the morale of the crews, since of the twelve aircraft from No. 405 Squadron detailed, one crew, commanded by Warrant Officer Robinson, was lost, but three also returned early, claiming airframe and engine icing as the cause. What Johnny Fauquier would have made of this we don't know, but on another occasion he is reported to have refused to let a crew who were on probation with the squadron land when they returned early from a mission. He did not think that the reason that they gave warranted an early return, and made them fly back to the base of their previous squadron – not suitable for Pathfinders. Part of the reason for his action may have been the reputation that No. 6 Group had earned earlier in the conflict for a higher than average number of crews returning early from missions, although it appears that the rate of early returns from many squadrons that were flying Lancasters was much higher when they were not accompanied by the more vulnerable Halifaxes and Stirlings.

It may have been a busman's holiday, but at least it was a break from the continual pounding of Berlin when Stettin was attacked on 5th January 1944, with, once again, departure being just before midnight. Thirteen aircraft from Gransden Lodge were detailed for the raid – all except one set out (its undercarriage collapsed on takeoff) and all returned safely, though two landed at other bases on their return. In one case this was due to fuel shortage, but one diverted to West Raynham in Norfolk due to an unexplained crew illness:

> Sgt. Daoust complained of extreme sleepiness when 15 minutes beyond Target, lost consciousness soon after, given artificial respiration by three of crew without effect. On landing at West Raynham found to be dead.
>
> [AIR 28/317]

There were no further operations for a few days, allowing a little time for the crews to recover, but on 14th January 1944 No. 405 Squadron went into action once more, and probably to the crews' relief, this time the target was Brunswick, not Berlin. Despite that, it was an expensive operation both for Bomber Command, which lost 38 aircraft, and for the squadron, as three of the fourteen aircraft that set off did not return, the crews lost being those of Flight Lieutenant Cloutier, Flying Officer Drimmie and Pilot Officer Floren. In 1950 a stream feeding a lake south of the town of Revelstoke in Canada was named Drimmie Creek in honour of the pilot of one of these downed crews.

All the heavy bombers of Bomber Command were stood down from operations following this attack until 20th January 1944, when the offensive shifted back to Berlin. Eleven aircraft were dispatched from Gransden Lodge, and on this occasion all returned. From this date onwards, should the inhabitants of the station have desired warmth, tea and buns, they had a new place in which to find them: the new N.A.A.F.I. building, which was handed over by the builders to the R.A.F. that day.

The crews had no opportunity for rest, however, as they were called upon the next day, 21st January 1944, to attack Magdeburg. Of the fourteen who departed only thirteen returned, the missing crew being that commanded by Pilot Officer Wilson. This also marked the last operation for No. 405 Squadron under the leadership of the tough and long-serving Johnny Fauquier, as on 22nd January 1944 he was succeeded, as was doubtless the plan, by Reg Lane. Fauquier had been posted to a desk job at No. 6 Group headquarters, but, as we will learn later, this was not the end of his outstanding operational career.

The personnel of No. 405 Squadron only had a few days to settle down under their new commander as on 27th January 1944 the assault on Berlin continued. Reg Lane summed up the state of mind of the crews as the battle wore on like this:

> *"Every time the crews came into the ops. room the route would be up on the map, and they'd look at the map and they'd say 'God! Berlin - again!' The old usual chit-chat that would go on had died, it was just not there. It was like walking into the jaws of death another night, because the losses on the Berlin raids were very heavy."*

Despite this, the fourteen Lancasters detailed for the mission set off as briefed, and all returned safely. While the squadron was preparing for this raid, the R.A.F.'s Regional Postal Officer visited to inspect the station's post office - he presumably gave it his stamp of approval.

THE BATTLE OF BERLIN

On the next night, 28th January 1944, the campaign against the German capital ground on, as once more fourteen aircraft left to plough the familiar furrow to Berlin. All returned safely, some early due to icing, and once more the crews taking part believed that this had been the best attack on Berlin that had been mounted. Since there was complete cloud cover over the target and thus no photographic evidence of the results, this assertion could not be put to the test.

The preparations for, and tense wait for the return from, this raid had had some no doubt eager witnesses, since earlier that day a number of aircrew cadets had arrived on attachment to Gransden Lodge. It would be interesting to know their impressions of life at the sharp end of bomber operations, and how it influenced their thoughts on their future careers. Another new arrival at the airfield that day was Squadron Leader J. Browne, who took up his post as Station Medical Officer; more detail of the health of the station's personnel appears in the records from this point onwards.

Even though the tension and stresses were high during this sustained campaign against Berlin, there were still those on No. 405 Squadron who managed to lift the mood, as Reg Lane later related:

> "This boy Mac, and Bennett … during that difficult time when every night it was Berlin, Berlin, Berlin and the morale was down. God, I can remember one occasion when they both came into the Ops Room - I was already there, they were both Squadron Leaders. They took one look at the map and realised, they could tell, you could hear a pin drop in the room, and old Benny put on his glasses and picked up one of the coffee mugs and grabbed a handful of pencils and put it in. Mac got into the act, and he grabbed a ruler and used it as a cane and put on dark glasses and they both came down

the aisle sort of saying, making like blind men, 'Can anyone tell us where we as going tonight and how we are going to find it?' Well, of course, it just broke the tension immediately and everyone roared with laughter and that was it, it was just great."

The characters referred to in this tale, 'Mac' and Bennett, appear to have formed something of a comedy double-act on No. 405 Squadron.

Following a day's rest, No. 405 Squadron was again on the road to Berlin on 30th January 1944, when thirteen of its aircraft joined yet another raid. This time they were unlucky, as one crashed at Coltishall in Norfolk, and three others, those of Flight Lieutenants Shackleton and Roberts and Flight Sergeant Bonikowsky did not return, but as we have seen, the latter survived and was able to recount his wartime experiences.

This was the final operation for the squadron for January 1944, and as the Gransden Lodge O.R.B. records, Harris's plans were proving costly, since the month resulted in ten aircraft missing, one crashed, seventy one missing personnel, one dead and four injured. This ongoing attrition meant that No. 405 Squadron had a numerical strength of only 421 at the end of January 1944, compared with around 650 the previous August. The level of losses, while possibly not as high on No. 405 Squadron as on some Main Force squadrons, led to a hardening in attitude on the part of Reg Lane as squadron commander that is chilling:

"Our losses got to the point where when a crew came down from 6 Group I didn't even bother with their last names, I just tried to catch their first names, that was all, because there was no point in trying to remember the last names, because they probably wouldn't be there two or three days hence. It

was a habit I got into that I never did really shake ... it was just not worth the effort. If they stayed around then I got to know their last names, if they lasted. But it was a question of 'Welcome to the Squadron', and probably two nights later I was writing a letter to his mother..."

The first two weeks of February 1944 brought about a much-needed respite for the crews of Bomber Command, since the weather and the full moon kept most heavy bomber squadrons on the ground. The attacks against Germany were continued by the Mosquito force however, with raids by a small number of these light bombers every night, and a few specialist flights and mine laying operations were also carried out. One such specialist raid was mounted in February 1944 by No. 617 Squadron, using its new low-level marking technique, on the Gnome-Rhone aero engine factory at Limoges. This target was largely undefended and the raid was very successful, but another using the same method against the Anthéor viaduct was less effective. Don Bennett was sceptical as to the merit of low-level marking, and its use added to the friction between him and its advocates, so the squadrons of No. 5 Group remained the only ones to utilise it. This scepticism may have been justified, since although the low-level marking could yield extremely accurate results in good weather, in cloudy conditions its value was limited.

While these activities were going on elsewhere, training continued at Gransden Lodge. One of these exercises illustrated the difficulty, as had already been seen at Bourn, of keeping quickly-built airfields in operation and good repair. Due to ongoing work only one runway was available, and the strong cross-wind on this runway meant that the exercise had to be abandoned due to the problems this caused the participating aircraft on takeoff.

During this stand-down period No. 405 Squadron also had an unrivalled opportunity to employ spit and polish, since on 10th

TRIALS AND TRIBULATION

February 1944 King George VI and Queen Elizabeth visited the station to inspect No. 405 Squadron.

After this inspection, their Majesties took tea with the assembled dignitaries, who included Don Bennett and the Station Commander in their number. According to Reg Lane, this tea party did not take place in one of the messes, but in the cottage close to the airfield previously occupied by the Yugoslav royal family. By this time it had been appropriated as more salubrious living quarters by Lane and the Station Commander, Group Captain Gordon Dunlop. As it lay so close to the airfield entrance, it was obviously passed many times a day by personnel going to and from their work, and Lane recalled, possibly apocryphally, that King Peter had once complained to a previous Station Commander that the passing troops never saluted him, even though he was the King of Yugoslavia. The Station Commander's response, as reported by Lane, was:

"Salute you, Sir? Hell, they don't even salute me, and I'm the base commander! With that, the Group Captain saluted, turned around and left!"

It appears that an accelerated building program at the station was coming fruition at this point, as during February 1944 many buildings were completed by the contractors and taken over by the R.A.F. Some of these were strictly utilitarian, such as pyrotechnic and bomb stores, latrines, ablutions, ration and produce stores etc., but some would have added to the comfort of Gransden Lodge's inhabitants, and increased its resemblance to a small, self-contained town. These included a new accommodation site, an airmen's dining hall, a gymnasium, a squash court, and barber's, tailor's and shoemaker's shops. One more notable addition was that of the Number 2 hangar. Despite its number, this must surely have been the third and final hangar on the airfield, since the second (the Type B1) was clearly under construction in March 1943, and a note in one of the No. 8 Group summary of events reports for mid-1944 indicates that two T2 hangars were probably standing by that date as:

> ... certain experiments were carried out at Gransden Lodge with a view to improving the access tracks to T.2. Hangars so as to facilitate the handling of heavy bombers. As a result the tracks of one T.2. Hangar at Gransden Lodge are being modified for test purposes.
>
> [AIR 14/540]

The long-running saga of the station's drains also began a new chapter during the month:

> **February 1st 1944.** Sample of Sewage Effluent taken for routine test from W.A.A.F. Sewage Plant.
>
> **Result:-** Unsatisfactory. High nitrate content. Immediate action taken to have the plant better maintained, and to have a defective syphon remedied. Action also taken to accelerate enlargement of main sewage plant which was grossly overloaded.
>
> [AIR 28/319]

The business of war continued on 15th February 1944, and, unsurprisingly, the target was Berlin, with a diversionary raid on Frankfurt an der Oder. Thirteen Lancasters from No. 405 Squadron were detailed for the former, three for the latter. Though there was one more attack on Berlin to come, this raid effectively ended the campaign against the city, but the crews did not know this, as more attacks on the capital were briefed then scrubbed.

TRIALS AND TRIBULATION

The next raid that actually took place was against Leipzig on 19th February 1944. All the fourteen crews taking part returned safely, and, in a telling slip, even the clerk recording events in the Gransden Lodge O.R.B. had become so used to the recent targets that at one point this raid is referred to as 'ATTACK ON BERLIN'. He or she got it right with the next raid, which took place on the following night, 20th February 1944, against Stuttgart. Once again, there were no losses from the thirteen Gransden Lodge based aircraft taking part.

There are some annoying gaps in the records at about this time, but it seems that No. 2784 Squadron R.A.F.R. probably arrived at Gransden Lodge in late February or early March 1944. The unit was certainly in residence by late March 1944, and we can speculate that this new squadron took over the defence of the airfield from No. 2955 Squadron R.A.F.R., but it is difficult to work out exactly what was going on with respect to which unit was where, and when.

A new tactic was introduced for the operation on 24th February 1944 when the target, Schweinfurt, was to be attacked in two waves, two hours apart, in another attempt to minimise the losses caused by nightfighters. This city, home of the major German ball-bearing factories, had been the scene of very heavy losses in previous American daylight raids. Five Lancasters from No. 405 Squadron were in the first wave, nine in the second, and from their point of view the new tactic was not entirely successful, as two crews from the first wave, captained by Flying Officer Christison and Flying Officer Jackson, were lost. The tactic was tried again the next night, 25th February 1944, against Augsburg, and this time the eleven and three aircraft sent in each wave respectively returned to Gransden Lodge. No more operations took place in February 1944, and perhaps the crews had realised that the worst of the battle for Berlin was over, as the O.R.B.

noted at the end of the month that the squadron spirit seemed to be 'very much improved'.

On 1st March 1944 Stuttgart was attacked again, and all the fourteen aircraft dispatched returned. Next day, Bomber Command borrowed a naval term and ordered that all heavy bomber squadrons should 'make and mend'. This meant that domestic activities should be undertaken and that there would be no operations. Some flying must have taken place, though, since on 2nd March 1944 one of the civilian contractors working at the airfield was hit and killed by an aircraft as it was taking off.

Over the next few days operations against München and Königsberg were planned then scrubbed, and it was then back to 'stand down' or 'make and mend' for the crews – probably few complaints about this were heard. It was also recorded that:

```
The New Station Sick Quarters was taken over
this month providing a total of 35 beds. It was
found necessary to have all patients food cooked
in the Sick Quarters owing to the distance from
the nearest Mess (1 6/10 miles). The coal stoves
supplied for heating the wards and offices were
found to be dirty and inefficient, so application
was made for slow combustion stoves to replace
them. The amount of labour involved in laying
and stoking fires and carrying coal was found to
be excessive, one male Nursing Orderly being
wholly employed on this, in the absence of
establishment of an ACH/G.D.

Considerable progress made with enlarging the
main sewage disposal plant.

Considerable improvement in the general
sanitation and hygiene of the Station.
```

[AIR 28/319]

TRIALS AND TRIBULATION

Once again we hear the old complaint that everything at Gransden Lodge was too far away from everything else, but it is heartening that the drains get an honourable mention.

The break from operations came to an end on 15th March 1944. Stuttgart was on the receiving end of a raid again that night, and despite the use of an unusual route that went almost to the Swiss border, there were losses, and among these was the crew of Flight Lieutenant Fyfe, one of the sixteen from No. 405 Squadron that took part. The squadron had better luck on 18th March 1944, when the aircraft dispatched to Frankfurt, sixteen in all, returned to base without loss. The cycle of raids planned then scrubbed continued, including one against Berlin on 21st March 1944. One notable event that did take place on that date was the return of fighter aircraft to Gransden Lodge, on a more permanent footing this time, when No. 1696 Flight arrived from Bourn.

This flight, whose full title was No. 1696 Bomber Defence (Training) Flight, was one of the many set up to provide the 'fighter' element in the 'fighter affiliation' exercises frequently undertaken by the bomber crews. The decision to form this and other Bomber (Defence) Training Flights had been taken in February 1944, using aircraft from the (Bomber) Gunnery Flights that were to be disbanded at the same time. No. 1696 Flight, to be available for use by No. 8 Group squadrons, was formed at Bourn, and at the time of its formation it was operating Spitfires, Hawker Hurricanes and Miles Martinet target towing aircraft, some of which were to be based at Ipswich.

There was one more raid to come for No. 405 Squadron before the next, and as it would turn out, final, heavy bomber attack against Berlin, and that took place on 22nd March 1944. The target was Frankfurt, and all of the fourteen Lancasters from Gransden Lodge returned home safely.

And so, the night of 24th/25th March 1944 saw one last raid by heavy bombers on Berlin, and within Bomber Command this became known as the 'night of the strong winds'.

The epithet was completely justified. Fifteen crews from No. 405 Squadron took part in the raid that night, with Reg Lane assuming the role of Master Bomber, and he recalled that, quite apart from the intrinsic dangers of attacks on Berlin, on this occasion a failure in operational systems contributed to Bomber Command's losses:

> "This was one of those nights when we ran into incredible winds ... there was a refinement of the Pathfinder technique where the lead Pathfinder airplanes would calculate the winds and would then transmit those winds back by W.T. to Bomber Command, and then Bomber Command would then issue a general broadcast to all the bombers of the wind that they should use at that given period of time, in other words on a certain part of the route.... The code that was used for wind speed only went up to 99 and there was no way of giving a wind speed of over 100, and on this particular night my navigator said 'I don't believe it', he said, 'I just don't believe it, but I'm picking up a wind of 115' - well of course, we were in the jetstream ... and he said 'But what is worse is it's about 90 degrees out from what was given to us at briefing' - and of course this is going to play havoc, so he said to the wireless operator 'Get this back' ... but the wireless operator said 'There's no way, I can't get that back, I can only go to 99', so he banged out 99. And nobody at Group, at Command rather, believed it, but they pushed it out, and of course the bomber crews didn't believe it, that there was this enormous change.... airplanes were all over the bloody place, they had been scattered by this strong wind, not forecast....

TRIALS AND TRIBULATION

I was there for about half an hour, I suppose, over Berlin, and we didn't have any trouble, then we started to go back, and by golly, as we went back, I called my navigator up. I said 'You don't need to navigate, just come up here', because, of course, by that time most of the bomber force was ahead of me, and I said 'We can map read our way home', and literally every defended area in Germany from Berlin west was alive. Searchlights, flak ... many of the bomber crews were shot down over the Ruhr, because they had drifted south in this wind, and they were all flying right over the most heavily defended area of Germany. So we did, he came up and he stood up beside me and we literally map read our way home.... I just flew in between the defended areas; I knew exactly where we were the whole damn time, with people being coned and being shot down. So it was a disaster, that particular raid ... if we had been able to go out and say the wind was 115 that would have been believed, but 99..."

Martin Middlebrook records that Reg Lane, as well as transmitting weather reports, also gave of his best in his role as Master Bomber by excitedly broadcasting general observations on the progress of the raid, since direction of the bombing was obviously impossible. Some of these distinctly Canadian remarks were apparently of a nature that renders them unprintable.

This raid marked the end of the Battle of Berlin for Bomber Command. Was that battle won or lost? Reg Lane, who was, as we have seen, often there in the thick of the action as Master Bomber, had no doubts:

"It was the one battle, historically, which the C. in C. Bomber Command, 'Bomber' Harris, did <u>not</u> win - as a *matter of fact, he lost the Battle of Berlin badly, if you use the casualties on each of those raids as a measure of success or failure."*

Whatever else is true, it is certain that Arthur Harris's confident forecast made before the battle had been proved wrong. It had undoubtedly cost the R.A.F. the predicted 400 or 500 aircraft, but just as clearly it had not cost Germany the war.

Later analysis of the campaign drew out many reasons for this failure, not least amongst them being the weather, which hampered both the bombing and the photo-reconnaissance that would have shown just how ineffective were the attacks. As the battle continued, the German defenses also became more deadly, in no small part due to the fact that the raiders often followed the same routes to the target. When the bombers did get through, they did not cause the devastation seen in the raids on Hamburg, which had so worried the Nazi High Command, as Berlin was of more modern construction and more sparsely populated.

Overall, 492 R.A.F. aircraft were lost in the Battle of Berlin, and over the whole duration of the campaign industrial production in the German capital actually increased, and the operation of the government was not materially disrupted. Harris was forced to concede that his long-held dream of winning the war through the use of air power was not to come true, and anyway, before long, Bomber Command would have another role to fulfil. It would soon be asked to provide support to the ground forces that were about to invade Europe.

INVASION

The invasion of the Continent, and the implied victory over the Axis forces that it would bring, had not yet taken place, but the sense that it was coming soon was growing. The preparations for this invasion were visible even as far away from the south coast of England as the region around Gransden Lodge. Vic Hutchinson, a lifelong resident of the Potton area (some 8 miles/12 km from Gransden Lodge), recalled the verges of the lanes in the district being stacked with munitions and supplies, ready to be brought forward once the invasion started.

The planning for the invasion, Operation OVERLORD, had begun in the spring of 1943 and, as is now well known, was to take place on the Normandy beaches. To give the operation the best chance of success, it was essential that the Axis forces were deceived over the timing and location of OVERLORD – Operation STARKEY, unsuccessful though it was, had been part of that strategy. Apart from aerial operations during the invasion itself, the Allied air forces had a vital role to play both in the deception plan and in the weakening of the defences and transport infrastructure that would be used by the German military to bring supplies and troops to the front. However, in late March 1944 the invasion was still some months away, and attacks on targets in Germany, part of Harris's strategic plan to bomb the enemy into submission, were still the order of the day.

INVASION

It was not unusual for aircraft from other units to land at Gransden Lodge due to bad weather or lack of fuel (or perhaps just because they were lost!), just as those from Gransden Lodge were occasionally diverted elsewhere. These visitors were generally aircraft from other Bomber Command squadrons, but sometimes they were more exotic, such as on the occasion around this time when three American Martin Marauders arrived from their base at Great Dunmow in Essex, their presence on the airfield harking back to the days some two years earlier when their aircraft were being tested by the B.D.U. for use by the R.A.F.

On 26th March 1944 No. 405 Squadron returned to battle by sending eight aircraft on that night's raid on Essen, and the losses on this raid were extremely light, around 1.3% of the aircraft dispatched, which may well have been because the German defence system was caught napping by the sudden switch of operations away from Berlin.

Some high-ranking officers were at Gransden Lodge on 30th March 1944, when Air Vice-Marshal C.M. McEwan M.C., D.F.C. came to visit. A.V.M. McEwen, known as 'Black Mike' McEwen, was a Canadian First World War fighter ace with 27 victories to his credit, who had been appointed Air Officer Commanding No. 6 Group a month before. While at Gransden Lodge he would have seen No. 405 Squadron's preparations for that night's attack on Nürnberg.

This was the full moon period, so operations would not normally have taken place, but early weather forecasts had predicted that cloud cover would protect the bomber stream but still allow the target to be visible. A later meteorological report indicated that these benign conditions were actually unlikely to occur, but the raid was allowed to go ahead anyway.

Compounding the crews' problems was the route used. Normally the route to the target would include many dog-legs and feints to make it difficult for the German defenders to anticipate the target and position their nightfighters accordingly. On this occasion, however, the route given to the crews included a 250 mile (400 km) straight run towards the target (Don Bennett claimed that he was overruled on its choice). This, coupled with the moonlight, badly forecast winds and the accurate disposition of the German nightfighter force, meant that the raid was a disaster. All the fourteen aircraft sent from No. 405 Squadron made it back to base, but 95 of the 795 bombers taking part were lost, and with a loss rate of 11.9% this was the most expensive raid undertaken by Bomber Command during the war. It is reported that 545 Allied aircrew lost their life in that single raid – around that same number as were killed in the whole of the Battle of Britain.

It would be well into April 1944 before No. 405 Squadron was called upon again, but during that period works were under way to improve flying facilities and keep the airfield operational, and at the end of March 1944 it was noted that:

> Large windows were installed in the front of the Control Room also the Perimeter Track was serviceable throughout after being under repair for many months.
>
> [AIR 28/317]

After the full moon, Bomber Command went back to work, and 9th April 1944 saw No. 405 Squadron's first participation in the raids of the Transportation Plan, which was designed to disrupt communications in advance of the invasion. Unsurprisingly, given his views on the value of strategic, as opposed to tactical, bombing, Harris was not in favour of the use of his forces in this way. In fact, he is reported to have said that, in his view, the only way in which Bomber Command could support the invasion would be to continue with his policy of attacking the industrial centres of Germany.

INVASION

Flying control, viewed through a window from the external balcony
(Bill Brown)

Harris was overruled, the raids on the French railway network went ahead, and so it was that on 9th April 1944 No. 405 Squadron attacked the rail marshalling yards at Lille. Only seven aircraft were required, and marshalling yards were the target again the next night, when seven Lancasters once more set out from Gransden Lodge for France, to Laon this time.

The raid on 11th April 1944 was on Germany again, and was originally planned to attack Osnabrück, but the target was later switched to Aachen. No. 405 Squadron was tasked to supply eleven crews, but there was a warning in the orders that they received:

TRIALS AND TRIBULATION

```
Target is now AACHEN - 11 Supporters required.
These must be genuine Supporters and not marker
crews on an easy outing.
```
                                                   [AIR 28/317]

Perhaps some skulduggery had been going on in the past, but in the event only ten suitable crews could be rounded up to be sent. On that day the vehicles belonging to No. 1696 Flight also arrived from Wyton. This arrival coincided with a note being sent to Bomber Command requesting that the number of Spitfires and Hurricanes on strength with the flight be brought up to the agreed levels, so obviously things there were still in a state of flux.

Several days of 'make and mend' and planned, then cancelled, operations against French targets followed, but finally on 18th April 1944 the operations were not scrubbed. Bomber Command was now, with increasing frequency, laying on raids against several targets on the same day, and on this occasion two of the raids were to be against the rail marshalling yards at Tergnier and Noisy Le Sec - No. 405 Squadron was called upon to supply eight aircraft for each raid. The battering of the rail network in France continued on 20th April 1944 when the squadron's target was the marshalling yards at Lens, which it successfully attacked with fourteen Lancasters.

22nd April 1944 saw No. 405 Squadron participate in two more raids, but this time one target was in France, Laon again, and the other was Düsseldorf in Germany. Seven aircraft left on each attack, but the crew of Flight Sergeant Saltzberry failed to return from Laon, the first loss for the squadron for a number of weeks. Operations switched back to Germany again on 24th April 1944, when the fourteen aircraft detailed for the attack raided Karlsruhe. Only eleven actually bombed the primary target as one returned early with equipment problems and two (aircraft 'H' and 'J') unintentionally bombed alternative targets, Heidelberg and

INVASION

Speyer, both well to the north of the planned aiming point. In the light of what we will soon discover was going on behind the scenes, it is informative to note that:

> Both 'H' and 'J' bombed on H.2.S. and thought they were on the primary.
>
> [AIR 27/1789]

It would have been a busy day for the operations staff at Gransden Lodge on 25th April 1944, as there were several potential targets for attack that day, but in the end the raids were cancelled. As part of the call from Bomber Command to No. 405 Squadron for crews, the order had been made that:

> All Backers Up to be on H.2.X. aircraft
>
> [AIR 28/317]

Strictly speaking, *H2X* was an American development of *H2S* that worked at the shorter wavelength of 3 cm (compared to the 10 cm of *H2S*), but this may also just have been shorthand for the 3 cm wavelength version of *H2S*, the Mk. III. Use of a shorter wavelength allowed a higher resolution picture of the ground beneath the aircraft to be produced - and thereby hangs a tale.

At about this time the scientists at T.R.E. were locked in a dispute with Bomber Command. On one side was Bomber Command, which was blaming deficiencies in *H2S* for its lack of success in the bombing campaign against Germany, and on the other side was T.R.E., which was convinced that the P.F.F. was not using the new 3 cm sets correctly. In an effort to obtain hard facts, Flight Lieutenant Len Killip, who was viewed as the most experienced *H2S* operator in the R.A.F and had been one of the founder members of the B.D.U., made a visit to No. 8 Group to investigate.

TRIALS AND TRIBULATION

His findings were damning. He discovered that the precious 3 cm sets were being used just like the standard *H2S* sets, and not being given any special consideration in terms of their use or the selection and training of specialist crews to use them. In fact, he thought No. 8 Group's internal organisation with respect to the 3 cm *H2S* appeared to be near chaos. This report by T.R.E. on No. 8 Group's misuse, in their view, of the 3 cm *H2S* eventually led to several of the P.F.F. squadrons, including Gransden Lodge's neighbours No. 97 Squadron at Bourn, being transferred to No. 5 Group to become part of that group's independent marking force. This reassignment, which had happened the previous week, undoubtedly did little to improve the already tense relations between No. 8 and No. 5 Groups. Perhaps the exhortation for all possible use to be made of *H2X* in the raid on the 25th was not unconnected. The positive outcome of these disagreements was that No. 8 Group reorganised its *H2S* training in order to achieve better results.

After the fruitless planning of the day before, on 26th April 1944 the operations actually came to pass, when two raids were sent against Essen (including eight Lancasters from No. 405 Squadron) and Villeneuve St. George (six crews from Gransden Lodge). Two targets were set again on 27th April 1944: Friedrichshafen, and Montzen in Belgium. No. 405 Squadron sent six aircraft to the former and eight to the latter, including Reg Lane as Master Bomber and Squadron Leader 'Teddy' Blenkinsop as his Deputy. No aircraft were lost on the Friedrichshafen raid, but this was not the case for those detailed for Montzen. Lane had directed the attack and sent all the aircraft home, including his Deputy:

"… and then it started. God, I could see ahead an aircraft, you could see the tracers, and then 'boom', an aircraft shot

down, and I didn't think too much about it .... And then another airplane was shot down, and then another airplane was shot down, and by this I thought 'My God, the fighters are into the stream', so I began to lose altitude .... I watched ten airplanes shot down ahead of me, and the tenth one blew up and out of it came the markers, and of course they were the Deputy Master Bomber's markers ... he was a hell of a good lad and I was basically bringing him along to take over the squadron..."

It later came to light that Blenkinsop had managed to escape from his aircraft and, after landing safely, did not try to get back to England but instead joined the French Resistance as he believed he could do more good there. He was later seen in a jail in Brussels, having been caught trying to blow up a house occupied by German forces, and was subsequently discovered in Hamburg as a slave worker. Here he escaped, but he was later recaptured and ended his days in the Neuengamme concentration camp. A 'hell of a good lad' indeed, and his sacrifice has not gone unnoticed in Canada, where a road in his native Victoria and an islet on the British Columbia coast have been named in his honour.

Sometime in or around April 1944, a rare bird had arrived on the Gransden Lodge runways – a Lancaster Mk. VI. We have seen that the Lancaster Mk. X had been produced in Canada for service in the R.A.F., but this was not the only development of the bomber that was in the pipeline. The majority of the Lancasters in service were the Mk. I and Mk. III variants, plus a smaller number of the Mk. II, which were quite different in that they used the Bristol Hercules radial engine instead of the Merlin. In mid-1943 Avro had embarked on a major redesign of the Lancaster, resulting in the Mk. IV and Mk. V, which had larger wings and fuselage and more powerful engines. These two marks were sufficiently altered that they were, in fact, no longer considered to be Lancasters. The designs became the Lincoln B1 and B2, but they did not see service until after the war. The Lancaster Mk. VI, of which there were only nine built, was a conversion of the Mk. III with more powerful Merlin engines and four-bladed propellers, both of which were fitted in an attempt to increase the aircraft's performance. Five of these were allocated to various squadrons for service testing and operational use, two of them to No. 405 Squadron between April and June 1944. Because of their superior speed and altitude performance, they were often flown by the pilot designated as the Master Bomber for a raid.

As well as the operations and other comings and goings on the station, the building program at Gransden Lodge was also still in full swing. During April 1944 more new buildings were taken on charge and occupied as the new W.A.A.F. officers' quarters were opened, the Servicing Wing moved into their new offices and the new transport offices were completed – and the sewage farm enlargements were finished. The go-ahead was received about now for another amenity to be added, when:

> 60. Authority was also obtained for a projector room to be built on to the new Airmens Mess at Gransden. All dispersed Stations will now, therefore, have properly equipped Station Cinemas. A longfelt need.
>
> [AIR 14/540]

On medical matters, the continual concern of the authorities over the prevalence of venereal disease apparently did not only apply to the station's male inhabitants, since during the month it was also recorded that:

INVASION

> Lecture given to all W.A.A.F. personnel on
> Hygiene and Venereal Diseases, by S/Ldr. Dovey,
> woman Medical Officer.
>
> [AIR 28/319]

A further note shows that the stresses of wartime were also experienced by those serving on the ground, though obviously to a lesser extent than by aircrew:

> Mess Personnel suffering a higher incidence of
> minor illnesses than remainder of personnel,
> probably due to long hours of work and shortage
> of staff.
>
> [AIR 28/319]

A possible explanation for this might have been found in a:

> Sample of water taken from Airmens Cookhouse for
> routine analysis. Result unsatisfactory – high
> bacterial count although no coliform organisms.
>
> [AIR 28/319]

The first raid of May 1944 for No. 405 Squadron came on the 3rd of the month, the target for its fourteen aircraft being the airfield at Montdidier in France. The squadron had originally been stood down, but at 11:15 this was countermanded and the attack was on. On occasions such as this the crews often had to be recalled to the airfield having been given the day off, which could lead to unforeseen consequences, as Reg Lane remembered:

> *"Being the squadron commander I had to sort of watch my Ps and Qs, but a lot of the aircrew didn't! We used to have an arrangement whereby if we had been stood down from*

operations, and we knew there was nothing on that night, we would, we would say, 'OK fellas, it's a stand down, bog off, do what you want.' Well, a lot of the lads would hop on bicycles or they would take a flight van if they were a flight commander, or the flight commander let them have the van, and they would all hop and go pub crawling or something like that. Well, it was not unusual for, although there had been a stand down for night operations, all of a sudden there would have been a change of heart at Bomber Command and there was a daylight raid the next morning and it was an early takeoff, so we had to get the crews back. So what we used to do was we would take one of the flight vans, and we had sort of a coded signal, this thing would run around the countryside, all around the area, just honking the horn, it was a certain letter in Morse code which meant 'recall'. We had one of our pilots, he was a hell of a big chap, and on one of these 'recalls' he was on top of a haystack with one of these W.A.A.F.s from the base and he was so excited when he heard this damn code – he knew what is was and he wanted to catch the van before it got by because he wanted to get on it and get back to base – and he pushed this gal off the top of this haystack! This poor girl broke her ankle when she hit the ground, so here was poor Mac worrying about getting back to base because he knew it was an op. recall, and worrying about this poor gal, who he'd just broken her ankle! That was the kind of thing that happened!"

Though the French targets were less heavily defended than some of those in Germany to which the crews were accustomed, there were still nightfighters to deal with, as Flight Lieutenant MacDonald and his crew found to their cost during this raid on Montdidier. Another crew, captained by Pilot Officer Borrowes, was lost in the next attack on 6th May 1944, when the squadron sent eleven Lancasters against the marshalling yards at Mantes-Gassicourt near Paris. On that raid, a crew noted that:

```
Only one "scarecrow" was seen near the target
and no searchlights.
```

[AIR 28/317]

These 'scarecrows' or 'scarecrow shells' were widely believed by bomber crews to be munitions especially designed to look like an exploding aircraft when they detonated. These were supposed to have been used by the Germans with the aim of lowering the morale of crews, by tricking them into believing that more aircraft were being lost than was actually the case. There has been debate on the subject since, but it is now thought that there was no such thing as the scarecrow shell, and that the reported sightings really were bombers blowing up, either due to *Schräge Musik* attacks or the aircraft's own bombs exploding prematurely. Given the number of real losses, such a weapon would probably have been ineffective anyway.

Bomber Command kept up the pressure on communications in France by mounting attacks on five targets on 8th May 1944, in addition to the customary nuisance and electronic warfare sorties it carried out almost daily. One of these raids, on which No. 405 Squadron sent fourteen aircraft once again, was on the rail yards at Haine St. Pierre. The squadron's bombs were accurate, but the crews reported 'considerable fighter activity over the target and homeward to the enemy coast'. The defences claimed two aircraft, those of Flight Lieutenant Chase and Pilot Officer Darlow, but the latter officer will, however, appear in our story again.

It was the turn of a Belgian city to come under attack from No. 405 Squadron on 10th May 1944, when it took part in the raid on Ghent, one of several on railway targets. The squadron

TRIALS AND TRIBULATION

provided the Master Bomber (not Reg Lane this time, but Squadron Leader Bennett), his Deputy and twelve other crews. Also on that day, back at base:

> The old N.A.A.F.I. block on No. 1 Communal Site was brought into use as a store and offices for "effects" work.
>
> [AIR 28/317]

This is a reminder of the grisly business, alluded to in the recollections of Sergeant 'Pee Wee' Phillips, that had to be carried out when crews did not return, and their personal effects had to be gathered, checked and sent on to their grieving families.

On 11th May 1944 Don Bennett visited Gransden Lodge to take part in the briefing for that night's operation, which was to be a short trip to France and the marshalling yards at Boulogne Sur Mer, and for which No. 405 Squadron was tasked to supply fourteen crews, including the Master Bomber and his Deputy.

Even given the pressure of operations, leave was still to be had, and the infamous 'Mac' had a reputation for riotous behaviour when on leave that went before him, so much so that others on the squadron would wait in eager anticipation for him and his crew to return from a break in London, all agog to find out what scrapes they had got themselves into this time. London was not the only place in which he could manage to get himself into trouble, as his squadron commander recalled:

> *"It was at this time, just before D-Day, there was an arrangement where aircrew could go to sea on a destroyer in lieu of going on leave; they could go to sea for a few days and spend time with the Navy and see how the Navy operated. There weren't many openings, but they were dished up, and Mac decided he was so whipped from the leave that he had been on that he just couldn't*

take another leave in London and that he needed a rest cure and he would go on the ship. So he went up somewhere up in Norfolk and boarded this destroyer, and they'd just got out to sea, they hadn't got out very far, oh, something like twelve hours, when word went out on the net that all aircrew were to be returned immediately, so the destroyer turned around and came back. By this time Mac, with that great personality of his, he was a member of the crew. So they decided that as soon as they'd tied up – I think they'd got in something like in the early afternoon and there were a number of trains that he could catch down to London to get back to base – well, they decided they'd have a party for him before he left. So they started, and they started pouring rum into him, using the old business of a new team every half hour coming and moving in. Well, of course, this went on and on and on and on, until Mac realised that if he was going to get to London and get back to the base, he was going to miss his last train – of course, by this time it was dark. So one of the officers who was to be the one who was to get him to the train, get him off the ship and to the train, they both got up on deck and of course everyone on the ship by this time was pretty well boiled, and this chap, who was a young Lieutenant, said to Mac 'The gangplank is over here, Sir', and of course with that immediately stepped off the side of the ship into the water, and left Mac dangling, trying to get his balance without falling into the drink. Well, Mac got on the train all right, got to London, but of course he'd missed the last train out of London to get back up to the base, and he decided that he'd go down to Covent Garden, which was about the only place where there'd be a pub open very early in the morning, so he went there and stayed there until he could catch a train. Got back to Gransden just about the time the bar was opening at lunchtime, and we were in the bar, having a beer just before lunch, and this apparition appeared in the doorway, looking like death warmed up. And he did, he literally stood in the door and then just fell flat on his face in the bar, and we had to carry him up and put him to bed. He was a wreck! And when he recovered later, he said, 'God', he said, 'that Navy! I thought I was going away for a rest from the usual type of leave we have in London! I think London is safer, and from here on in I'm going to go to London!"

Following the operation against Boulogne, there was no further trade for No. 405 Squadron until 19th May 1944, when two targets were designated. These were the marshalling yards at Le Mans, which received the attentions of six of the squadron's Lancasters, and a 'special target' for ten more, the radar jamming station at Mont Couple near Calais. According to R.V. Jones, the jammer at Mont Couple, about which he had known for some years, was one of several that could, it was feared, jam the *Gee* signals to be used for navigation during the forthcoming invasion, so putting it out of action was obviously vital. Unfortunately, this raid did not achieve it, since the marking seems to have gone awry and none of the seven crews from No. 405 Squadron who actually dropped their bombs saw any markers – the remaining three crews did not bomb at all.

Over the next few days operations were divided between targets in France and Germany, with five aircraft from No. 405 Squadron raiding Duisburg on 21st May 1944, and seven attacking Dortmund and nine Le Mans on 22nd May 1944. This was the start of a busy time for Bomber Command, as the invasion, although obviously this was not generally known, was only a matter of a few weeks away. No. 405 Squadron took a full part in this build-up, sending seven Lancasters against Aachen on 24th May 1944, but this raid saw the end of the road for one crew, as Squadron Leader Bennett and his crew-mates did not return.

In spite of the losses the attacks rolled on, and on 27th May

INVASION

1944 the target for No. 405 Squadron's fifteen crews was the airfield at Rennes (St. Jacques), which was dangerously close to the invasion beaches. Next day it was the turn of a coastal gun battery at Mardick to be raided, Gransden Lodge supplying fourteen aircraft.

While all this airborne activity was going on, more domestic matters were not being overlooked on the ground. Slightly bizarrely:

> Mrs. L.M. Henderson gave the first of a series of lectures on Mothercraft.
>
> [AIR 28/317]

It is hard to believe that the hard-bitten bomber crews would have shown much interest in this, so we must presume that the station's W.A.A.F. contingent was the intended audience. At about this time French and German classes were also started, and were likely to have attracted a larger attendance.

Another attempt was made to knock out the jammer at Mont Couple on 31st May 1944, and No. 405 Squadron supplied the Master Bomber and Deputy, along with eight more crews. This time the markers straddled target within a few hundred metres, and by ordering the crews to bomb between them, the raid was successful. At the same time the squadron also put up another five aircraft for an attack on the rail marshalling yards at Trappes.

With only a few days to go until the invasion, there was no operation on the board for No. 405 Squadron, but as June 1944 began the fuel supply for the airfield was improved when:

> The Equipment section took over the newly completed 48,000 Gallon Petrol Installation from the Contractor.
>
> [AIR 28/317]

When one considers that with full tanks a Lancaster could carry 2,154 gallons of fuel, 48,000 gallons would be enough to fill only

TRIALS AND TRIBULATION

about 22 aircraft to the brim - around the number of bombers that No. 405 Squadron had on strength at this time (the airfield would eventually have two such bulk petrol installations). Having that much petrol close at hand must have been a sore temptation to those unable to get rationed fuel for their car or motorcycle.

Trappes was once again the destination on 2nd June 1944 for six crews from No. 405 Squadron, but the aircraft of Squadron Leader Coldrey did not return. Today, there is a monument to the lost crew near to the spot where their aircraft crashed. 4th June 1944 saw three of No. 405 Squadron's aircraft in action, taking part in an attack on a coastal gun battery at Calais, and a

A W.A.A.F. driver and her lorry in the M.T. yard (Pathfinder Collection)

INVASION

similar target at Longues, almost overlooking the invasion beaches, was attacked by sixteen the next day, the day before the invasion.

And so the long-awaited day came when the Allied forces returned to continental Europe, when on 6th June 1944 the invasion of the Normandy beaches began, and with it Bomber Command's Battle of Normandy. Amazingly, the invasion itself is not mentioned in either the Gransden Lodge or the No. 405 Squadron O.R.B., but the squadron's operations now switched to supporting the ground troops. On D-Day itself No. 405 Squadron's participation was limited to the provision of the Master Bomber and Deputy for a raid on Condé-sur-Noireau, well to the south of the invasion beaches, a location described as a 'choke point' - one assumes that the aim was to hinder supplies being brought forward to the front.

Next day, 7th June 1944, saw a more concerted contribution, when No. 405 Squadron took part in two attacks, the first by three aircraft against the railway junction at Achères, just north of Paris, and the second by twelve (a thirteenth cancelled due to instrument failure) against a target much closer to the front, in the Forêt de Cerisy between Saint-Lô and Bayeux. Following a day's rest, on 9th June 1944 eight Lancasters from Gransden Lodge were dispatched to attack the airfield at Rennes once more, the ninth getting bogged down on takeoff and not making it aloft.

There was a change in command at No. 1696 Flight on 10th June 1944, when Squadron Leader A. Lynch D.F.C. and Bar took over after service on No. 97 Squadron. His predecessor, Squadron Leader T.E. Dodwell D.F.C. and Bar, left to join a Mosquito squadron, No. 571 at Oakington.

That day also saw a return to railway targets for No. 405 Squadron, not marshalling yards this time but the locomotive depot at Versailles/Matelot on the outskirts of Paris. One of the seven crews dispatched, Flight Lieutenant Stronach's, did not make it home. Next day, 11th June 1944, the target was the railway junction at Tours, and again there was a loss for No. 405 Squadron, as Pilot Officer Melcombe and his crew failed to return from the thirteen that set off.

The night of 12th June 1944 saw the start of a new campaign by Bomber Command against the Axis oil industry, when the synthetic oil plant at Gelsenkirchen was attacked, but No. 405 Squadron did not take part as it was still heavily involved in support of the ground troops. On this night its aiming point was at a railway junction east of Amiens and all the eight crews marking the target returned safely. Following a day's stand down, they were back in action on 14th June 1944, again against a railway junction, this time at Cambrai, and once more eight aircraft took part.

No. 405 Squadron was requested to provide sixteen crews for bombing on 15th June 1944 – not marking or controlling the raid this time – as part of another attack on the Lens marshalling yards. The weather was not suitable for high level bombing, the cloudbase being only 7,000 feet, and of the crews from Gransden Lodge that participated, two, captained by Flying Officer Keenan and Flight Sergeant Stewart, did not make it back home.

The raid against Peenemünde on 17th August 1943 had been an attempt to prevent the German forces developing the V-2 rocket, and it had succeeded in slowing that program down, but another weapon, the V-1 flying bomb, popularly known as the 'doodlebug' or 'buzz bomb' because of the sound made by its pulse-jet engine, was also being prepared to strike against Britain. Operations to bomb the launching sites for these pilotless aircraft, christened 'ski sites' due to their distinctive shape, had begun in December 1943, but in spite of this on 13th June 1944 the first V-1 attack was launched against London, and the bombardment began in earnest a few days later. British military intelligence had long expected this development and had identified the V-weapon construction works and storage sites as targets for Bomber Command, and these joined the list for attack along with those in the oil campaign and tactical targets to support the invading troops.

Given this new turn of events, on 16th June 1944 No. 405 Squadron set out on two raids. One was against the synthetic oil plant known as Sterkrade (Holten) at Oberhausen (three aircraft) and one against the V-weapon construction works at Renescure near St. Omer (eleven aircraft). There were no losses, though one Lancaster landed at Manston in Kent with engine and instrument failure. Another construction works, at Oisement/Neuville-au-Bois west of Amiens, was attacked on 17th June 1944, and the raid (to which No. 405 Squadron contributed seven crews, including the Master Bomber and Deputy) was deemed accurate, even though the target was completely covered in cloud. However, this may not have been the case, as this target was attacked again on 21st June 1944, the Master Bomber and Deputy being supplied from Gransden Lodge, but the cloud cover was once more extensive and these two were the only aircraft to bomb, and they ordered the Main Force to abort. The raid took place in daylight this time, Bomber Command having restarted daylight raids some days previously for the first since May 1943, and quite probably in expectation of this, on the day before the order had gone out for the squadron's aircraft to be painted with 'special white recognition markings'. These would probably have been the black and white 'invasion stripes' applied to Allied aircraft operating in daylight over the continent.

No. 405 Squadron went back to night bombing on 23rd June 1944, the construction works at Coubronne being raided by seven of its crews. That day also saw another piece of the infrastructure needed to make Gransden Lodge a fully operational station put into place when the new machine gun and cannon firing range was taken over from the airfield's Clerk of the Works.

There were two raids on 24th June 1944 in which No. 405 Squadron took part, both again on construction works. The first was in daylight, directed by the two crews supplied by the squadron, against Bonnetot on the Cherbourg peninsular, and the second was a night attack on the works at Middel Straete by fourteen crews, all of which bar two appear to have bombed very accurately. A similar combination of raids was scheduled on 27th June 1944, but both at night this time, when thirteen crews took part as bombers on a return visit to Oisement/Neuville-au-Bois and two acted as markers in a raid on the works at Wizernes. The latter target was a huge underground construction facility for V-2 rockets that had been reinforced early in 1944 with a concrete dome over 70 metres in diameter and 5 metres thick, and the munitions commonly used by Bomber Command barely scratched the surface of such a fortress. This works is now a museum, known as La Coupole.

In a change from the continuing raids against the V-weapon sites, on 28th June 1944 No. 405 Squadron was switched back to attacks on the French rail network, when it put up fourteen crews to mark the night operation against the marshalling yards at Metz. It cost the squadron one aircraft, as the crew of Pilot Officer Smitton failed to return. On the last night of June 1944, a busy month for operations, No. 405 Squadron sent ten aircraft on a successful dusk raid against a road junction at Villers Bocage, south-west of Caen, in order to prevent German tanks passing through for a planned attack against British and American forces. Given the intense pace of operations, it is perhaps unsurprising that a gentle rap over the knuckles was delivered by No. 8 Group, which noted around this time that No. 405 Squadron's (along

INVASION

with No. 7 Squadron's) level of errors when carrying out visual bombing was much higher than for any other P.F.F. unit. The report did go so far as to allow that the squadrons 'do not lack keenness', but included the reprimand that they were not being thorough enough in their practice bombing.

Quite apart from the damage that aircraft from Gransden Lodge were wreaking on their targets, the facilities at the airfield itself were in danger of causing upset, literally and figuratively, to the locals. The medical report for the station at the end of June 1944 tells us that:

> The central percolating filter in the Main Camp Sewage Farm has been brought into service without adequate rest. The resultant effluent contains quantities of organic matter and constitutes a potential source of danger to the villages of Great and Little Gransden. Action has been taken to rest this filter for a further three months.
>
> [AIR 28/319]

From the summary in the Gransden Lodge O.R.B. for the same date we also find that another unit was based at the airfield at this time, No. 9405 Servicing Echelon, six members of which were mentioned in dispatches on the 19th of the month. This unit would have been attached to No. 405 Squadron to carry out the maintenance of its aircraft.

The second half of 1944 brought no let-up in the relentless attacks against the V-weapon sites, oil targets and the occasional foray into Germany. In fact, as the following table shows, July 1944 was a frantic month for No. 405 Squadron, with up to three targets being attacked on the same day, and hardly any days when it was not required for operations:

TRIALS AND TRIBULATION

Date	Target	Crews
1st July 1944	Oisement/Neuville-au-Bois	2
2nd July 1944	Oisement/Neuville-au-Bois	16
4th July 1944	Biennais	2
5th July 1944	Watten	2
	Wizernes	10
6th July 1944	Croixdalle	2
	Coquereaux	8
7th July 1944	Caen	16
9th July 1944	Mont Candon	2
	L'Hey	7
10th July 1944	Nucourt	12
12th July 1944	Vaires	12
	Bremont	2
	Acquet	2
15th July 1944	Anderbelck	2
	Nucourt	10
18th July 1944	Caen	5
	Cagny	11
	Acquet	2
19th July 1944	Rollez	8
20th July 1944	Bottrop	4
	Courtrai	4
22nd July 1944	Acquet	8
23rd July 1944	Kiel	16
24th July 1944	L'Hey	2
	Stuttgart	14
25th July 1944	Stuttgart	9
	Forêt du Croc	2
27th July 1944	Les Hauts Boissions	6
28th July 1944	Hamburg	7
	Stuttgart	9
30th July 1944	Battle area aiming point 'C'	2
	Battle area aiming point 'E'	10

INVASION

That is the bald summary, but let us now put some meat on the bones. Firstly, the losses. Two aircraft were lost from these missions – Flight Lieutenant Virtue and his crew on 20th July 1944, and that of Flying Officer Townsend on 28th July 1944, which might be considered light losses given the intensity of the operations.

Some of the targets we know of from previous raids, but some are new. The majority were V-weapon construction, launch and storage sites in northern France, the one at Watten being on a par with Wizernes and similarly resistant to damage. Of the remainder, Caen and the 'battle area' targets were obviously attacked in support of the ground forces, as was Courtrai; the raid on the synthetic oil works at Bottrop was part of the oil campaign; and Kiel, Stuttgart and Hamburg were the strategic targets beloved of Arthur Harris. It was during this campaign against the V-weapon sites, especially the highly toughened ones like Watten and Wizernes, that No. 617 Squadron used the 12,000lb (5,440 kg) *Tallboy* 'earthquake' bomb with notable effect.

On 6th July 1944 two new members were posted in to No. 1696 Flight, at least one of which was an example of a comparatively rare breed in the U.K. – an officer of the South African Air Force. Two days later a needless death on the airfield was recorded:

> F/O. Pearson - Navigator - 405 RCAF. Squadron was admitted to Station Sick Quarters at 00.30 hours after being involved in a collision with a heavy truck whilst cycling to his billet, he was suffering from a Compound Fracture of skull. After emergency treatment at Station Sick Quarters, he was transferred to R.A.F. Hospital, Ely, where he died at 20.30 hours the same date.
>
> [AIR 28/317]

TRIALS AND TRIBULATION

There is a tragic irony in the fact that this officer had survived his bombing missions only to be knocked down and killed in a mundane road accident on the way to his bed. It appears that this might have been a multiple accident, as another victim of a motorcycle crash (a member of the U.S. Air Force) was admitted to the sick quarters at the same time.

The invasion was only the first step towards the end of the war, but some people were looking ahead to the future and the problems and opportunities that it might bring. In early July 1944:

```
A lecture was given by Mr. D.R. Hardman, J.P. in
the Information Room on "The Challenge of Japan".
Approximately 50 Officers, N.C.Os. and airmen
were in attendance.
```

[AIR 28/317]

There was another lecture a week or so later on the subject of 'China in the 20th Century', which was similarly well attended. It is also cheering to note that amidst all the death and destruction, even on an active airfield a new life could be brought into the world, when a baby girl was born to one of the station's W.A.A.F. contingent in the Station Sick Quarters. Elsewhere the athletes of No. 405 Squadron took part in the Inter-District R.C.A.F. Field and Track Meet at R.A.F. Digby in Lincolnshire. The six participants achieved good results, gaining several first and second places, and two qualified to take part in the finals in London.

The raid against Nucourt on 15th July 1944 was a new departure for No. 405 Squadron, and to a certain extent for Bomber Command, as the squadron used a new technique known as 'Heavy *Oboe*' or '*Oboe* Leader' for the first time. This method of attack had been debuted earlier that week, and instead of a target being marked by a Mosquito using *Oboe*, an *Oboe*-equipped aircraft was used to lead a formation of bombers, and when the leader dropped his bombs as directed by *Oboe*, the formation followed suit. This technique was used several times in the following days, though it could plainly only be used in daylight.

20th July 1944 saw mention of another radar innovation known as *Village Inn*, when instructions as to when it was to be switched on and off during that night's raid were received. This device was an automatic gun-laying radar system, fitted beneath the rear turret of an aircraft, which projected an indication onto the rear gunner's sights that showed him where he should aim his guns to hit an attacker being tracked by the radar. It is not completely certain that No. 405 Squadron was equipped with *Village Inn* (this may have been a general instruction), but the squadron was introducing other defensive technology at about this time – the *Carpet* system, which could be used to jam the German *Würzburg* fighter interception and flak fire control radars. The plan was for half the squadron's aircraft to be fitted with *Carpet*; but although it was successful for a while, the protection it offered was soon nullified by modifications to the *Würzburg* systems.

The theme of self-improvement for the staff at Gransden Lodge also continued, but with a slightly different audience in mind this time, when:

> The first of a series of cookery demonstrations was given to WAAF. personnel by a representative of the Food Advice Centre, Cambridge.
>
> [AIR 28/317]

Further lectures on topics looking outward towards the world would follow, including one entitled, presciently, 'Poland and Russia'.

Sometime during July 1944 the various specialists on No. 405 Squadron produced a publication aimed at new arrivals:

TRIALS AND TRIBULATION

```
UNIT PUBLICATION:- A new pamphlet "Calling All
Pathfinders" has just been put into use in the
Squadron for issue to all Captains of aircraft,
and the general knowledge of the other crew
members. This pamphlet deals with nearly every
subject from signing in to flying, and helps very
much to put the newer crews into the picture
regarding the functions of the Path Finder Force.
```
[AIR 27/1789]

This pamphlet is an informative and sometimes amusing document, and gives an interesting insight into how the aircrew of the squadron lived and worked, and what was required of them. It begins with a pep-talk, signed by the squadron C.O., outlining the history of the squadron and its achievements and stressing the need for the squadron's high standards to be upheld in the future. This is then followed by a number of chapters, each of which is dedicated to a different crew role in an aircraft. Some of these include technical details of how the newly-arrived crew members should best perform their duties, and all emphasise the need to seek out and heed the advice of the ground crews. However, they also contain useful snippets of information such as at what time aircrew should report for roll-call and work in the morning, the fact that there were three pubs 'within crawling distance' of the airfield, and instructions on how to book a seat on the nightly bus to Cambridge or Bedford (coupled with a stern injunction not to be shot down by 'blonde night fighters' while on a night out!). Naturally enough, the pressing need to obtain a bicycle - by legal means, mark you - looms very large in all the chapters.

As July 1944 drew to a close, it had been an exhausting month for the aircrew, but don't let us forget the concentrated effort put in by those ground crews during this intense period of operations. They would have been literally working day and night, mostly in the open, to keep the requisite number of bombers ready for operations.

INVASION

A new month brought no let-up in the unremitting tempo of day and night attacks. On 1st August 1944 the Master Bomber and Deputy for the raid on Belle Croix les Bruyères were supplied by No. 405 Squadron, but the weather was so bad when they arrived that they ordered the mission to be abandoned. On 3rd August 1944 the weather over France was better, and eight Lancasters from Gransden Lodge attacked the V-weapon site at L'Isle Adam near Paris, and a further three that in the Forêt de Nieppe. Five aircraft went back to L'Isle Adam the next day, and eleven more went to Trossy St. Maximin, another V-weapon dump.

On 5th August 1944 an attack was made on Noyelles-en-Chaussée, but there was complete cloud cover and icing, and only one of the four No. 405 Squadron aircraft detailed actually bombed. The eight sent against the oil dump at Bordeaux Bassens fared slightly better, though cloud was a problem there too, and matters were not helped by a lack of radio discipline when:

```
One Pilot (believed Australian) gave much back-
chat from H-12 thereby interfered with the
Master Bomber's bombing run and broadcasting.
```
[AIR 27/1789]

This doubtless gave rise to some salty language on the part of Squadron Leader J.W. Perry, the Master Bomber from No. 405 Squadron.

Following this, there was a day off for Bomber Command's heavy bomber squadrons, but on 7th August 1944 raids in support of Operation TOTALISE, a series of attacks by mainly Canadian ground forces against the area near Falaise, commenced. No. 405 Squadron took part in operations against two aiming points in the area that day; the raid against the first was abandoned just before the squadron's two aircraft were due to arrive, but the twelve sent against the second carried out their task successfully.

TRIALS AND TRIBULATION

The 'Woodie' McDonald crew of No. 405 Squadron preparing for flight
(Pathfinder Collection)

Next day's TOTALISE operations were cancelled, but instead fifteen aircraft were sent from Gransden Lodge to attack a 'GAF and Army Dump and Tank Lorry Garage' in the Forêt De Lucheux between Arras and Abbeville. On 9th August 1944 No. 405 Squadron supplied two Master Bomber/Deputy Master Bomber pairs for raids on the sites at Coulonvilliers and Forêt du Croc. Both these raids were quite small in terms of numbers of aircraft, there being only twenty Main Force bombers taking part in each, and the attack at Coulonvilliers lasted only two minutes.

INVASION

No. 405 Squadron re-joined to the oil campaign on 11th August 1944, specifically to attack the 'oil installation on the water edge' at La Pallice. All ten aircraft sent returned safely, as did the four that went back there for a repeat attack the next morning, but this time the target was the port's submarine pens. Later on 12th August 1944 eleven crews were detailed for a raid in Germany, on the Opel factory at Rüsselsheim near Maintz, and to round off a busy day a further four were dispatched in the early hours of the next morning, after a last-minute request for their services, to Falaise. Not undeservedly, the squadron was stood down next day.

Operation TRACTABLE, another push against Falaise by Polish and Canadian forces, began on 14th August 1944 and No. 405 Squadron supported its countrymen by sending fourteen aircraft to attack two aiming points. This close-support raid was a risky business for those on the ground, as:

> The two Aiming Points were very close together and very near the front line troops who were withdrawn to 1500 yards of the Aiming Point for safety.
>
> [AIR 28/317]

It says much for the improvement in Bomber Command's accuracy that 1,500 yards (less than 1,400 m) was now considered to be a safe distance from the aiming point of a bombing raid, but even so some casualties were caused among the friendly forces by bombs dropped short.

There was no such danger in the next operations on 15th August 1944, as these were against two Luftwaffe airfields, Volkel in Holland and Brussels/Melsbroek, the latter today the site of Brussels Airport. None of the aircraft dispatched from Gransden Lodge on these raids, numbering two and nine respectively, were lost. These airfields, far from the front lines, were not attacked to

161

TRIALS AND TRIBULATION

support the ground forces, but rather in preparation for the resumption of the night offensive against Germany, for which Arthur Harris had been impatiently waiting.

NIGHT STRIKERS

No. 405 Squadron's return to strategic German targets was not long in coming, as on the night of 16th August 1944 four Lancasters were ordered to Stettin and twelve to Kiel. Unfortunately for the squadron, these targets were not as lightly defended as those in France, and Pilot Officer Walters and his crew failed to return from Stettin, as was the case for Flying Officer Fisher and his crew on the Kiel raid. No crews were lost on the next night's raids, though, as the twelve aircraft sent to Bremen and the three dispatched to Sterkrade came back safely, but one pilot, as the jargon of the day had it, 'put up a black' by attacking what he described as an unidentified town in the Bremen area, only to find that the attack proper opened up at another position some distance dead ahead. Not what was expected of Pathfinders at all.

There was then a welcome break from operations for some days, and during that time No. 405 Squadron got a new leader, as on 23rd August 1944 the squadron's new C.O., Wing Commander C.W. Palmer D.F.C., took over from Reg Lane, who, like Johnny Fauquier before him, was being posted to No. 6 Group headquarters. During the party that inevitably took place to mark the change in command, Lane arranged for a phone call to be placed for Palmer to a lady-friend in Leeds in Yorkshire. Just by chance, Lane kept the scrap of paper on which the phone number was written, a seemingly minor event that was to have a major effect on his later life.

TRIALS AND TRIBULATION

The squadron's rest came to an end on 25th August 1944, when it went back into the fray with a sixteen-ship attack on Rüsselsheim. All came back safely, although, as had happened before, some members of one crew had taken to their parachutes without orders during an attack by a nightfighter. On the next night Kiel was the target once more, and thirteen aircraft from Gransden Lodge took part in the raid without loss, but there were some injuries, as the medical report for the month end shows:

26th August, 1944.

W/O. Martin (405 Squadron) sustained flak wounds of the right ankle while on operations and after emergency attention at Station Sick Quarters was transferred to R.A.F. Hospital, Ely, for X-ray and surgical treatment.

Cycle Accidents continue to be the cause of many avoidable wasted man hours on the Station, this in spite of the fact that the hours of darkness are comparatively few at the present time. Injuries sustained range from superficial cuts and abrasions to serious head wounds necessitating prolonged hospital treatment. No doubt the enforcement of Station Standing Orders regarding carrying of front and rear lights, pillion passengers, etc., will help to minimise accidents for the future.

There was a small outbreak of food poisoning on the Station during the hot early days of the month. This was probably fly-borne and steps were immediately taken to deal with the situation and bring it under control.

V.D. Lectures.

V.D. Lectures have been given to incoming crews as it has been found that the percentage of V.D. among aircrew was unduly high.

[AIR 28/317]

Regarding the last point in the report, it has been suggested that at least some Canadian crews in No. 6 Group may have become infected with venereal disease intentionally, as a way of avoiding operations.

Be that as it may, on 27th August 1944 a notable raid took place, as for the first time since 1941 a daylight attack was mounted by the R.A.F. against a major German target: Homberg, and its oil refinery. No. 405 Squadron sent just three aircraft, but the raid as a whole was well protected as it was escorted by nine squadrons of Spitfires on the outward flight and seven squadrons on the withdrawal – the R.A.F. had learned well from the experiences of the Americans. The next evening the squadron's numerical contribution to attacks on three tactical targets was small, only six crews, but it was nonetheless important as they made up the three 'Master Bomber and Deputy' pairs for the raids on the construction works at L'Hey and Fromental and the Île de Cezembre coastal gun battery. As it would turn out, these were among the final raids against the V-weapon sites in northern France, since they would soon be overrun by the ground forces, but the V-1 and V-2 threat was far from over.

The last operation for No. 405 Squadron in August 1944 came on the 29th of the month, when fifteen of the sixteen Lancasters requested (one returned early with engine trouble) attacked Stettin again. There were no losses, but some aircraft were diverted to other airfields on their return due to low cloud back at base.

A wartime bomber station covered a considerable area of countryside that would once have been agricultural land, and it had a large number of mouths to feed at a time when supplies were short. It is not surprising, therefore, that the residents of Gransden Lodge did their best to supplement their rations by growing some of their own food. They were assisted in this undertaking by an advisor from the Air Ministry, who came to the airfield at the end of August 1944 in order to offer some tips on the station's horticultural efforts.

The approach of autumn, with its longer nights and poorer weather, would make night raids against Germany more common, but at the beginning of September 1944 the next targets allocated to No. 405 Squadron were back in France, when in the early morning of 1st September 1944 three aircraft raided the V-weapon storage dump at La Pourchinte. On 5th September 1944 it was the turn of Le Havre to receive the bombers' attentions, with four aircraft from No. 405 Squadron in the fourth wave of the attack, but when they arrived they found that almost all the buildings around the aiming point had already been obliterated.

Two targets were identified for No. 405 Squadron on 6th September 1944. One was back in Germany, but only just, as seven aircraft were sent to raid the facilities at the port of Emden, just over the Dutch border. The other, for four aircraft, was the unfortunate Le Havre again, but this time the weather was so bad, with cloud and rain, that the Master Bomber, whom the squadron had supplied, ordered the mission to be abandoned.

We have not heard much about the activities of No. 1696 Flight; this is not due to lack of interest, but rather to the fact that the flight's O.R.B. seems not to have survived. From the O.R.B. accounts of other Bomber Defence Training Flights we can piece together roughly the sort of activities that it was carrying out, and occasionally we can find snippets of information elsewhere. One such is that in September 1944 the decision was made that six Bomber Defence Training Flights should no longer operate a mixture of Spitfires and Hurricanes, but each would be solely equipped with six Spitfires. Or that was the plan.

Whether it was in a Spitfire or Hurricane, one of the pilots of the flight is reported by a veteran of No. 405 Squadron to have indulged in a rather too exuberant 'beat-up' of the airfield that resulted in him touching the runway with his aircraft's propeller – luckily, he managed to retrieve the situation and land, probably to hear a few home truths from his C.O.

On the morning of 8th September 1944 five Lancasters from No. 405 Squadron took off to raid Le Havre again, but once more the weather thwarted them and the mission was abandoned. While they were airborne an aircraft from No. 218 Squadron landed at the airfield from the same raid, and the crew were probably as surprised as those in flying control, as they had mistaken Gransden Lodge for the airfield to which they had intended to divert. Shortly afterwards four of the local crews arrived back, but Wing Commander Morrison and his crew were reported missing – but oddly enough he also managed to write up an account of the attack! The explanation was simple: he and his crew had baled out from their aircraft near the Allied lines, and they were repatriated within a few days.

Le Havre's luck ran out on 10th September 1944 when the weather there was at last clear, and that day's attack, led by a Master Bomber from No. 405 Squadron along with four other crews, was finally pressed home.

The call on 11th September 1944 was for No. 405 Squadron to make available four crews for a raid on the synthetic oil plant at Castrop Rauxel. These were supplied, and though two bombed accurately, the other two did not cover themselves in glory since they managed to bomb two different targets, both many kilometres away from the aiming point, although in fairness at least one had suffered a mauling from flak. Also on that day, back at base and looking towards the location of their likely future deployment, the R.A.F. Regiment members began classes in German.

Another synthetic oil plant, this time the one at Wanne-Eickel, was the target on 12th September 1944, and twelve crews

TRIALS AND TRIBULATION

from No. 405 Squadron took part. Only ten made it back home, as the Lancaster of Flying Officer Sovran went missing, and another crew crash-landed at Woodbridge by the skin of their teeth:

> ... after gliding 4/5 miles over the sea following flak holing the tanks.
>
> [AIR 28/317]

Later that day another nine aircraft were sent on what would turn out to be the last major attack on Frankfurt of the war, and all arrived home safely in the early hours of the next morning. Another crew ended up at Woodbridge next day, when one of the six aircraft dispatched on that afternoon's raid on the Nordstern synthetic oil plant at Gelsenkirchen landed there owing to flak damage.

Seven aircraft from No. 405 Squadron were requested for the attack on 14th September 1944, but while they were on their way to the target (Wilhelmshaven) the raid was called off due to 'bad weather at base.' Perhaps 'Black Thursday' was still in the mind of the planners. It was not the weather but the German defences that claimed one the squadron's crews on 15th September 1944, as Flight Lieutenant Long's aircraft was shot down in the attack on Kiel. The remainder of the twelve Lancasters that had set out returned home, two of them engaging in combat with nightfighters but surviving the experience.

After these raids into Germany, attention was switched back to support for the ground forces. On 17th September 1944 No. 405 Squadron supplied a Master Bomber, Deputy and three other crews to lead an attack (ironically) by No. 5 Group on Boulogne, and later that day they put up just the 'Master and Deputy' pair for a raid on Biggekereke in Holland, which was designated as 'a defended locality', a description that could probably have been applied to many places at that time.

Following this, there would be no operations for No. 405 Squadron for the next two days, during which a:

```
Party of WAAF. paid Educational Visit to Kings
College Cambridge and attended Cookery Lecture
at a Post War Kitchen Exhibition.
```
[AIR 28/317]

While this was going on, preparations were being made back at Gransden Lodge for twilight raids on two aiming points at a target identified as the 'Calais defence area'. The twelve aircraft requested from No. 405 Squadron were airborne by 16:54 on 20th September 1944, and all of them had returned by 19:09. Two days followed when operations were planned then aborted, and the stood-down crews could, if they were so inclined, have taken part in a:

```
Discussion Group - "Should Family Allowances be
Introduced after the War".
```
[AIR 28/317]

These discussion groups and other lectures were becoming increasingly common, and no doubt broadened the horizons of the personnel of the station, some of whom may not have left their home town until the war.

The reason for the attacks on Calais became clear on 23rd September 1944 when three crews from No. 405 Squadron were briefed to support another operation by the Canadian ground forces (Operation UNDERGO), which was intended to take the port of Calais. In the end the raid was postponed, so they were instead sent to attack the Domburg coastal gun batteries. The squadron's attacks on Calais commenced on 24th September 1944, though this raid was seemingly not considered part of Operation UNDERGO. Nevertheless, the crews of the three aircraft dispatched did as they were ordered and directed and supported the raid.

There was an early start next morning for three crews on No. 405 Squadron, as the briefing for their participation in Operation UNDERGO was at 05:30 and they were airborne two hours later, but the mission was aborted due to bad weather. Within minutes of their return, a further five were on their way to the same destination, and by the time they arrived the weather had improved slightly, but again the Master Bomber gave the order to abandon the raid. Orders for the next day's operations had already been received by the time they landed, including the instruction that any aircraft that still had bombs on board when they returned were to remained bombed-up, as it was possible that they would be needed again the next day.

Two operations were indeed mounted on 26th September 1944, not against Calais this time but on gun batteries in the Cap Griz Nez area. All three aircraft sent on the first raid got back to base unscathed, but in the second, one of the five taking part failed to return. The aircraft was that of No. 405 Squadron's C.O. of only a month, Wing Commander Palmer. News was received on the same day that Wing Commander H.A. Morrison D.F.C., who had been shot down and quickly returned home a few weeks earlier, had been awarded the D.S.O., and with the loss of Palmer he assumed immediate, if temporary, command of the squadron.

At No. 6 Group Headquarters, Reg Lane heard that his replacement Charlie Palmer had been lost, and happened to find the scrap of paper on which the phone number of Palmer's friend in Leeds was written. There was no name on the note, just a phone number. Lane called the number to pass on the sad news, and the person answering the phone told him that she would tell the intended recipient, one Barbara, what had happened. While this phone call was going on, a female photo interpretation officer who chanced to be in Lane's office overheard the conversation, and asked whether he had been trying to contact Barbara Andrews. When Lane said that he had, it turned out that by a huge coincidence Barbara had once been a dance pupil of the photo interpretation officer, who immediately asked Lane whether he would like to meet her. The rest, as the saying goes, is history, and Lane married Barbara in 1944.

No. 405 Squadron soon buckled down to work under its new commander when it was detailed for an attack on another oil campaign target, the Bottrop synthetic oil plant, on 27th September 1944. All nine of the crews taking part returned safely, though there was some wayward bombing in the poor weather, with bombs dropping some miles from the aiming point. On 28th September 1944 two 'Master and Deputy' pairs plus a backer-up returned to Cap Griz Nez, which was suffering under 'a concerted attack on 6 different aiming points'. However, the weather was on the side of the German forces and both the attacks controlled by the Gransden Lodge crews were aborted. Following a day's stand down, on the last day of September 1944 the squadron returned to Bottrop for a daylight attack, but only two of the nine crews taking part bombed the oil plant, and the remainder bombed Bottrop town; to what good purpose is not clear, since the aiming-point photographs taken by those seven crews showed only cloud.

The first four days of October 1944 gave the crews on No. 405 Squadron a chance to draw breath after the concentrated run of operations that had been taking place, but on the night of 5th October 1944 a full effort of sixteen crews was called for to take part in a raid on Saarbrücken. This attack was made at the request of the American ground forces, and the intention was to cut the railways and block supply routes through the town. The call was again for sixteen aircraft on 6th October 1944, this time to be split into two groups. One group of nine would make a daylight raid on Sterkrade, and another seven a night attack on Dortmund. This second raid saw the largest contribution by the Canadians of No. 6 Group to any attack in the war – they sent forth 293 aircraft – and marked the beginning of a second Battle of the Ruhr.

In the early hours of 10th October 1944 there was proof for those at Gransden Lodge that, despite the best efforts of Bomber Command and the ground forces, the V-weapon menace had not yet been beaten, as at 00:18 a buzz-bomb passed over the airfield. Although they were not common, this would not be the last time that a V-1 would be seen overhead the airfield.

Next day, undaunted, five aircraft were sent on the night's mission to bomb the guns at Fort Frederik Hendrik, a Napoleonic fort on the Dutch coast that guarded the approaches to Antwerp, and just as had been the case on the same day the previous month, on 12th October 1944 the target was the Wanne-Eickel synthetic oil plant, when just four crews were requested from No. 405 Squadron to act as Supporters.

14th October 1944 must have been an exhausting one for both air and ground crews. The target was Duisburg, and in the morning thirteen aircraft were requested to attack four different aiming points. They all returned safely before noon, but while they were still on their way back orders were received for a second raid on two further aiming points in the same city, and by a few minutes to midnight fifteen Lancasters were on their way back to the Ruhr. The reason for this all-out effort against Duisburg was that the previous day Arthur Harris had been directed to begin Operation HURRICANE, the intention of which was to demonstrate to the enemy the overwhelming superiority of the British and American air forces. This was to be achieved by mounting 'maximum effort' attacks on objectives in the Ruhr.

There was to be little rest for the weary personnel of No. 405 Squadron, as on 15th October 1944 fifteen aircraft were once more called up for a raid on Wilhelmshaven, but it would be 19th October 1944 before the Gransden Lodge squadron was called into action again, though it was not for want of trying on the part of the planners as several missions were planned and scrubbed. Eventually the squadron was 'on', and sixteen of its crews were sent on one of the two raids mounted on Stuttgart that day.

As Angus Robb recalled, there were lighter moments even during this period of intense effort:

> "Before I leave the month of October, there was an incident which caused embarrassment to some and a great deal of amusement to others. For some reason, which I cannot now recall, the H2S radar in our aircraft had been giving trouble, requiring the attention of the radar mechanics. The WAAFs were now doing this job, and as was the practice, had asked if they could fly with us to check that everything was now OK. They arrived at the 'plane, complete with parachute, parachute harness and Mae West in their arms wanting someone to show them how to wear them. All very well you may say, but one of our female passengers was wearing a skirt and as the harness has to come up between your legs, tightly, you can see the difficulty."

The efforts of the crews that culminated in this gruelling round of attacks had obviously not gone unnoticed in high places, as during a break between operations fourteen officers and N.C.O.s from No. 405 Squadron were awarded the D.F.C. or D.F.M.

The squadron welcomed a new commanding officer when on 22nd October 1944 Group Captain Newson D.F.C. and Bar arrived and assumed command. This appointment was recorded as being a temporary command, but it was made permanent the following month.

TRIALS AND TRIBULATION

One of Bill Newson's first jobs would have been to oversee the planning of his new squadron's next operation, which took place the day after he took over. The target was the rail junction close to the Krupps works at Essen in the Ruhr. 'Happy Valley' was never an easy target, and on this occasion it was noted, with some understatement, that:

```
The route out and home was mostly through cloud
of a front reaching to approximately 22,000ft.,
and with over 1,000 aircraft on the route, the
crews found it quite a tough trip.
```
[AIR 28/317]

In spite of this, all the fifteen aircraft sent returned safely.

We have seen that in September 1944 it had been decided that all Bomber Defence Training Flights' fighter aircraft should be Spitfires. A month or so later this had still not happened, and so a representative of the A.O.C. No. 8 Group wrote a slightly tetchy letter to Headquarters Bomber Command regarding the state of No. 1696 Flight's aircraft, in particular the replacement of the Hurricanes with old, sub-standard Spitfires. Whether this letter caused a change of heart is not clear, but what we do know is that at the end of October 1944 it was agreed that No. 1696 Flight should operate twelve Spitfires, six Hurricanes and a single Oxford. At the beginning of the month the plan had been for the flight to continue operating six Martinet target tugs, but complaints had been raised that these were too slow to be useful, so the Hurricanes were to be retained to replace the Martinets.

This replacement of the fighters was not the only change in the aircraft operating from Gransden Lodge that was taking place. When No. 192 Squadron had been in residence at the airfield in 1943, the majority of its operations had been carried out in the Wellington, but it also had on strength several examples of de Havilland's superlative Mosquito. The B.D.U. had also used the Mosquito, or 'Mossie' as it was affectionately known, in some of its trials. On 25th October 1944 Gransden Lodge was about to become home to the Mosquito again, when No. 142 Squadron was formed at the airfield.

The entry in No. 142 Squadron's O.R.B. states that the squadron was formed on this day in October 1944, but that is not strictly true, as it had a long history prior to that date. The squadron was first formed in 1918 as part of the Royal Flying Corps, the predecessor of the R.A.F., in Egypt (the squadron's badge carried a winged Sphinx to mark the association). After the original squadron was re-numbered as No. 55 Squadron, a new incarnation of No. 142 Squadron came into being in 1934 when it re-formed as a bomber unit, after which it served in the European and North African theatres of war until it was disbanded in Italy. This occurred only a few weeks before it was again re-formed at Gransden Lodge to become part of the Light Night Striking Force of No. 8 Group.

The Light Night Striking Force (L.N.S.F.) was formed around the units within the Pathfinder Force that were operating the Mosquito. No. 109 Squadron had been part of the P.F.F. from its inception, and had been instrumental in the development of *Oboe*. For maximum range, *Oboe* required the receiving aircraft to operate at as high an altitude as possible, since it required 'line of sight' from the transmitter to the receiver. No. 109 Squadron was thus, for a short time, equipped with the high-flying pressurised Wellington Mk. VI, but it switched to using the Mosquito as it became available, as the Mosquito could operate at similar altitudes and was much better suited to the task. In June 1943 two more Mosquito squadrons joined the P.F.F. These were No. 105 Squadron, which operated alongside No. 109 Squadron in marking and bombing using *Oboe*, and No. 139 Squadron, which was used by Bennett as a supporting squadron to accompany target marking units and also to carry out diversionary raids to draw defenders

TRIALS AND TRIBULATION

away from the main attack. This latter tactic proved very effective, and as more crews and aircraft became available further Mosquito squadrons were formed and added to the growing Light Night Striking Force. These diversionary and nuisance raids were by no means the only operations for which the L.N.S.F. was used, as it was also employed very successfully as a pure bomber force, often operating in weather conditions that kept the majority of Bomber Command on the ground. It was noted for frequently being used in attacks against Berlin, raiding the 'Big City' 170 times, include on 36 nights in succession. Berliners, Don Bennett recalled, regarded these raids as anything but a mere nuisance, and although they were not on the same scale as the attacks during the Battle of Berlin, they were never taken lightly.

This, then, was the role for which No. 142 Squadron was re-formed. To make room for the new arrivals, the assorted fighters of No. 1696 Flight returned to Bourn.

No. 405 Squadron, of course, continued operating while its new neighbours were setting themselves up on the station. On the same day that No. 142 Squadron arrived, it sent sixteen aircraft, including the raid's Master Bomber, in a repeat attack on the oil plant at Homberg. No operations took place next day, but No. 142 Squadron was nonetheless busy, as:

> Today we moved into our offices with all the usual bother and hustle of getting equipment and phones in and setting ourselves up as an establishment, complete with our own briefing room etc. The Navigation Officer, 134026 F/Lt. C. Hassall arrived and we had news of the Squadron Commander coming in the next day. The Adjutant went to Group Headquarters in the afternoon and arrived back with the happy news that some aircraft could be expected the next day.
>
> [AIR 27/975]

True to their word, next day Wing Commander B.G.D. Nathan, the new commanding officer, arrived, along with the first two Mosquito Mk. XXV aircraft. These, like the Lancaster Mk. X, were products of the growing Canadian contribution to aircraft construction for the R.A.F.

On 28th October 1944 Gransden Lodge's own Canadians dispatched ten Lancasters on a raid on Köln, as well as six to join an attack aimed at the island of Walcheren and the gun positions there. The raids on this island, which guarded the vital approaches to Antwerp, were designed to soften up the defences before the invasion of Walcheren a few days later.

No. 142 Squadron had little time to settle in, since on 29th October 1944 it began operations with an attack by the squadron's only two aircraft on Köln, while No. 405 Squadron sent four aircraft on a return visit to Walcheren.

On the next day, No. 142 Squadron began the unit's association with Berlin by sending its two Mosquitoes there for the first time,

A Mosquito of No. 142 Squadron photographed from the cockpit of another (Bill Brown)

while No. 405 Squadron went to Köln with eleven aircraft, and sent nine there again on the last day of October 1944, along with two of the station's Mosquitoes. By the end of the month, at less than a week old, No. 142 Squadron's strength had already grown to twelve aircrew and 63 ground crew, and it would continue to increase quickly in the coming weeks.

It seems that that ubiquitous form of transport at Gransden Lodge, the bicycle, had started to claim sufficient victims to be worthy of note. In No. 405 Squadron's O.R.B. for October 1944 'cycling accidents' (there were five) were recorded alongside the normal 'venereal diseases' and 'other infections' in the summary of the squadron's state of health. Other medical matters were also causing concern, as the station's medical reports noted that a large number of new personnel had been posted in to No. 2784 Squadron R.A.F.R., but of these a great proportion were deemed unfit for field training.

With the coming of the new month, it was No. 142 Squadron's turn to attack Köln on 1st November 1944, but its contribution was minimal as it had only one aircraft available to send to carry out this spoof raid.

Both the Gransden Lodge squadrons were detailed for the raid on Düsseldorf on 2nd November 1944. The two Mosquitoes that were dispatched returned successfully, but only fifteen of the sixteen Lancasters from No. 405 Squadron made it back home. The last of them crashed close to the American fighter airfield at Debden, near Saffron Walden in Essex, after a traumatic flight. The station O.R.B. noted the bare facts:

> 405/K. jettisoned on the target area with the pilot F/O. Hannah wounded in the shoulder by flak and the R/G. Sgt. Perini baled out N. of the target. The aircraft was flown back and successfully belly landed at DEBDEN by the NAV/SET. Operator F/Lt. Martin G.A. D.F.C.
>
> [AIR 28/317]

Behind this, however, was a remarkable story. The pilot, Harold Hannah, was hit by shrapnel from flak on the run up to the target, and slumping forward onto the controls, pushed the bomber into a steep dive. One of the crew, George Martin, an ex-Metropolitan Policeman, took charge and with the aid of the rest of the crew managed to get the pilot out of his seat. In the confusion, the rear gunner thought that he had been ordered to bale out, and did so. Eventually Martin, who, like the rest of the crew, had no piloting experience, managed to get onto the controls and recover the Lancaster from its dive. Being in the target area the crew dropped their bombs, and they, after refusing to bale out when given the choice by Martin, managed by a combined effort to fly their aircraft back to the U.K. The radio operator succeeded in raising the airfield at Debden, only some 35 miles (55 km) from home, and Martin was talked down to a landing, but the Lancaster was far too high and overshot to belly-land in a field beyond the runway. Miraculously none of the crew were seriously hurt, but Hannah died later. Flight Lieutenant Martin was awarded the D.S.O., and the crew's exploits were later dramatised in a B.B.C. radio program, aptly titled *'The Pilot Who Couldn't Fly'*.

Only the Mosquitoes of No. 142 Squadron were required for duty on 3rd November 1944, and both those available made the trip to Berlin and back without incident, but on the next night aircraft from both squadrons were sent on the raid on Bochum, two (still the entire complement) from No. 142 Squadron and eight 'heavies'. On Guy Fawkes Day, 5th November 1944, just No. 142 Squadron was operating from Gransden Lodge, with its two aircraft taking part in a Mosquito-only mission against Stuttgart.

The Nordstern oil plant at Gelsenkirchen was meant to take another pounding on 6th November 1944, in a daylight raid, and No. 405 Squadron sent nine crews. One returned early with engine problems, but four bombed the target and the remaining

TRIALS AND TRIBULATION

four had trouble identifying the target due to cloud and bombed, as instructed, 'any built-up area'. Of these last four, it is instructive to note that, in spite of being the élite of Bomber Command and having navigational aids available, two crews were not 100% sure of where they had actually attacked, as they had bombed what they described as a 'built-up area which may have been Gelsenkirchen', on the basis that wherever it was, it was being bombed and was covered with smoke. No. 142 Squadron contributed two aircraft to the raid, and on their return one crew enjoyed the hospitality of the Americans at Hethel in Norfolk, as they had had to divert there due to icing.

A further Mosquito-only raid was mounted against Hannover on 8th November 1944; No. 142 Squadron was still only able to send two aircraft, which actually departed a few hours after midnight, but more Mosquitoes and crews were arriving and they would soon be able to play a bigger part in operations. Next day it was the turn of the station's Lancasters, and No. 405 Squadron joined the raid on Wanne-Eickel with ten aircraft, but this was another attack where the cloud played a big part, as despite sky-marking being used, the target could not be identified accurately so the order was again given to bomb 'any built-up area' and little damage was done to the actual target.

Neither of the squadrons at Gransden Lodge were required on 10th November 1944, and No. 142 Squadron celebrated the fact that there was a:

```
General stand down today. Hence, everybody who
could be spared disappeared into the unknown
with a becoming promptitude.
```

[AIR 27/976]

The squadron was in action the next day, though, and it could now muster three aircraft for the attack on a new oil campaign target, the Hoesch Benzin synthetic oil plant in Dortmund. Two encountered no problems, but the pilot of the other had some unusual problems to sort out over the target, as his navigator's oxygen pipe had come adrift and rendered him unconscious, but the pilot was able to re-connect the pipe and revive him. No. 405 Squadron also took part in this raid, sending seven Lancasters.

Following these missions there were a few days without operations for either squadron, but they were not idle, as No. 142 Squadron was taking part in LORAN training – so LORAN was now operational – and:

> Welcome news was received of some officers' beds, mattresses, etc., at Gamlingay Station, so after having collected a further instalment of furniture from the Main Stores for our Crew Room, these beds, etc., were fetched, so that comfort in a small way is gradually becoming apparent in our quarters.
>
> [AIR 27/976]

On 15th November 1944 No. 142 Squadron sent two Mosquitoes to Berlin, and on the following day No. 405 Squadron went back into action in a raid against the town of Jülich, near Aachen, in support of the ground forces. The aim of the attack, to which the squadron contributed twelve crews, was to cut communications behind the German front lines that the Americans were about to attack.

The progress of war had become promising enough for those in high places to begin to think about the time when the conflict would be over. In particular, the fate of the many airfields built over the preceding few years would need to be decided. The Post-War Airfield Requirements Committee had begun this task in August 1944, and was in the process of evaluating the literally hundreds of airfields then extant. To help with this, each airfield

TRIALS AND TRIBULATION

was assigned a score in each of three categories: 'A' for suitability for flying, 'B' for ground support facilities and 'C' for extension possibilities. In November 1944 the committee met at the Air Ministry for the eighth time, and Gransden Lodge was among the airfields under consideration. Its score in all three categories was acceptable, though the rating for its ground facilities was significantly lower than for a number of the others, but overall it was good enough for it to be recommended for retention by the R.A.F. after the war was over.

That happy state was, however, some way in the future. No. 142 Squadron was sufficiently up to strength by 18th November 1944 for it to be asked to provide crews to participate in two operations that day, but neither went exactly as planned. Two aircraft were sent on the first raid on Wanne-Eickel but one arrived late as its undercarriage was down, and the other suffered a generator failure, lost all its navigational aids and crashed-landed at Watton in Norfolk with its bombs still on board. Four aircraft were scheduled for the other attack on Hannover, but only three took part as one had been damaged in an earlier test flight. No. 405 Squadron also took part in the Wanne-Eickel raid with twelve aircraft, and earlier had sent four on a raid on Münster.

It was not all plain sailing for No. 142 Squadron on its next operation on 20th November 1944 either, when seven Mosquitoes set off for Hannover. Only five returned to Gransden Lodge, and of these, one crashed on landing at base with only one functioning engine. Another, flown by the same crew that had crashed at Watton, landed at Woodbridge and ran into the F.I.D.O. pipeline, and a third crew landed at Ford in Sussex due to self-inflicted navigational problems after the navigator lost his charts and navigation log through the *Window* chute.

The squadrons fared better on 21st November 1944. The first raid, in which six of No. 405 Squadron's aircraft took part – it was on Koblenz - was unusual, in that it was conducted solely by 43 aircraft from No. 8 Group, and it was carried out as a training *H2S* attack. Later, six of its crews, along with two from No. 142 Squadron, took part in a more conventional raid on the oil plant at Castrop Rauxel, this time without incident. No. 405 Squadron then departed for its third raid of the day. This one was directed against two targets, and had a twist. All ten aircraft flew over the first target, Aschaffenburg, and five attacked the railway yards there, supported by the others. The remainder carried on to bomb Worms 'blind' – perhaps this was another test of blind bombing techniques, like the first of the day's missions? To round off a very busy day on the airfield, No. 142 Squadron's second operation was by four Mosquitoes against Stuttgart, but again one returned early and landed at Tangmere, close to the Sussex coast, on only one engine.

After a well-deserved day off for all concerned, No. 142 Squadron was back in action on 23rd November 1944 when it sent six aircraft against Hannover once more. The squadron was now approaching full strength in both aircraft and crews, and was able to field ten of each on its next operation, on 25th November 1944 against Nürnberg.

The break from operations had lasted longer for No. 405 Squadron, and it was not until 27th November 1944 that it was back in action again. Its seven aircraft were sent against Freiburg, which was not an industrial town but had been singled out for its first raid of the war as it was a railway centre and German troops were believed to be present there. The other target on that day, for seven more Lancasters, was definitely an industrial one as they were to attack the inland port town of Neuss, hard by Düsseldorf. Twelve Mosquitoes were plying their trade too, taking part in what was becoming known as the 'Milk Run', a raid on Berlin, but one of these ended up bombing Osnabrück and returning early after mechanical problems.

TRIALS AND TRIBULATION

Most of the crews, though, would not have been back in time to enjoy the entertainment laid on for that night, which was provided by the cast of the R.C.A.F. Gang Show 'All Clear'.

Ten Mosquitoes from No. 142 Squadron were detailed to act as part of the Main Force in the raid on Nürnberg on 28th November 1944, but only nine managed to get airborne, as one swung on takeoff causing damage to its undercarriage. A previously unheard-of unit based at Gransden Lodge got a mention on that day as well, although only as it was leaving:

```
J.1803. F/Lt. G.C.Smith and J. 83463 P/O. Barton
of No. 6 Grp. Diversion Unit were posted to
R.A.F. Woodbridge with all the personnel of the
unit.
```

[AIR 28/317]

This Diversion Unit, which would shortly have access to two aircraft of its own, would provide repair crews, supplies and spares to assist aircraft from No. 6 Group that had been diverted to airfields in the south of England.

Twelve crews from No. 142 Squadron flew again as part of the next night's raid on Hannover, during which one pilot had an embarrassing experience as, through no fault of his own, he managed to broadcast his intercom chatter over the radio due to a faulty switch, which was, apparently, heard by all the squadron's other crews.

30th November 1944 saw both squadrons engaged in operations. Each provided two aircraft for an attack on one aiming point in a raid on Duisburg, and No. 405 Squadron sent another nine to hit a second aiming point in the same city. In addition, No. 142 Squadron dispatched ten Mosquitoes against Hamburg. During the day the welfare of the many female inhabitants of Gransden Lodge had also been assured by a visit from Group Officer Beecroft, one of the Inspectors of W.A.A.F, who expressed her satisfaction with the amenities that the airwomen of the station enjoyed.

Another visitor that day was one Squadron Leader Hailstone of the Air Ministry. He was looking into servicing matters, but with a name like that he should surely have been a weather man!

By the end of November 1944 No. 142 Squadron was up to fighting strength, as it now had 185 air and ground crew and nineteen aircraft on charge. No. 405 Squadron obviously had a larger population, but this was in a constant state of flux, as can be seen by the fact that in the month of November 1944 alone 32 personnel were posted in and 43 posted out, from a total of about 580 souls.

December 1944 arrived accompanied by cloud, strong winds and drizzle at Gransden Lodge, and No. 142 Squadron sent twelve crews off into the overcast for an attack on Karlsruhe, all bar one returning to the airfield, the other having diverted to Tangmere. The winter weather obviously made conditions even more uncomfortable for those working on the ground, but their combined ingenuity arrived at a solution, as the ground crews of both squadrons employed a highly unofficial (and potentially lethal) modification to the coal stoves used to heat the huts on the airfield. This involved a device that allowed used engine oil to be drip-fed onto house bricks arranged in the base of the stove. These would previously have been heated by burning a can of petrol in the stove, and when the oil was dripped onto them it would burn merrily and in a short time the flue of the stove would become red-hot and the hut as warm as toast. As one can imagine, this was not without its perils, and a delay in ignition of the petrol could cause the fumes in the stove to explode and send blazing petrol running across the floor, and the clouds of black smoke caused by letting the oil drip onto the bricks before they were sufficiently hot could result in the rapid and unsympathetic appearance of the airfield's fire crews.

Angus Robb of No. 405 Squadron remembers other liberties being taken with stoves, and the related pranks that lightened the mood in trying times:

TRIALS AND TRIBULATION

"The trips to the local hostelry's meant that there was quite a lot of energy to be expended when these establishments closed their doors and the Mess President had decided to close the Mess bar. It was considered a good idea to find a billet with all the people inside asleep and then take as many of the beds as possible outside without awakening the incumbents. It is surprising how proficient we became at this exercise, and could manage a few beds before someone blew the whistle. I awoke many a night to find a clear blue sky above me. Coins inserted into the light fittings of an empty hut was another favourite pastime. When the occupiers returned, switching on the lights made a very satisfying noise blowing the bulbs, at the same time blowing the fuses. A more dangerous affair was the placing of the internal contents of a Very cartridge down the chimney stack of the stove which was situated in the centre of each hut. I say dangerous because one took the risk of falling off the roof trying to complete the task. Bullets were also put down the chimneys, but this was considered very bad form as this could cause serious damage to life and property, and this, of course, was not the aim of any these games; but they did help to pass the time."

On 2nd December 1944 several of the personnel from No. 2784 Squadron R.A.F.R. were recorded as being posted to Oakington. This is the last definite evidence that we have of the presence of the R.A.F. Regiment at Gransden Lodge, although it seems probable that defensive cover of some sort would have remained. No. 2784 Squadron R.A.F.R. had converted to become a rifle squadron in October 1944, so would no longer have been able to contribute to the anti-aircraft defences of the station.

Ted Ruthglen and Bob McWhirter of No. 405 Squadron play-acting after being issued handguns (Pathfinder Collection)

Later on that night two Mosquitoes and sixteen Lancasters took off for Hagen in the Ruhr. The attack caused major damage, including, unbeknownst at the time to the planners, the destruction of a factory making batteries for U-Boats. In the early hours of the following morning a larger force of ten aircraft from No. 142 Squadron was deployed as a contribution to a raid on the railway yards at Giessen. Only 66 Mosquitoes took part in this attack, but a much heavier raid by over 250 aircraft a few days later caused massive destruction to this small university city.

No. 8 Group made its first attempt at 'dambusting' on 4th December 1944. The target was the Urft reservoir dam in the Eifel, but unlike the famous attack by No. 617 Squadron in 1943, the aim of this raid was not to cause damage to the German war machine, but rather to deny the German defenders the ability to

TRIALS AND TRIBULATION

release water to flood areas through which advancing forces would pass. No. 405 Squadron provided eight aircraft for the attack, but it was not successful in breaching the dam, despite causing it some damage. Later in the day six further crews from the squadron took part in a raid on Karlsruhe, and No. 142 Squadron also put up twelve Mosquitoes to join another attack on Hagen.

The progress of the Allied troops into continental Europe that the destruction of the Urft dam was meant to assist was clearly demonstrated on 5th December 1944. On that day, twelve Mosquitoes of No. 142 Squadron took off for a raid upon Nürnberg. One of these landed back at base almost immediately with electrical problems, and another suffered engine failure and diverted to another airfield - Brussels/Melsbroek. It will be remembered that this airfield had been a target for No. 405 Squadron only four months previously. While some of their number were on their way back from their unexpected continental leave, on 6th December 1944 No. 142 Squadron participated in three raids, when two aircraft flew against Osnabrück and seven against Berlin. On the third raid two Mosquitoes were joined by sixteen Lancasters from No. 405 Squadron for an attack on the oil plant at Leuna, west of Leipzig, over 500 miles (800 km) from base. All returned safely, the Lancasters taking about six and a half hours for the round trip.

On the 7th and 8th December 1944 No. 142 Squadron took part in two raids, dispatching four crews to Köln and eight against the Meiderich oil plant near Duisburg in an *Oboe* Leader attack. Next day saw the squadron on the Milk Run again, with ten crews taking off for Berlin. Only seven of them got to the target, however, as three landed early: two had suffered mechanical problems, and a third had managed to hit a tree on takeoff, smashing the transparent nose of the Mosquito.

There were no heavy bomber operations on the day following this raid, and No. 142 Squadron was stood down too. Any aircrew left on the station in the evening would have needed to be ready to take to the shelters with their ground-based comrades, as at 18:55 an air raid message was received warning of a flying bomb. Wherever the V-1 landed, though, it was not at Gransden Lodge.

No. 142 Squadron was slated to take part in two missions on 11th December 1944. In the first of these, twelve aircraft returned to Duisburg in another *Oboe* Leader attack, and later in the day another twelve raided Hamburg. It must have given the Mosquito crews pause for thought when one of those taking part in the Hamburg attack reported that a jet fighter had been sighted. Their unarmed Mosquitoes relied on speed and altitude to escape interception by German nightfighters, and now they had been made painfully aware that the opposition had aircraft that could challenge them.

No such threats were in evidence on their next raid, on 12th December 1944, when thirteen aircraft from No. 405 Squadron accompanied two from No. 142 Squadron took part in what would turn out to be the last heavy night raid by Bomber Command on Essen. The crews were doubtless thankful to be able to report back that they had found that the defences were very moderate – for Essen. To draw the defending nightfighters away from this attack, ten more Mosquitoes from No. 142 Squadron had joined 39 others in a spoof raid on Osnabrück.

Two days of poor weather then followed, meaning no operations took place, but on 15th December 1944 twelve of No. 142 Squadron's aircraft made the trip to Hanover. Next day its operation was cancelled, even as some of the crews were taxying out for takeoff.

The city of Ulm had escaped Bomber Command's attentions up until this point, but on 17th December 1944 it received what was to be its only attack of the war. Ten Lancasters from No. 405 Squadron took part in the raid, which was aimed at the Magirus-Deutz and Kässbohrer lorry factories and other military installations, but in the process the majority of the medieval centre of the city was destroyed. Six more crews from the squadron made the familiar trip to the unfortunate city of Duisburg, and once more No. 142 Squadron was taking part in a supporting spoof raid, with twelve aircraft raiding Hanau, although one returned early with a broken oil pipe but managed to make a good landing even though it still had a full bomb load on board and only one functioning engine.

The weather on 18th December 1944 was good enough for ten crews from No. 142 Squadron to take part in the night's raid on Nürnberg, but next day there was a change to foggy conditions with visibility down to around a few hundred metres, and by 20th December 1944 a familiar weather pattern had begun, with foggy days and nights predominating. Neither squadron was operating that day because of the conditions, but on No. 142 Squadron there would probably have been an interested audience when a Major from No. 8 Group headquarters lectured them on the latest developments in German anti-aircraft and nightfighter defences.

The weather on 21st December 1944 was slightly better during the day, but the fog closed in again during the evening. Eight aircraft of No. 405 Squadron and three from No. 142 Squadron nevertheless took part in a raid on the Nippes rail marshalling yards in Köln, but three aircraft ended up at Graveley on their return due to the fog.

A different set of marshalling yards was the target on 22nd December 1944, and fourteen Lancasters from No. 405 Squadron were assigned to the raid on Bingen. In a foretaste of what was to come, they took off in very bad visibility, and things only got worse, as:

> On the return the aerodrome was in fog. 4 landed at Gransden, 7 at Downham Market, one at Graveley and one at Warboys. 405/J attempted to land at Graveley but hit a tree, they managed to carry on to Downham Market and made a successful Belly Landing.

[AIR 28/317]

It sounds like this had the potential to be to a repeat of 'Black Thursday', except that now there was also a F.I.D.O. installation at Downham Market in Norfolk to help. For one crew all this was immaterial, as Flying Officer Tite and his crew did not return, one of only three aircraft lost on the raid, and the first loss for No. 405 Squadron for some months.

1944 was drawing to a close, and soon another wartime Christmas was to be celebrated at Gransden Lodge – and although those present did not know it, it was to be the last. In Europe, other events were concentrating minds. Since mid-December 1944 the German counter-attack in the Ardennes, 'The Battle of the Bulge', had been under way in some of the worst winter weather seen for many years. By the 20th General Eisenhower had begun his own counter-offensive in the area around Bastogne; General Anthony McAuliffe, the senior officer of the American units surrounded at Bastogne, when offered the chance to surrender, gave a famous one word reply - "Nuts!"

On 23rd December 1944 the weather cleared sufficiently for the Allied air forces to assist by attacking the German supply routes. Even though the conditions in the U.K. were questionable, No. 142 Squadron was tasked to dispatch eight of its aircraft on a raid on Seigburg, and a further six to Limburg. By the time of their return the Gransden Lodge weather had again taken a hand, as the conditions had worsened to thick fog. The first of the Seigburg aircraft to return attempted a beam approach, but undershot and burst into flames, with both the crew suffering serious burns. The remaining aircraft were diverted to Ford, and the crews on the Limburg raid were sent to Downham Market. The weather stayed bad, and the diverted crews did not make it back to Gransden Lodge until after Christmas. The ground crews and the remainder of the station staff were obviously not affected, and in the evening an airman's dance was held to get the Christmas celebrations under way.

TRIALS AND TRIBULATION

The Officers' Mess, Christmas 1944 (Bill Brown)

Next day, Christmas Eve 1944, No. 405 Squadron was put on alert to supply ten crews for operations, but this was later cancelled. No. 142 Squadron was also stood down, although with thirteen of its aircraft away from base and another burned out this was hardly surprising. It was confirmed that there would be no operations next day, so festivities could continue unhindered.

Christmas Day 1944 was a busy one, with, once again, service customs being upheld in the serving of Christmas dinner, and plenty of entertainment was laid on. As the entry in the No. 405 Squadron O.R.B. recounts:

> CHRISTMAS DAY ENTERTAINMENTS,
> 25TH DECEMBER, 1944
>
> A big entertainment program was scheduled for today. At 1030 hours, the Officers entertained the Senior N.C.O.'s in the Officers' Mess. Liquid refreshments were in abundance as well as an excellent buffet lunch. The Officers' Mess was gailey bedecked with Christmas decorations and mistletoe and, on many occasions,

advantage was taken of the significance of the mistletoe. At 1200 hours, the airmen were served an excellent turkey and ham dinner with all the trimmings by the officers of No. 405 Squadron. In the afternoon the E.N.S.A. concert scheduled had to be cancelled but in its place an "Abbott and Costello" cinema was shown.

In the evening, the Officers and Senior N.C.O.'s had a Christmas Dinner similar to that of the airmen. This was exceedingly well-prepared and served. After consuming their food like real epicures, Officers and Senior N.C.O.'s served the hard-working waitresses.

At 2030 hours, an all-ranks dance was held in the N.A.A.F.I. building. This was very well attended. Refreshments were served and music supplied by the Station Dance Band. Everyone joined in the Christmas festive spirit and thoroughly enjoyed themselves.

All in all, considering the fact that the majority of the Squadron boys are a long way from home and are particularly lonesome at this time of the year, they seemed to have thoroughly enjoyed themselves, and much credit is due to all personnel who assisted in making their Christmas as happy a one as it could possibly be under the circumstances.

[AIR 27/1789]

The station O.R.B. also mentions a six-a-side rugby tournament taking place on Christmas afternoon, but this seems not to have figured large with the Canadian contingent.

To make up for the cancelled E.N.S.A. concert, on Boxing Day 1944 a concert party from the Canadian Army gave a performance. No. 142 Squadron's wanderers also returned from

Ford that day, and those from Downham Market made it back the day after. Ian McLeod, an Australian navigator who spent the enforced break at Downham Market, remembered the occasion like this in an interview for the Australians at War Film Archive:

"Well, we were guests of another station and of course we had no money so we couldn't buy any liquor, but they put on a good spread for us, you know it was a real good English Christmas. Like poultry, the puddings, everything went well with it. They really did us fine.... but it was strange being away and it was our first sign of snow and hoar frost and we were cold.... I think we spent most of the time at this station Downham Market sitting in front of a big fire and then we had learnt the system of mulling beer, you know you put the hot poker in the fire and pull it out and shove it in your pot of beer but we remained sober, we didn't overdo it because we were being shouted by friends."

Both the Gransden Lodge squadrons were back in action in the few days leading up to the year's end. No. 405 Squadron attacked the railway yards at Rheydt (four crews) on 27th December 1944 and those at Bonn (sixteen crews) on the next night; No. 142 Squadron contributed four aircraft to a raid on Opladen and a further fourteen to one on Frankfurt. On 29th December 1944 sixteen Lancasters again set off, this time as part of the oil campaign, to participate in an attack on the Scholven-Buer synthetic oil works at Gelsenkirchen. Unfortunately, only fifteen returned, since the crew of Flying Officer Wilsher was posted missing. No. 142 Squadron was meanwhile attacking the marshalling yards at Troisdorf with three of its aircraft. Next day the squadron continued operations when ten Mosquitoes were sent to Hannover, and two on a spoof attack on Duisburg; No

405 Squadron also sent nine Lancasters against the rail marshalling yards in Köln.

On the last day of 1944, No. 142 Squadron rounded off its first year as part of the L.N.S.F. by taking part in two raids, ten aircraft going to Berlin and two to attack the marshalling yards at Osterfeld. This attack brought to an end a year that had seen changing fortunes, both for the units based at Gransden Lodge and for the Allies, who now had the prospect of victory before them.

THE FINAL PUSH

> New Year's Day passed very quietly on the Station. A special meal was had by the Airmen and the Officers somewhere along the lines of the Christmas dinner. In the evening an All Ranks Dance was held and was very well attended. Everyone seemed to have thoroughly enjoyed themselves and by the looks of determination on their faces, one would gather that they intend to make 1945 the last year of this conflict, if at all within their power.
>
> [AIR 27/1790]

With those words, No. 405 Squadron's O.R.B. recorded the start of a new year, and after the festivities the squadron went immediately back into action on 2nd January 1945. One of the sixteen crews participating in that day's attack on Nürnberg did not get a chance to take any further part in shortening the war, however, as the aircraft of Wing Commander Lawson was posted missing from this, his 93rd, operation.

Even though No. 142 Squadron was no stranger to Berlin, in the new year it would visit the German capital even more frequently. 2nd January 1945 saw nine of its aircraft over the 'Big City', and in addition another two were sent to Hanau. The night of 2nd/3rd January 1945 also saw the demise of an old acquaintance of the station, as the 'Ruhr Express', now serving with No. 419

THE FINAL PUSH

Last stop for the 'Ruhr Express'. KB700 after crashing on 2nd January 1945 (Bomber Command Museum of Canada)

Squadron, crashed after running off the runway at the end of its 49th operation. This was especially unfortunate as KB700 was scheduled to return to Canada after its 50th mission, to become a memorial to the Canadians who built and flew Lancasters.

It was the Mosquitoes that were next in action and the target was again Berlin, with six aircraft from No. 142 Squadron scheduled to take part in each of two raids on 4th January 1945.

The Lancasters of No. 405 Squadron were not called upon until the following day, and the fourteen that took part in the mission to Royan brought their crews back safely. This was a controversial attack as Royan, near Bordeaux, was being besieged by the French Resistance in an attempt to dislodge a die-hard German garrison in the town. The German commander had given the local civilian population the chance to leave, but over 2,000 chose to remain. Due to a series of misunderstandings, the raid was ordered to soften up the town in the mistaken belief that the

TRIALS AND TRIBULATION

only civilians remaining there were collaborators. It is said that an attempt was made to cancel the raid at the last minute, but if that is so then it did not succeed, and over 85% of the town was destroyed and more than 500 French civilians were killed.

The missions carried out by No. 142 Squadron on 5th January 1945 were less contentious. Three crews were sent in the late afternoon to Hannover, and a little later nine of the squadron's Mosquitoes went once again to Berlin. There seems to have been a certain element of farce to one crew's mission, as:

> ... when crossing the Dutch coast on way out lost VHF and inter-com. Hand signals and shouting were very unsatisfactory ...
>
> [AIR 27/976]

Far more serious was the fact that Flight Lieutenant Eichler and his navigator were killed when their aircraft crashed at Hatley Park, just south of Gransden Lodge, after they ran out of fuel while approaching to land. This Czech pilot and his navigator were not unaccustomed to accidents, as it was they who had crashed on two consecutive raids the previous November, on the second occasion colliding with the F.I.D.O. pipeline at Woodbridge. That they ran out of fuel highlights how necessary it was to economise on petrol on longer missions. One pilot on No. 142 Squadron, Bill Brown, had the reputation for exercising extreme economy, with the result that he was often back from operations much later than the other aircraft, but with fuel to spare. His ground crew, with tongue in cheek, named his aircraft 'Rambler' in recognition of the time it spent rambling around the countryside.

On 6th January 1945 eight Mosquitoes from No. 142 Squadron took part in a spoof raid on Kassel, and the squadron also had trade at Hannover on 7th January 1945, sending nine crews. Another three crews, in the company of fourteen from No. 405

THE FINAL PUSH

Squadron, took part in the final major raid of the war against München, but the Lancaster of Flying Officer Sparling and his crew failed to return from this mission.

Operations then came to a grinding halt, once again owing to the weather, but not the usual fog this time as:

> Due to heavy snow-fall which is most unusual in this part of the country, operations have been completely hampered. An excellent snow-clearing plan has been put into operation but despite this fact, the runways are not sufficiently suitable for take-off of heavy aircraft.
>
> [AIR 27/1790]

One can imagine the disgruntled mutterings of those put onto snow-shovelling duties, but their labours paid off and within a few days No. 405 Squadron was able to announce that the runways were now free from snow and that the squadron was ready to undertake operations again.

Notwithstanding these noble efforts, the weather remained depressingly miserable, and it would be some days before operations could begin again. For No. 142 Squadron an:

> Official stand-down for the squadron was confirmed at 10.00 hours and with the exception of those personnel attending the funeral of F/L Eichler, everyone retired to the warmth and comfort of the mess.
>
> [AIR 27/976]

It sounds as though drink may have been taken, as subsequently it was noted with relief that:

> Group gave us a pleasant surprise today by informing us we were not required for operations

TRIALS AND TRIBULATION

> – a welcome diversion, enabling all to recover from the previous day's stand-down.
>
> [AIR 27/976]

No. 405 Squadron used this break to carry out various housekeeping chores. These included the Navigation Section taking up new quarters, the establishing of a training room for the squadron's Visual Air Bombers, and:

> **P.F.F. Board:-** A P.F.F. Board was held for Navigators and Air Bombers. Five Navigators and three Air Bombers successfully passed the board although it is pointed out that two of the Navigators needed special attention.
>
> [AIR 27/1790]

Passing this examination board was, seemingly, one of the hurdles that aspiring aircrew had to jump in order to be awarded the coveted 'Pathfinder Eagle' badge to wear on their tunic.

By 14th January 1945 the weather was deemed suitable to go to war, and No. 142 Squadron responded by sending six crews to join the spoof raid on Berlin that was diverting attention from the No. 5 Group attack on Leuna, and later in the day another six returned to Berlin. No. 405 Squadron was also working, sending nine crews in daylight against the Saarbrücken marshalling yards, and later seven to Merseburg, accompanied by two of the station's Mosquitoes. The weather had not finished its tricks, though, and three Lancasters were diverted to Exeter in far-off Devon on their return, and a 'Mossie' ended up at Woodbridge. Conditions must have been worse elsewhere, as two aircraft from No. 608 Squadron, normally based at Downham Market, were actually diverted *to* Gransden Lodge. During this day of hectic activity the preparations of No. 405 Squadron's crews would have been disturbed, but their morale possibly improved as:

THE FINAL PUSH

> Flight Lieutenant Shields, Public Relations Officer, No. 3 District Headquarters, visited the Unit for the purposes of interviewing aircrew with a view to obtaining from them some of their experiences on operations and subsequent publication of their experiences in the daily journals back home. Due to its special function, this Squadron has not received very much publicity in any of the Service periodicals, so his visit has done much to indicate to the aircrew that they are not forgotten about by higher authority and that at long last their folks back home will have an inkling of the very important part they are playing in the general war effort.
>
> [AIR 27/1790]

Although they no longer lived on the edge of the airfield, the Yugoslav royal family had maintained links with their former neighbours, and on 15th January 1945:

> This Station was honoured by the visit of Her Majesty, Queen Mother Marie of Jugo-Slavia. She was accompanied by her two sons, Aide-de-Camp, Lady-in-Waiting, the Air Officer Commanding No. 8 Group (P.F.F.), Station Commander, 405 Squadron Commander, 142 Squadron Commander and the R.A.F. and R.C.A.F. Public Relations Officers. Her Majesty expressed her satisfaction with everything she viewed and hoped that she would be able to make an official visit again in the near future. The itinerary of her visit is as follows:-
>
> | Time | Place |
> | --- | --- |
> | 1500 | Commanding Officer's Office |
> | 1510 | Intelligence Library (speak to aircrew) |
> | 1520 | Crew Rest Room (405) (speak to aircrew) |
> | 1540 | Maintenance Hangar (speak to ground crew) |

TRIALS AND TRIBULATION

1600	Lancaster Dispersal (speak to ground crew)
1610	142 Squadron Dispersal (speak to aircrew)
1625	Sick Quarters (speak to patients and staff)
1650	Information Room
1700	Station Club (tea served)
1730	Visit ends.

[AIR 27/1790]

After their day of hob-nobbing with the gentry, it was then back to reality with a bump for both the Gransden Lodge squadrons. Nine Mosquitoes went to Mannheim, and No. 405 Squadron took part in two missions, the first against the oil plant at Zeitz with nine aircraft and the second to Magdeburg with seven. Flight Lieutenant Payne and his crew went missing from the Zeitz raid, and 57 years after the event his brother Cecil visited Gransden Lodge from his home in Calgary to see the place from which his brother had taken off on his final mission. The researches of his family into Flight Lieutenant Payne's death indicate that his aircraft was lost through a mid-air collision, ironically with a Lancaster flown by a crew from the third Payne brother's squadron.

It was No. 142 Squadron's turn to take part in a raid on Magdeburg on 18th January 1945. Twelve crews set off in the early hours, but two were 'unable to maintain operational height and airspeed' due to icing, so turned and bombed Emden instead. Very late on the same day another twelve were dispatched against Sterkrade, and all of them made it there and back this time. The squadron was briefed for operations then scrubbed for a couple of days, but was back in action on 21st January 1945. This raid was against Kassel, with twelve crews departing, but Squadron Leader Don, the 'B' Flight commander, and his navigator Flying Officer Allen, the squadron bombing leader, failed to return.

THE FINAL PUSH

No. 405 Squadron had been rested from some days now, but on 22nd January 1945 both it and No. 142 Squadron were called upon for the day's operations. The first of these was against Hannover, and only the Mosquitoes took part, nine departing to return safely later. Shortly afterwards a further three, in the company of thirteen Lancasters, raided Duisburg.

Next day, in a vaguely sinister-sounding development, a member of the R.A.F. Police's Special Investigation branch paid a visit 'in connection with an Investigation'. Exactly what had prompted this visit is not recorded, but two Courts Martial would take place in early February 1945, so perhaps it was related to these.

The squadrons on the station were not required for duty for a few days, and they did not miss the opportunity afforded by the break to have some fun. Many of the aircrew of No. 142 Squadron had missed out on the Christmas celebrations when they were stuck away from base due to the weather, but they were able to make good for this omission when:

> ... the Squadron threw its first party in the Old Officers' Mess under the prendonym of "The Saints". Thus, all aircrew and all of the ground-crew that could be spared spent the day decorating the Mess and getting everything ready. The party was a huge success and thanks must be given to all who took part in the organisation.
>
> [AIR 27/976]

On 28th January 1945 No. 405 Squadron was sent back into action again, when eleven aircraft took off into snow showers to take part in a raid on Stuttgart. The crew of one of these claimed to have damaged an Me. 410 nightfighter, but Flying Officer Cummer (another American serving in the R.C.A.F.) and his crew were downed by either another fighter or flak, and failed to return.

TRIALS AND TRIBULATION

Flying Officer Hannah, the injured pilot of the Lancaster that had been flown back from Germany by its remaining crew members, had by now died from his wounds, and at the request of his sister, who was serving in the U.K. with the Canadian Women's Army Corps, he was interred at the R.A.F. Regional Cemetery at Harrogate in Yorkshire on 1st February 1945. No. 142 Squadron was also busy that day, but in a very different way, with two raids scheduled. Five crews acted as 'window openers' (dropping *Window* ahead of the main body of the attack) in the raid on Stuttgart, and another seven made the now-familiar trip to Berlin and back.

The Stuttgart raid completed No. 405 Squadron's operations for the month, but No. 142 Squadron had one more to go, as it was detailed to send eight Mosquitoes back to Berlin on 29th January 1945. One landed early at Woodbridge, and was later joined by the remainder as snow and bad visibility at Gransden Lodge meant they could not land back at base.

A new month brought slightly better flying weather, as on 1st February 1945 there was only an overcast and light rain, albeit with strong winds. Two Mosquitoes and thirteen Lancasters were launched into these conditions to a join a mission against the city of Ludwidshafen, and later in the day ten more of No. 142 Squadron's Mosquitoes were once again over Berlin. In the early hours of the following day six more were sent to the German capital. The scene was thus set for a very intense period of operations that would last for some months, and the sites producing fuel for the German war effort were to be among the early targets. The first of these operations to involve the squadrons from Gransden Lodge took place on 2nd February 1945 when seven aircraft from No. 405 Squadron and two from No. 142 Squadron were among the force attacking the well-known target of the Wanne-Eickel oil plant. On the same day, ten more Mosquitoes were sent to Magdeburg.

THE FINAL PUSH

The Prosper benzol synthetic fuel plant at Bottrop was the target on 3rd February 1945. Two Mosquitoes and eight Lancasters from the station took part, and one Lancaster crew claimed to have destroyed a Ju. 88 nightfighter. Eight of No. 142 Squadron's crews were supporting the raid by taking part in a spoof attack on Wiesbaden, but they almost got a taste of their own medicine, as

> The dummy fire site 5 miles N. of the town was in action with realistic street lighting and rows of houses on fire, but attracted no bombing.
>
> [AIR 28/318]

The next few days saw the pressure on the Reich's cities and fuel supplies being maintained, Gransden Lodge's contribution being nine Mosquitoes to Hannover and three to the Nordstern synthetic oil plant in Dortmund on 4th February 1945, then nine on the Milk Run to Berlin two days later. A tactical target was on the board for No. 405 Squadron on 7th February 1945, when it assigned fifteen aircraft to an attack on Kleve (Cleeves), which was carried out in order to assist the units of the Canadian army that were advancing on the Dutch/German border. No. 142 Squadron was similarly involved and sent eight crews as 'Early Windowers' in support of a raid on Goch, just south of Kleve; they then carried on to bomb Düsseldorf. Another four aircraft were deployed against Magdeburg.

Both squadrons were in action against more familiar targets on 8th February 1945, when No. 142 Squadron sent eight aircraft to Berlin, and No. 405 Squadron dispatched eleven to attack the Pölitz oil plant. The raid was rated as 'extremely accurate' and put this important facility out of action. The attack was cited by Albert Speer, the German Minister of Armaments and War Production as a major setback to the German war effort, but it was not without cost, and Flying Officer McIntyre and his crew did not return to base. In the early hours of the next day a small contingent of just four crews from No. 405 Squadron took off at the highly antisocial hour of 04:06 to attack, once more, the Wanne-Eickel oil plant.

There was no call for aircraft for operations on 11th February 1945, but on the ground, an enterprising member of No. 405 Squadron saw his ingenuity come to fruition when notification was received that:

> The installation of a new blackout curtain in aircraft equipped with Loran has been adopted after trial from the design developed by CAN/R.172039 LAC Hayes.
>
> [AIR 27/1790]

Another innovation that seems to have originated at Gransden Lodge is mentioned in the film *'Prelude to Victory'*, which was produced at about this time. This film depicts an operation by squadrons of No. 1 Group based at Hemswell in Lincolnshire, and in one scene a gun turret that is said to bear 'the Gransden Lodge Modification' is shown. The film's commentary says that this modification removed some of the Perspex glazing from the turret in order to improve visibility for the gunner. The addition of a clear view panel to many types of rear gun turret, often in the field, was common, but quite how Gransden Lodge came to be associated with the modification is not clear. Perhaps it may have been a field modification developed by No. 405 Squadron that was adopted elsewhere.

Next day the only call was for twelve of No. 142 Squadron's crews, who were destined for Stuttgart, but the day after, 13th February 1945, was a date that was later to become infamous, as that was the day on which Bomber Command mounted a raid that has divided opinion ever since. There were several missions

THE FINAL PUSH

that day for which the Gransden Lodge squadrons supplied crews. Two of them, against the Böhlen oil plant near Leipzig (two Mosquitoes and six Lancasters) and Magdeburg (eight Mosquitoes) were as uncontroversial as any bombing raid could be. The third, however, was different. No. 142 Squadron sent two aircraft to take part in the spoof raid on Bonn that was designed to deflect attention from the main attack – the first raid on Dresden.

For several months the British had been planning a series of especially heavy raids on German cities in the hope that these would finally break the enemy war machine and civil administration and bring about the end of hostilities. This scheme, code named Operation THUNDERCLAP, was to be put into operation when the situation on the German side had reached a critical point, and with the Germans fighting on two fronts thanks to the Russian advance from the east, it was deemed that the time had come. Berlin, Leipzig, Chemnitz and Dresden were all earmarked as targets, as they were considered vital communication and supply centres, and it was for the last of these, Dresden, that ten crews from No. 405 Squadron departed. All but the aircraft of Flight Lieutenant Fredericks returned again safely.

The controversy over this raid began almost immediately, as the German authorities claimed that the city contained no war industries and that the attack was an example of British barbarism. In fact, it would appear that there were indeed factories making munitions, bombsights etc. in the city, but the raid, sanctioned by Churchill, has become a byword for destruction. Estimates of the number of civilian casualties vary widely, but recent researches by German authorities have put the figure at around 25,000.

Operation THUNDERCLAP continued on 14th February 1945 and this time the target for No. 405 Squadron was Chemnitz. It took part in two raids there that day, sending seven and nine crews respectively. No. 142 Squadron was again part of a spoof when six of its aircraft went on a Mosquito-only raid on Duisburg, and another six were sent to Berlin once more.

Another five days would pass before Gransden Lodge went to war again, and when it did so a new hand was on the tiller, as on 15th February 1945 Group Captain G.H. Womersley D.S.O., D.F.C. assumed command of the station when Group Captain Dunlop was posted away to R.C.A.F. Headquarters. The new station commander was a highly experienced bomber pilot who had worked at No. 8 Group headquarters, and had later been commanding officer of No. 139 Squadron before attending Staff College in the U.S.A.

The first operation under his command came on 19th February 1945, when the target was Erfurt. The twelve crews from No. 142 Squadron taking part were warned in advance of the risk that a diversion to another airfield might be required on their return, and they were advised that economising on fuel on the trip back from the target would be prudent. The techniques of the crew of 'Rambler' would therefore have been very useful, but in the end all the Mosquitoes returned to Gransden Lodge.

Next day an officer with a deliciously appropriate name came visiting the station to check on the state of provisioning:

> S/Ldr. Salmon H.Q. Bomber Command Staff Catering Officer visited the Station and discussed the question of the Messes and the possibility of additional equipment.
>
> [AIR 28/318]

While he was so engaged, the daily business of going into battle continued around him. No. 142 Squadron was again sent to Berlin, nine of its aircraft making the round trip, while three more were called upon for a raid on Mannheim. Two Lancasters from No. 405 Squadron took part in the raid on the Rhenania Ossag

THE FINAL PUSH

refinery at Monheim near Köln, while seven more attacked Dortmund. One of these was carrying a Monroe *Nickel* bomb, packed not with explosives but propaganda leaflets - *Nickel* was the code name for a leaflet-dropping attack. Unfortunately, there was another loss for the squadron on this operation, as Squadron Leader Marcou and his crew were posted missing.

The regular stream of Mosquitoes from No. 142 Squadron making the trip to Berlin continued over the next few days: six on 21st February 1945, twelve the next day and four on 23rd February 1945. As well as these missions, the squadron also sent six crews on a spoof attack on Worms on the 21st, and on that day eleven aircraft from No. 405 Squadron also took part in what was to the final large-scale raid on the long-suffering city of Duisburg.

Another city that had been taking a severe battering throughout the war was Essen, and on 23rd February 1945 No. 405 Squadron added to its woes by sending ten Lancasters to take part in a daylight raid there, which resulted in more damage to what remained of the Krupps works. Six more of the squadron's crews

Planning a sortie in No. 142 Squadron's Briefing Room (Bill Brown)

were among those who raided, for the first and only time, the town of Pforzheim. This was a particularly devastating attack, and it is recorded that 1,825 tons (over 1,650 tonnes) of bombs were dropped there in 22 minutes, and an estimated 83% of the town's built-up area was destroyed. No. 142 Squadron's other contribution to the day's events took the form of spoof raids on Frankfurt-am-Main and Darmstadt by eight of its Mosquitoes.

Though they had seen through the previous attempt to deceive them with dummy targets, the ten crews from No. 142 Squadron who were bound for Berlin on 24th February 1945 were given some extra assistance by a special briefing on 'spoofs' before they departed.

No. 405 Squadron put up three Lancasters for that day's oil campaign target, the plant at Kamen, but No. 142 Squadron's other 'op' of the day was slightly out of the ordinary. There was nothing special about the target (Neuss), but its two Mosquitoes were among the eighteen sent in the company of the Consolidated Liberators and Halifaxes of No. 100 Group (by now the home of No. 192 Squadron), which was Bomber Command's dedicated electronic counter-measures unit. Five of the specialist crews from No. 100 Group were lost that night, it is presumed to nightfighters.

In contrast, the operations over the next few days were almost mundane, if such life-threatening activities could ever be considered as such. On 25th February 1945 No. 142 Squadron sent twelve crews to Erfurt, then two days later a further twelve to - no surprise - Berlin, while No. 405 Squadron's task was to supply three crews for a raid on Mainz. On the closing day of February 1945 Berlin was once again the target for twelve crews of No. 142 Squadron. The city must have become very familiar to them by now.

If we jump forward by a month and look at the summary of operations carried out from Gransden Lodge in March 1945, we

THE FINAL PUSH

can see that it continued to be a busy time for the air and ground crews of the squadrons. No. 405 Squadron carried out 208 sorties, flew over 1,100 hours and dropped just under 560 tons (over 500 tonnes) of bombs, plus target markers and flares etc. The figures for No. 142 Squadron are similar; it flew over 1,200 hours in 281 sorties, and dropped over 250 tons (over 220 tonnes) of bombs. It would be a little tedious to recount each and every raid in detail, and in truth most were similar in character to those that had been carried out up until this time, so let us summarise the operations in the following tables. Firstly, those carried out by No. 405 Squadron:

Date	*Target*	*Crews*
1st March 1945	Mannheim	10
2nd March 1945	Köln	9
5th March 1945	Chemnitz	16
7th March 1945	Dessau	16
8th March 1945	Hamburg	15
11th March 1945	Essen	14
12th March 1945	Dortmund	7
13th March 1945	Erin	6
14th March 1945	Zweibrücken	12
15th March 1945	Misburg	16
16th March 1945	Nürnberg	14
19th March 1945	Witten	16
21st March 1945	Heide	15
22nd March 1945	Hildesheim	13
27th March 1945	Paderborn	14
31st March 1945	Hamburg	15

And next, the operations carried out by No. 142 Squadron:

TRIALS AND TRIBULATION

Date	*Target*	*Crews*
1st March 1945	Berlin	12
2nd March 1945	Berlin	3
	Kassel	9
3rd March 1945	Berlin	12
4th March 1945	Essen	3
	Berlin	9
5th March 1945	Gelsenkirchen	3
	Berlin	9
6th March 1945	Wesel	6
	Berlin	6
7th March 1945	Berlin	9
	Frankfurt	3
8th March 1945	Kassel	3
	Hannover	3
	Berlin	6
9th March 1945	Berlin	12
11th March 1945	Berlin	12
12th March 1945	Berlin	12
13th March 1945	Erin	2
	Berlin	6
	Frankfurt	2
	Dahlbruch (Gelsenkirchen)	2
14th March 1945	Homburg	3
	Berlin	9
15th March 1945	Berlin	6
	Mannheim	6
16th March 1945	Berlin	6
	Hanau	6
17th March 1945	Berlin	5

THE FINAL PUSH

Date	Target	Crews
19th March 1945	Witten	2
	Kassel	8
20th March 1945	Berlin	6
	Berlin	6
21st March 1945	Bremen	4
	Berlin	14
	Berlin	1
22nd March 1945	Berlin	8
23rd March 1945	Berlin	10
26th March 1945	Berlin	12
27th March 1945	Berlin	10
30th March 1945	Berlin	6
	Berlin	6
	Erfurt	6

One thing that is immediately apparent from these statistics is the concentration of effort by the L.N.S.F. on Berlin. On 11th March 1945 the station O.R.B. recorded that this was the twentieth night in succession that Mosquitoes had raided the German capital. In fact, as noted earlier, Berlin would eventually be attacked by Mosquitoes on 36 consecutive nights.

The raid on 17th March 1945 was short of one aircraft, since that navigated by Ian McLeod, one of the No. 142 Squadron crew members marooned at Downham Market over the previous Christmas, suffered an engine failure on takeoff and ended up in a ditch off the end of the runway, having ploughed through a hedge. The occupants were unhurt but shaken, so they were taken to hospital as a precaution, where they were cheered by a medic announcing "I've got the cure for you", at the same time producing a bottle of brandy.

TRIALS AND TRIBULATION

The operations carried out by No. 405 Squadron, while fewer than those undertaken by the Mosquito squadron, brought casualties of a more serious nature, as on 15th March 1945 the crews of Flight Lieutenant Laing and Flight Lieutenant Parkhurst were lost, as was that of Flying Officer Peaker on 19th March 1945. The first of these days must also have seen parking space for Lancasters at a premium on the airfield, as fifteen from other squadrons were diverted to Gransden Lodge.

The records for March 1945 tell us that a major reorganisation of the ground personnel of the squadrons had been carried out, the result of which was that almost all the ground crew were now managed centrally by the station, instead of by the squadrons.

The station medical reports for the month also hold a couple of interesting entries. One of these records that another baby had been born in the Sick Quarters, and another that a cautionary film entitled 'Pick Up' on the subject of venereal disease had been shown (but to 'males only'). Obviously V.D. was still a problem

Ground crew of No. 142 Squadron (Bill Brown)

on the station, as the same reports show that there had been an increase of three new cases in the month.

We have seen from the B.D.U. days that scientists from all the allied countries were using their expertise to try to shorten the war. In March 1945 some researchers from closer to home came visiting the airfield, bringing with them a device of their devising that was designed to improve the accuracy of No. 405 Squadron's bombing:

> <u>Bombing Leader's Report:</u>- The whole of ground training during this period was devoted to the Cambridge Machine for Visual Centring Training. This machine from the Psychological Laboratory Cambridge arrived on 20th March and under the supervision of F/O Horn (W.A.A.F.) each Visual Air Bomber carried out 7 training and one test exposure, or a total of 148 plates. Everyone showed a tendency to improve with practice and final results compared very favourably with those of the other P.F.F. squadrons previously visited.
>
> [AIR 27/1790]

Not to be outdone, some of the pilots also tried their skill, and reputedly did a better job than their bomb aimers.

This intriguing machine was intended to measure and improve the ability of bomb aimers to assess the mid-point of a pattern of target markers and so train them to place their own loads accurately. It involved the trainee viewing a simulated pattern of target markers on a photographic plate, and guiding his 'pilot' (the assessor) to release her bomb load in the centre of the pattern. The accuracy of the position in which the bombs would have fallen could then be calculated and the bomb aimer's performance scored.

The weather on the previous day had caused the operations for No. 142 Squadron to be cancelled, but on 2nd April 1945 the weary trail back to Berlin called for fourteen of its crews. In an indication of changing times, the Gransden Lodge O.R.B. once more starts recording things other than operations, such as on that day, when, it was noted, 'The Streamliners', an R.C.A.F. dance band, played for the enjoyment of the station's W.A.A.F. contingent at their Invitation Dance.

The attack in which No. 405 Squadron took part on 3rd April 1945 had deadly unintended consequences. The squadron's twelve Lancasters formed an element of a daylight raid on Nordhausen, which was targeted on what were believed to be barracks occupied by Nazi officials fleeing from Berlin. In fact, these buildings were the living quarters for slave workers from the nearby V-2 manufacturing plant, and many hundreds of these unfortunates were killed. No. 142 Squadron's mission that night was to send twelve Mosquitoes to Berlin yet again, and the B.D.U.'s work was proving to be useful, as there were reports of some *Boozer* indications from nightfighter radar systems over the target.

There was no such confusion about aiming points on 4th April 1945. Sixteen aircraft from No. 405 Squadron attacked the synthetic oil plant at Leuna, as they had done before. No. 142 Squadron also had an oil campaign target, and six crews were sent against the Lützkendorf refinery.

Another six were dispatched on a spoof raid on Magdeburg, but the operation was real enough for Flight Lieutenant Pudsey and his navigator, who did not return. The remarkable thing about these fatalities is that this was only the third loss of an aircraft and crew in action by No. 142 Squadron since its reformation. This says much for the merits of the Mosquito.

For three days the Gransden Lodge squadrons did not operate, though raids were planned then cancelled, then on 8th April 1945 ten Lancasters and four Mosquitoes attacked the shipyard areas of Hamburg. Ten more of No. 142 Squadron's crews raided Dessau,

THE FINAL PUSH

and, in an unusual departure, seven crews from No. 608 Squadron who had been diverted after a raid on Berlin were debriefed on the station, and their reports appear in the Gransden Lodge O.R.B.

While the day's work had been going on back at base, some of the station's sportsmen had enjoyed a day at the seaside, when:

> At Bournemouth, the Gransden Lodge Basket Ball team played in the R.C.A.F. o/s Championships finals. After a hard struggle against Bournemouth R.C.A.F. the match was lost by 42 points to 26 points.
>
> [AIR 28/318]

No such frivolities were in evidence next day, as on 9th April 1945 No. 405 Squadron dispatched sixteen crews to raid Kiel, which No. 142 Squadron supported by sending six Mosquitoes to take part in a spoof raid on Hamburg, while six more raided the railway yards at Plauen.

There was a day of 'make and mend' for No. 142 Squadron on 10th April 1945, but No. 405 Squadron was in action. It sent nine aircraft on a raid on Plauen, and another four to participate in an attack on Leipzig. Three of these got back home safely, but the other suffered badly after being attacked by an Me. 163 fighter over the target.

The aircraft that inflicted the damage on this Lancaster was a Messerschmitt Me. 163 *Komet*, a swept-wing, rocket-powered interceptor that had phenomenal speed and altitude performance but an endurance that was measured in minutes. It could climb to 12,000 m (over 39,000 feet), and accelerate to over 950 km/h (about 590 mph) to attack a bomber stream and outrun any defending fighters. Its speed often acted against it, though, as it was difficult to manoeuvre into a firing position against its slow-moving targets. However, one managed it on this occasion, and

TRIALS AND TRIBULATION

shot away the Lancaster's rear turret and one rudder, killing the rear gunner. The pilot managed to get his aircraft back to Woodbridge, where four of the crew baled out before he landed safely with the remaining injured crew member on board.

The operation for No. 405 Squadron on 11th April 1945 had a Wagnerian feel to it, as it was called upon to send four bombers to join the daylight raid on Bayreuth, although it was the railway yards not the opera house that was the aiming point. Twelve of the station's Mosquitoes, in two waves, made the trip to Berlin that day, and twelve more put on a repeat performance on the next, followed by another twelve-strong contingent attacking Hamburg on 13th April 1945.

It may have brought back memories of the dark days of the Battle of Berlin for some of the fifteen crews from No. 405 Squadron when they took part in the attack on Potsdam on 14th April 1945. This was the first time that heavy bombers of the R.A.F. had entered the Berlin defence zone since March 1944, but now the opposition was meagre and only one aircraft from the entire raid was lost. The Lancasters had the company of twelve of No. 142 Squadron's Mosquitoes on the journey, as they were raiding Berlin. When the crews returned, they could unwind after the long mission by enjoying the entertainment provide by yet another R.C.A.F. dance band, which was playing at a dance laid on in order to drum up support for a Canadian Victory Loan Drive.

This trip was repeated on the next two days, when No. 142 Squadron sent twelve aircraft back to Berlin each day.

On 17th April 1945 sixteen aircraft from No. 405 Squadron were detailed to attack the railway yards at Schwandorf, and twelve from No. 142 Squadron should have taken part in the operation against the airfield at Ingolstadt, but only eight managed to get airborne. This was not the fault of the weather or unserviceability, but something rather more spectacular:

THE FINAL PUSH

> The night operation was marred by an unfortunate accident during take-off. The ninth A/C with F/L Nolan as pilot and P/O Green as navigator swung at the beginning of the take-off run. The undercarriage collapsed and the aircraft burst into flames but the crew managed to get out of the aircraft in time. Little could be done to extinguish the fire as the petrol tanks caught fire and, as the A/C was bombed up, it was not safe to approach. The bombs exploded 2 or 3 minutes later but no injuries were sustained by anyone. The three A/C waiting to take off were ordered back to dispersal points.
>
> [AIR 27/976]

This accident had echoes that rang down the years. In 2004 the British T.V. company Channel 4 produced a documentary series entitled *'Bomber Crew'*, in which grandchildren of World War Two aircrew were brought together to see how they would cope if they, too, had to crew a bomber, and Flight Lieutenant Nolan's grandson was among the participants.

The airfield must not have sustained serious damage from the exploding ordnance, as on 18th April 1945 six crews from No. 405 Squadron were able to take off to participate in the raid on the naval base, airfield and town on the small island of Heligoland. No. 142 Squadron was able to put up crews on the 19th and 20th April 1945 to join the raids on Schleissheim airfield and Berlin (twelve crews on each on the first day, then eight on Berlin and four on Schleissheim on the second), and there would certainly have been sighs of relief if the crews had known that this was to be the last attack of the war on Berlin. The squadron was also busy next day, when it sent six aircraft against Kiel.

On the same date, wireless operator Sergeant Henderson of No. 405 Squadron made an exciting-sounding entry in his log book when he recorded that he had taken part in an air test of a new super-bomber. In fact, he seems to have flown as a passenger in an Avro Lincoln B1, although neither the station nor squadron records mention that this new aircraft type, which would not enter squadron service for some months, had visited Gransden Lodge. Even more mysterious than the presence of the Lincoln at Gransden Lodge is its identity, as its number, clearly recorded in Henderson's log book, relates to no known R.A.F. aircraft.

No. 405 Squadron was in action again on 22nd April 1945 when it supplied nine aircraft to attack Bremen, which was designated as 'a tactical target, in direct support of the Army', and next day No. 142 Squadron sent fourteen Mosquitoes to attack Travemünde.

For one Mosquito crew at Gransden Lodge, 25th April 1945 turned out to be a really bad day, as:

```
F/O D.R. Maguire (152019) was involved in two
flying accidents during the day. He was air-
testing Mosquito KB.450 in the morning and on
landing, overshot the runway. The undercarriage
collapsed, rendering the A/C Category 'B' - for
repair at contractor's works. In the afternoon,
F/O Maguire was air-testing Mosquito KB.613. On
landing, he stalled the A/C. It bounced, swung
to starboard, the undercarriage collapsed and
the drop tank went up in flames. The A/C was
extensively burned and was beyond repair. The
crew were uninjured.
```

[AIR 27/976]

But for many other crews, it was quite the opposite of a bad day. At twelve minutes past six on the morning of 25th April 1945, nine Lancasters of No. 405 Squadron took off as part of a force raiding Hitler's 'Eagle's Nest' retreat at Berchtesgaden, presumably with the intent of finishing off the German dictator. By early afternoon they were all back, and a few hours later four more attacked the gun positions on the island of Wangerooge that

THE FINAL PUSH

guarded the approaches to Wilhelmshaven and Bremerhaven. They were not to know it, but when the last of them had touched down at a few minutes before seven o'clock in the evening, the squadron's fighting war was finished. It would take part in more missions of a decidedly different character before the conflict was over, but it would drop no more bombs. Appropriately, on the same day two officers from the R.C.A.F. District Headquarters visited in order to interview the Canadians on the subject of post-war resettlement and rehabilitation.

No. 142 Squadron was still in the firing line, though, and on the day of No. 405 Squadron's last 'op' it sent twelve Mosquitoes to bomb Pasing airfield near München, then on 26th April 1945 twelve more to join the attack on the airfield at Eggebek.

In a sure sign that things were returning to a more normal footing, by the end of the month the station O.R.B. was able to record that:

> At Upwood the Gransden Lodge Soccer team was beaten by Upwood in the Bomber Command Challenge Cup. The score was 1 - 3.
>
> The 8th Canadian Victory Loan was successfully concluded. The grand sum of 46,950 dollars being subscribed.
>
> [AIR 28/318]

The Victory Loan drive was not the only call upon the pockets of the Canadians. Fred Davies, a No. 405 Squadron veteran, recalls that on pay-day one of the station's medical officers would join the other gamblers shooting dice on the Sergeants' Mess pool table, and such was his prowess that he was known to 'clean out' the other players. This would often lead to a heartfelt cry of "How can we save money when the doc. wins it all?" from the recently impoverished...

TRIALS AND TRIBULATION

In keeping with the lighter atmosphere on the station, on the last few days of April 1945 'The Streamliners' got to play return gigs, and a couple of days later another R.C.A.F. Gang Show, 'The Tarmacs', performed before a large audience. This audience, quite apart from the quality of the show, would have had an even greater cause for merriment, as by the time of the concert newspaper headlines were proclaiming 'HITLER DEAD', the Führer having committed suicide on 30th April 1945.

While hangovers were being nursed on the station, an event that foreshadowed the future use of Gransden Lodge occurred next day, when on 3rd May 1945:

> A Glider towed by an aeroplane from Gt. Dunmow crashed near Gransden. Pilot received fractured pelvis, the other occupants minor injuries.
>
> [AIR 28/318]

That, though, would have been far from the thoughts of the crews of No. 142 Squadron. On the previous night, that of 2nd/3rd May 1945, sixteen of its Mosquitoes had taken part in the last operations of the European war: two raids against the port of Kiel. At 02:21 on 3rd May 1945, when all the aircraft had landed back safely, Gransden Lodge's life as a combat station came to an end.

MANNA, EXODUS AND COOK'S TOURS

By the winter of 1944 the conditions under which the people of Holland were living had become almost intolerable. Fuel, power and especially food were in extremely short supply, so much so that this became known to the Dutch as the *hongerwinter* ('hunger winter'). Despite attempts by Sweden and Switzerland to supply aid, the continuing fighting on the continent made this difficult, and the much-needed supplies did not reach all of the areas where they were required. In some places, the Dutch were reduced to eating tulip bulbs in order to survive, and in January 1945 Queen Wilhelmina of the Netherlands requested help from the U.K. and U.S.A. With the agreement of Churchill and U.S. President Roosevelt, by April 1945 General Eisenhower was in a position to ask Air Commodore A.J.W. Geddes to formulate plans for an operation to supply food by air to 3,500,000 Dutch civilians.

Geddes rose to the challenge and the result was Operation MANNA, the mass dropping of food supplies by R.A.F. bombers. Later in April 1945 Eisenhower was given permission to negotiate a truce with the German forces in Holland in order to allow the operation to go ahead and, following broadcasts by the B.B.C. to alert the Dutch civilians to what was about to happen, on 29th April 1945 Operation MANNA and the U.S. equivalent, Operation CHOWHOUND, were launched.

TRIALS AND TRIBULATION

On 30th April 1945 No. 405 Squadron flew again to take part in Operation MANNA, when five Lancasters backed up the marking of the aiming point at the racecourse of The Hague where the remainder of the crews taking part were to drop their supplies. The operation was repeated next day by six crews, and on 2nd May 1945, when the last raids of the war were taking place, five more marked the racecourse again. On the 4th and 5th May 1945 the squadron once more marked at The Hague, with three aircraft each day, but on 7th May 1945 its eight aircraft were switched to Rotterdam to carry out the same task.

Three days before this, German officers had signed a document at Field Marshal Montgomery's headquarters on Lüneburg Heath surrendering their forces in north-west Germany, Denmark and Holland and on 7th May 1945 General Eisenhower, with representatives from the Allies, accepted the unconditional surrender of all the German forces. At last, the fighting in Europe was over, Victory in Europe Day, V.E. Day, had arrived, and the celebrations could finally begin. Unaccountably, this gets no mention in the No. 405 Squadron or station records, but No. 142 Squadron's O.R.B. noted the event on 8th May 1945:

```
This is a historic day. V.E. Day was announced
and the whole station took part in celebrations.
No special leave or pass was granted and there
was a travel ban for distances exceeding 20
miles from the station. The Squadron A/C are
grounded for 2 days.
```

[AIR 27/976]

So it appears that jubilation was not unconfined at Gransden Lodge, but there are stories of a number of hayricks on local farms being set ablaze in the evening to mark the occasion. This alleged pyromania was laid at the door of the more exuberant spirits in No. 405 Squadron, and even though there were some among the

MANNA, EXODUS AND COOK'S TOURS

The V.E. Day service at Gransden Lodge (Pathfinder Collection)

R.A.F. personnel who took a slightly dim view of the behaviour of the Canadians – the latter being referred to by the former, somewhat disparagingly, as 'The Log Rollers' – it seems as if this time the attribution of the mischief may have been correct. Residents of nearby Gamlingay also remember hayricks being set alight by flares fired by revellers from No. 405 Squadron; they also recall that some squadron members had previously earned a dubious reputation by fighting in the Hardwick Arms in that village, on one occasion a pugilist finding himself in the street after being smashed through the pub's glass door. Even so, on this occasion any high jinks would have been completely justified, given what the squadron had been through over the preceding years. The squadron clearly had a better reputation in the pubs in the Gransden villages, though. Angus Robb recalls that on V.E. Night:

> *"The owners of the Crown & Cushion gave us the keys of the establishment the previous day, saying they were off to London and when all the stock had been consumed, make sure the place was clean."*

TRIALS AND TRIBULATION

Although not specifically related to V.E. Night, Ian McLeod tells a story that shows that No. 142 Squadron's standing in the eyes of the habitués of the local pubs was good, too:

> "... the squadron stood down one day in the month and then we might adjourn to a hotel, a pub. We used to go to a little pub, place called Eltisley up the end of one of the roads. You'd say to one of the locals, 'What's up the end of that road?' – 'Never been up there mister.' Never been up that far, and that was the English, they never travelled anywhere. So we went up to this little pub at Eltisley and it was run by an ex-Navy fellow and we, on the second time we went up, we had a fellow that played the double bass, one of our fellows, he was a double bass champion of Northern England, Geordie Richardson, and one of the fellows was a beautiful pianist too, so we used to have a sing-song and everything, you know, with a few beers. On the second occasion an old farmer - I'm going in there ordering the beers - and this old fellow came out as if he's going to leave. I said, 'You're not going to leave?' He said, 'I'm going home to get my wife.' He enjoyed our company so much, and a sing-song ..."

Not all the members of No. 405 Squadron were participating in the V.E. Night celebrations. Early in April 1945 Operation EXODUS, an operation to bring home ex-prisoners of war by air, had begun, and on V.E. Day itself, 8th May 1945, ten Lancasters of No. 405 Squadron were part of this operation and flew newly-released prisoners from Brussels to R.A.F. Westcott near Aylesbury in Buckinghamshire.

Edwin Horner, a flight engineer with the squadron, remembered that day's operation. He recalled that there were thousands of ex-P.O.W.s waiting at Brussels for a flight home, of which the crew from Gransden Lodge picked up 24. One of these was, unusually for a released prisoner, wearing fine pair of boots. When asked how he had come by them, he replied that for months he had seen them being worn by one his guards, from whom he had demanded them when he was released. When the crew and their passengers arrived at Westcott the ex-prisoners were given a warm welcome and a buffet meal, but when the flyers from No. 405 Squadron got back to base in the late afternoon they found that not only had they missed the victory celebrations, but that there was nothing left for them to eat. Despite this, Horner remembered the day as one of the most satisfactory of his life.

At least one of the squadron's own was also repatriated during Operation EXODUS. Arthur Darlow, a self-described 'kriegie' (prisoner of war, from the German), who had been shot down a year before almost to the day, came back by air. His diary, parts of which appear in his grandson Stephen Darlow's book *'Lancaster Down!'*, records that, following a heavy night, things almost went awry at the last minute on the return trip from Rheims, but that he finally made it home safely:

> "Up this morning at 7.30 am, and had good breakfast. Am feeling drunk from fumes of last night's 'binge'. Travelled to aerodrome this morning, in charge of 24 men. Waited for quite a time, but finally took off in Lancaster. Ropey crew, DR compass went u/s and pilot and navigator didn't notice it. Brought their attention to it and found ourselves 80 odd miles off Norfolk coast, en route for Norway. Turned onto 270 and crossed Norfolk coast, instead of at Dover. Arrived RAF Station, Wing, about 8 pm. De loused again, given meal, then waited till 1 am for train to Cosford. Arrived 3 am, sent telegram, interrogated and re-equipped with battle

TRIALS AND TRIBULATION

dress etc. Had a bath (beautiful) and got to bed at 7 am. Up again at 8 am and finally caught train home at 2.25 pm. Arrive home at 9 pm and nearly got squeezed to death by Anne. <u>Boy oh boy, what a marvellous woman.</u> Cheerio to kriegie life, and now for 42 days leave."

No. 405 Squadron took part in EXODUS flights again on 9th and 10th May 1945, on both occasions sending eight aircraft to Lübeck. There was no call for EXODUS on 11th May 1945, but on that day a number of low crimes and misdemeanours were dealt with when a Court Martial was held. There were also other indications that the normal conditions of life on a peace-time R.A.F. station were beginning to be seen for the first time. The number of parades undertaken by the station's personnel started to increase, at the same time as their working hours began to decrease. We can see the evidence for this in No. 142 Squadron's O.R.B.:

> The Squadron took part in a Station parade held as a rehearsal for the expected visit to the Station of the A.O.C. There was no flying during the day or night. In view of the cessation of hostilities in Europe, the Station reverted to peace-time working hours. Skeleton staffs were available in all sections.
>
> [AIR 27/976]

The Gransden Lodge cricket team was also in action, playing matches against local opponents such as the area's electricity supply company.

On 15th May 1945 No. 405 Squadron flew its last missions of the war, when it sent two waves of eight then seven Lancasters on EXODUS operations to evacuate 360 prisoners from Juvincourt in France to Wing in Buckinghamshire. Though it was detailed for further EXODUS operations, these were all cancelled before

MANNA, EXODUS AND COOK'S TOURS

they took place, and No. 405 Squadron did not fly operationally from Gransden Lodge again.

V.E. Day had brought an end to the war in Europe, but the Allies knew that they still faced a formidable foe in the Japanese. In order to increase the pressure against Japan from the air, the British Commonwealth nations planned the formation of the Very Long Range Bomber Force, known as 'Tiger Force'. This force, originally intended to be up to 1,000 heavy bombers in strength and made up of squadrons from the British, Canadian, Australian and New Zealand air forces, would be transferred to the Far East and used in bombing operations to support a planned invasion of Japan.

No. 405 Squadron was earmarked to be part of the Canadian element of Tiger Force, and was re-equipped during May 1945 with Canadian-built Mk. X Lancasters, the siblings of the original Mk. X delivered by Reg Lane. The intention was that these would be replaced in turn by the new Lincoln bomber before the Tiger Force squadrons departed for operations in the Far East.

Like their Canadian counterparts on the station, No. 142 Squadron also received another aircraft, but in this case a pre-owned example. Possibly with Tiger Force in mind, a Lancaster was transferred to the squadron from No. 405 Squadron so that the Mosquito crews could receive some instruction in flying the heavier aircraft, but, probably wisely, they were not allow to carry out the takeoff or landing.

Another use was soon to be found for all the aircraft of the squadron, as in the closing weeks of May 1945:

> Authority received from No. 8 (P.F.F.) Group H.Q. for "Cook's Tours" to be carried out over Europe for the purpose of enabling aircrews and maintenance ground staff to see the damage inflicted by the bomber offensive. The Squadron is allowed to send the Lancaster and 2 Mosquitoes

TRIALS AND TRIBULATION

> daily for this purpose. Not more than 10 persons
> are to fly in the Lancaster and not more than 3
> in the Mosquitoes. A/C engaged on these flights
> are not permitted to fly below 1,500 feet and
> detailed routes must be adhered to.
>
> [AIR 27/976]

One feels that there is a good chance that the last instruction in this entry may have been honoured more in the breach than in the observance. These Cook's Tours, the name of which is a reference to the guided tours operated by the Thomas Cook travel agency since the early 20th century, began next day, and were to become a regular feature of squadron life at Gransden Lodge. On 22nd May 1945, in a swan song for No. 405 Squadron:

> A parade of all ranks was held in the Lancaster
> Hangar, Gransden Lodge, at 1600 hours. The
> parade was addressed by Air Vice-Marshal Bennett,
> C.B., C.B.E., DSO, Air Officer Commanding Path
> Finder Force, who thanked the squadron personnel
> for their part in the War Effort and wished them
> "Bon Voyage". Personnel were excellently turned
> out and the parade went well, which was remarked
> upon by Staff Officers.
>
> [AIR 27/1790]

This date also marked the passing of the baton of A.O.C. No. 8 Group from Bennett to Air Vice-Marshal John Whitley, who would oversee the running down and eventual disbandment of the group.

Within a few days another departure took place, when on 26th May 1945, following a reportedly riotous party, the personnel of No. 405 Squadron left the station for their new base at Linton-on-Ouse in Yorkshire, and a return to the Canadian No. 6 Group:

MANNA, EXODUS AND COOK'S TOURS

> The move of the Squadron from R.A.F. Station
> Gransden Lodge, No. 8 (PFF) Group to R.C.A.F.
> Station, Linton-on-Ouse (No. 62 Base, No. 6
> (RCAF) Group), was effected. A road party of 26
> which left Gransden Lodge at 0600 hours arrived
> Linton at 1700 hours. The rail party departed
> Gamlingay Station at 1100 hours amid cheers and
> tears of R.A.F. personnel of Gransden Lodge and
> the local village of Great Gransden.
>
> [AIR 27/1790]

The members of No. 405 Squadron had been the longest serving residents at Gransden Lodge, having been there for over two years, and they had suffered the highest losses of the units based there. Although most of the squadron had now left, a few members remained behind to deal with the inevitable bureaucracy, but by the end of the month the Station Commander was able to declare himself satisfied with the results of a marching-out inspection, though there was a charge against the departed squadron for some panes of broken glass. This may not have been unconnected to those parties...

With the departure of No. 405 Squadron, No. 142 Squadron was, if only briefly, the sole major unit based at Gransden Lodge. Being enterprising individuals, its members did not let the grass grow under their feet, and shortly after the Canadians had left they bagged living accommodation that they had vacated, it being closer to the messes and having the luxury of running water laid on.

The medical teams on the station, who may have hoped that demand for their services would decrease now that hostilities had ceased, were called into action again on the last day of May 1945 when they had to deal with the aftermath of the crash of an American Mustang in the vicinity of the airfield. The unfortunate pilot was killed in the accident, and the Gransden Lodge sick quarters staff arranged for his body to be returned to the American authorities. A sad end for a pilot who had survived the war.

TRIALS AND TRIBULATION

No. 142 Squadron's exclusive occupancy of the airfield was only to be short, since at Graveley No. 692 Squadron, a sister squadron in the Light Night Striking Force, was also preparing to move. This was because No. 227 Squadron had moved to Graveley to join the resident No. 35 Squadron, both of which were intended to become part of Tiger Force. With the new squadron's arrival, No. 692 Squadron and its aircraft had to leave Graveley for Gransden Lodge, so on 4th June 1945 the squadron's nineteen Mosquitoes and one Lancaster were flown over to their new base, and within the next few days the remainder of No. 692 Squadron had made the short road journey from Graveley and were ensconced at their new home. It is interesting to note that the squadron's aircraft included a Lancaster as well as the Mosquitoes, probably for the same reason that one was issued to No. 142 Squadron.

Brought into being on 1st January 1944, No. 692 Squadron's equipment was in part funded by a South American organisation formed to raise money to aid the war effort in Europe. Because of this support the squadron acknowledged its benefactors in its name, so it was officially known by the splendid title of 'No. 692 (The Fellowship of the Bellows) Squadron'. At least two other R.A.F. squadrons also carried the name of this organisation in their title.

Despite undoubtedly having been formed with a serious intent, it is also clear that The Fellowship of the Bellows, whose stated aim was 'to raise the wind' to buy aircraft for the R.A.F., had a whimsical side too. The members advanced in the Fellowship, based on their financial contributions and the progress of the war, through ranks such as Puff, Gust and Hurricane before being awarded the Order of the Bellows. The Cashier was known as the Receiver of Windfalls, the Treasurer as the Keeper of the Windbag and the President was, naturally, known as the High Wind.

No. 692 Squadron, which like the latest incarnation of No. 142 Squadron had only been in existence for a relatively short time, nonetheless had a notable war record. In February 1944 it had operated the first Mosquito to carry a 4,000lb (over 1,800 kg) 'cookie' bomb; this capability allowed a Mosquito to carry a larger bomb load to Berlin than the B-17 Flying Fortress could at that time. In another operation, with minimal training, the squadron had successfully dropped mines into the Kiel Canal, becoming the first Mosquito squadron to carry out a mining operation. Don Bennett was unable to resist the opportunity to make a none-too-thinly veiled dig at No. 5 Group by recalling that this operation was carried out without weeks of specialised training and with no briefings to the Public Relations department. He contrasted this with previous operations that had been carried out, including one that had involved dropping weapons into 'a fairly vast sheet of water'. One can easily imagine what he may have had in mind as a structure that might hold back a 'fairly vast sheet of water', and the famous No. 5 Group squadron that had, with great fanfare, dropped things into it…

Back in London, the deliberations of the Post-War Airfield Requirements Committee had been continuing, and on the same day that No. 692 Squadron finished its move to Gransden Lodge, the committee issued the draft of an interim report on its recommendations. By this time it had concluded its mammoth task of assessing 586 airfields, and of these it proposed that 326 should be retained. These were graded into five classes, mainly based on their runway length and the possibilities for runway extension. Those in Class 1(A) were the most desirable, and Gransden Lodge figured in the 123 so classified.

The newly-arrived squadron joined No. 142 Squadron in participating in numerous training exercises during the remainder of June 1945. It was also a time of many comings and goings, as

TRIALS AND TRIBULATION

personnel were leaving the squadrons for new postings or to depart the service altogether, and new faces were still being posted in from Operational Training Units. In some cases, personnel were just transferred between the two squadrons on the station. Recreation and relaxation were still available to those remaining though:

> R.A.F. Gransden Lodge took a prominent part in a Sports Day held at R.A.F. Upwood. In Athletic events we took first and second places in the 100 yds. Sprint, we were first in the Mile Relay Race and took third place in the Officers' 100 yds. sprint.
>
> [AIR 28/318]

In addition to the sporting events, concerts and dances were also still being organised and enjoyed.

In a change from the training regime, both squadrons were soon to be involved in a more unusual and important exercise. No. 142 Squadron's O.R.B. for 1st July 1945 records:

> 5 special exercises were carried out in the early morning to-day. The Squadron had been detailed to fly Mosquitoes on a route out across the North Sea in order to test the efficiency of the German radar system. This was done by detailing our navigators to log either Gee fixes or D.R. positions every 15 minutes and sending logs of trips in to Group for comparison with fixes taken by the radar operators. The exercise was given the name of "Post Mortem".
>
> [AIR 27/976]

This Exercise POST MORTEM was a major undertaking. In an effort to find out just how effective the German radar system had been when tackling a raid by the R.A.F., a whole section of the

Reich's radar chain in Denmark was re-activated, and, with R.A.F. observers taking careful notes, their former enemies once more carried out their wartime procedures as the attacking aircraft approached. Alfred Price, in his book *'Instruments of Darkness'*, notes that the Germans considered it to be in their own interest to co-operate in this exercise, as they freely admitted that they expected that another war might soon break out against the Russians, and that it would be to Germany's benefit to make sure that Britain was in as strong a position as possible should that happen. So once again, though in a smaller way, crews from Gransden Lodge were involved in radar intelligence gathering, as those of No. 192 Squadron had been almost three years before.

The threatened inspection by the new A.O.C. eventually took place early in July 1945, and No. 142 Squadron noted that he was impressed with the high standards of efficiency that he saw on display. Gratifying as this praise must surely have been to the inhabitants of Gransden Lodge, the realities of life in a world outside the narrow confines of an R.A.F. base were brought into focus a few days later on 5th July 1945:

> To-day was polling day for the general election and every effort was made to ensure the convenient registration of votes by all personnel.

[AIR 27/976]

It was at this General Election, the first to be held after V.E. Day and, in fact, the first to be held since 1935 due to the war, that Winston Churchill's Conservative Party was voted out of office, despite Churchill's success as a wartime leader. Churchill was succeeded as Prime Minister by Clement Attlee. One of the first acts introduced by his Labour Party government was the Family Allowances Act, the rights and wrongs of which had been the

TRIALS AND TRIBULATION

subject of a discussion group at Gransden Lodge the previous September.

This change of government did not affect the duties being undertaken by the squadrons on the station, since July 1945 continued the previous round of exercises and Cook's Tours. At about this time, a W.A.A.F. officer, Edith Heap (after her marriage, Edith Kup), was serving at Bourn alongside No. 105 Squadron. As she recalled in her memoirs, she had a slightly unsettling experience at Gransden Lodge after she had been posted there:

> *"The WAAF quarters were about ½ mile from the mess, & down one side, barbed wire between, was an Italian P.O.W. camp. Who on earth had decided that, I wondered, our own forces were kept at a further distance. Letters & Lord knows what else, passed through the wire, & one day, being alone in our hut, I was changing for dinner. There was a rattling, & on looking up, there was an Italian trying to open my window. I ran & locked the front door, & rang for S.P.s who took an age to arrive, & by the time they did the Eyetie had gone."*

There was no prisoner of war camp in the villages around Gransden Lodge, but there was a camp for captured Italians at Therfield Heath, near Royston, which is about 10 miles (16 km) from the airfield. In all likelihood the Italian intruder was a prisoner working on the land, some of whom were considered trustworthy enough to be accommodated on the farms where they worked. Perhaps he lodged next to the W.A.A.F. billets for some of the time.

Earlier in her career, Heap had served at R.A.F. Pocklington in Yorkshire, where Johnny Fauquier, erstwhile C.O. of No. 405 Squadron, had also been based during his first period as the squadron's commander. She recalled that he drove his crews so hard that one, albeit drunken, crew member threatened to shoot him (obviously the threat was never carried out). She also saw evidence of Fauquier's down-to-earth personality when, after a few drinks, he ate the flowers that were decorating his dinner table.

Like many others, Heap was able to take part in a Cook's Tour, and she recalled her flight in No. 692 Squadron's Lancaster like this:

"It was a gorgeous day, & outward bound we flew over Margate – the beach was packed with people sitting cheek by jowl, the first time they had been able to bathe & enjoy the sea for six years. We flew to the Hague & Neimegen, absolute wrecks. Wesel with the bridge in the water, & scene of a desperate land battle & up the Rhine, to Cologne & round the Dom at a few hundred feet. Up the Rhine to look at blown bridges & what a sight of devastation it was. One could only feel how terrible it must have been on the receiving end. Then Duren, Aachen & Dunkirk & home via Manston. I particularly remember the roads, shining in the sun like so many icebound rivers, caused by glass driven in hard by blast, & cows grazing peacefully in the fields. We were all rather quiet on landing, & though I, for one, had seen lots of photographs, both bombing, recce & those taken low level after V.E. day, to actually see rows & rows of empty shells, once houses, with the odd church spire standing high and bleak was quite a shaker. It was far worse than London & Coventry etc., & frankly I just don't know how the Germans stood it so long."

The program of parties, concerts and sports events on the station continued, including one musical performance at which, in a

TRIALS AND TRIBULATION

reversal of the usual order of things, the band may have supplied the beer, since the entertainment was being supplied by the Northampton Brewery Concert Party.

Now that the crews on the Gransden Lodge squadrons were engaged in exercises and Cook's Tours, the dangers of operational flying were obviously a thing of the past. This did not mean that aviation had become a risk-free occupation, as No. 142 Squadron found when one of its aircraft crashed at the airfield while attempting a single-engine landing after a night cross-country exercise. The crew escaped without injury, but their aircraft was destroyed by fire.

Dealing with this accident must have been one of the final administrative chores for No. 142 Squadron's C.O., as on 25th July 1945 Wing Commander Nathan ceased command of the squadron in preparation for release from service. Wing Commander Nathan had been commanding officer since the squadron was re-formed at Gransden Lodge, and his departure was another sign that the end of hostilities was getting closer. The squadron's new C.O., Wing Commander Gray, arrived from No. 608 Squadron on 31st July 1945.

Away from Gransden Lodge, preparations were still under way for Tiger Force, and the politicians and planners were looking even further ahead to the depressing possibility of fighting another war, probably against Russia. In July 1945 discussions on the subject of future Very Heavy Bombers (V.H.B.s) – even larger and heavier than the Lincolns slated for Tiger Force – were minuted. In the light of what actually happened post-war, the hoped-for airfield upgrading program, which called for 27 V.H.B. airfields, one to be built every year for 27 years, seems remarkably optimistic. The expectation was that eighteen airfields would be required by the end of 1960, and Bomber Command recommended that the next six should include Gransden Lodge, which was third in their order of priority. The planners were not convinced of the correctness of Bomber Command's recommendations, and favoured building new three new V.H.B. airfields in Scotland, Northern Ireland and south-west England, so it was not clear even then that Gransden Lodge would 'make the cut' and see a continuing operational future.

However, before any of these plans for fighting the next war would be required, the current conflict had to be brought to its end, and there was still a real possibility that crews would be required to put Tiger Force into action. No. 142 Squadron called for fifteen crews to volunteer for service in the Far East, and those that did so were given the requisite inoculations and sent off on embarkation leave.

These preparations being put in hand to send forces to the Far East were about to be rendered unnecessary, though. The O.R.B. of No. 142 Squadron contains a reflective entry for the fateful day of 6th August 1945:

> All flying cancelled owing to unfavourable weather conditions. But there was news of aerial activity in the Far East which threatened to alter not only the course of the war in that theatre of operations but probably of the whole world in post-war science. Scientists have for years been attempting to split the atom and today their efforts have borne fruit in the dropping of the first atom-bomb on the naval port of Hiroshima. No reports were available at the time to decide the amount of damage but later information showed that the bomb had wrought complete devastation to over fifty per cent of the city. On the squadron, everybody knows that victory is near and becomes apprehensive as to his future.
>
> [AIR 27/976]

TRIALS AND TRIBULATION

This was followed on 9th August 1945 by the dropping of the second atomic bomb on Nagasaki, and the implications of these events for the continuing need for their services was clearly not lost on the aircrew at Gransden Lodge. Next day:

> In the evening, in the Officers' Mess, a party was held by the 2 Squadrons on the station, for it was deemed that with the rapid closing of activities in the Far East and the apparent subsequent disbanding of these units, some celebration was called for - with most successful results.
>
> [AIR 27/976]

Finally, on 15th August 1945, the long-awaited day arrived, to be greeted, as:

> Another historic day. Victory was declared in the Far East with the total unconditional surrender of the Japanese. Today and tomorrow have been declared 'VJ' days. The Squadron A/C have been grounded for these 2 days and the whole station stood down for celebrations. No special leave or pass was granted and there was a travel ban for distances exceeding 20 miles from the station. The whole station was invited by the people of the village to share their celebration with them.
>
> [AIR 27/976]

At this distance in time we can only begin to guess at the huge relief felt by those involved in the fighting. It was over. They had made it. In celebration a Victory Dance, surely well attended, was held at the airfield.

After the festivities on the airfield and in the villages, which Derek Daniels, a local resident from whom we have heard before, remembers involved bonfires and blazing hayricks once again, late August 1945 saw the return of familiar faces to No. 142 Squadron, as the fifteen crews who had volunteered for service with Tiger Force arrived back after their posting to the Far East had been cancelled. So these volunteers had escaped any further combat, and had enjoyed some embarkation leave without the subsequent bother of having to embark, but at the cost, presumably, of sore arms from the inoculations!

Life on the station, with the return of peacetime conditions, began to live up to the description of the R.A.F. as the 'world's best flying club', as we can see from this report:

SPORTS REPORT. – AUGUST 1945.

CRICKET. Bad weather reduced the number of Station games to two, but both of these games were won. Warboys were narrowly beaten at home by three wickets, whilst Tempsford lost by the margin of 32 runs. 692 Squadron triumphed over S.H.Q. in both games played between these two Sections.

SWIMMING. The Swimming runs to The Leys Baths on Wednesday afternoons proved as popular as ever and F/L. Lidstone, F/L. Elliot and Sgt. Ford, were called upon to represent No. 8 Group.

TENNIS. Organised games of tennis were held at St. Neots each week, F/L. Godrich representing No.8 Group.

ATHLETICS. F/L. Alford repeated his double on the Inter-Command Athletic Meeting, by winning the 1/2 mile and mile. Later on in the month he ran second in the mile for the R.A.F. versus A.A.A.

CYCLING. Interesting cycle runs were held weekly and were well attended.

[AIR 28/318]

TRIALS AND TRIBULATION

The established routine on the squadrons continued into September 1945, when we can find confirmation that the Oxford, formerly the property of No. 1507 B.A.T. Flight, was still operating from Gransden Lodge, as a pilot from No. 692 Squadron took on the duties of B.A.T. Flight instructor.

Other crews from No. 692 Squadron were still visiting Germany on a regular basis, but now with a less hostile intent. Some of these trips seem to have been remarkable prosaic, including, for instance, one that involved the squadron's Lancaster acting as a flying delivery truck, picking up an engine to deliver to Schleswig then collecting a number of airmen and flying them back to Wyton. On another occasion one of the squadron's aircraft ended up stranded at Kassel after engine problems.

On 13th September 1945, No. 692 Squadron received a new commanding officer, Squadron Leader F.C. Young, whose duties, we must assume, were mainly to be the management of the disbanding of the squadron (especially given his relatively junior rank). On 15th September 1945, Battle of Britain Day, both resident units provided aircraft for display at R.A.F. 'At Home' days at various airfields around the country, while at Gransden Lodge there was a parade and a church service to commemorate the Battle.

These were to be almost the final outings for No. 692 Squadron, since on 20th September 1945, with little obvious fanfare apart from a party the previous night, the squadron was disbanded.

Having marked the passing of No. 692 Squadron, the members of the remaining Mosquito squadron were looking to their own unit's imminent dissolution. On 27th September 1945:

```
3 A/C carried out Cook's Tours in the morning.
Added to this, 9 personnel from the squadron
flew as passengers in a Lancaster from R.A.F.
```

MANNA, EXODUS AND COOK'S TOURS

> Graveley to Berlin, where they put down for the day. On arrival there they were taken on a conducted tour of the city in the afternoon and in the evening, were permitted to survey Berlin 'free-lance'.
>
> [AIR 27/976]

These visits by aircrew to Berlin were collectively known as Operation SPASM, and the crews from No. 142 Squadron were transported to Berlin and back by an aircraft and crew from No. 115 Squadron. While there, the visitors were able to liberate fragments of marble panelling from the *Reichskanzlei* (Reich Chancellery) as souvenirs, despite being under the watchful eye of Soviet soldiers. Unfortunately, the activities of the members of No. 142 Squadron when going 'free-lance' are not known.

On the next day, 28th September 1945, the end came for the squadron:

> In the morning, 4 A/C carried out day cross-country exercises and bombing. The Station Commander also flew one A/C on a local flying trip. The personnel on visit to Berlin, returned to the station in the afternoon.
>
> Today, the squadron is official disbanded.
>
> [AIR 27/976]

Thus, with little ceremony, Bomber Command's operations at Gransden Lodge came to a close, some three and a half eventful years after they had begun. Flying was to continue at Gransden Lodge, but the uses to which it would be put were to become steadily less warlike.

AFTER THE BOMBERS

With the disbanding of the Mosquito squadrons, a process of reduction in numbers on the station began.

The virtual cessation of flying obviously removed the need for some previously essential functions, and in the first week of October 1945 the airfield's meteorological office closed, meaning that any forecasts required would now have to be obtained from Graveley. In addition, a number of staff from Flying Control were being posted out, but this process was not all one way, as a number of administrative posts were being filled by postings in. Further evidence of the changed status of the station can be seen from the fact that it was thought necessary for a vocational advice service to be instituted.

Though the flying facilities on the airfield were being scaled back, and help was being given to those seeking to plan their return to 'civvie street', the administration and support side of the station was still operating (in all senses), as was noted later in the month when the medics had to deal with a road accident involving one of the resident sergeants who managed to drive his motorcycle into the side of a lorry in Little Gransden.

Details are scant, but another itinerant unit passed through Gransden Lodge a few days later, when on 30th October 1945 a formation named as 'Bomber Command Unit France' arrived from Lille Vendeville. Quite what job this unit had been carrying out on the Continent, the number of personnel assigned to it and how long it remained on the station are unfortunately lost in the mists of time, but whatever its role, it does not seem to have been a flying unit, as the Gransden Lodge O.R.B. states that there was no flying for November 1945.

This may not be strictly accurate, however, as other documents record that another unit based on the airfield was indeed flying at this time. This unit was first mentioned in the O.R.B. in late September 1945, when it was noted that:

> Lt. Col. A.H. Dowson and Major S.A. Hart visited R.C.A.S.U. on the Station.
>
> [AIR 28/318]

The initials R.C.A.S.U. stand for the Radar Controlled Air Survey Unit, which, as its name indicates, was a unit whose task was to use radar navigation techniques and equipment to assist in airborne mapping. There was also evidence of Australian interest in the activities of the R.C.A.S.U., as two members of the R.A.A.F. and another from the Australian Scientific Research Liaison Office are recorded as visiting in November 1945.

Earlier in 1945, discussions had been taking place as to how to improve the coverage and accuracy of photo-reconnaissance in the South East Asia theatre of war. By May 1945 the minutes of the War Office Survey Research Conference were able to record that agreement had been reached to make available four Mosquitoes equipped with *Gee-H*, together with two mobile *Gee-H* ground stations and associated personnel, to form the basis of this new unit. One of the participants at the conference was Major Hart, which explains his visit to Gransden Lodge. The meeting of the committee in July 1945 was informed that creation of the new unit to carry out this mapping task, the R.C.A.S.U., had been approved and was in hand. The conversion of the aircraft for the unit, and initial trials, had been carried out at R.A.F. Defford, but the unit was intended to be part of No. 60 Group; the Group's No. 72 Wing was, from mid-May 1944, responsible for the technical control of the mobile *Gee*, *Gee-H* and *Oboe* ground stations deployed following the invasion. No. 60 Group agreed with the recommendation that Wing Commander R.S.J. Edwards, who was carrying out the trials at Defford, should be the commanding officer of the new unit, but frankly stated that it did not know where it would assemble the unit, and that there was no suitable airfield available.

By the end of August 1945, of course, the war in the Far East was over, which was causing some re-thinking of plans, including whether the survey work in South East Asia should be carried out, and, indeed, whether such a specialised unit was actually required. Despite this, it was agreed that further development of the techniques was still worth pursuing. This left the problem of where to base the new unit, but as we know, the R.C.A.S.U. found a home at Gransden Lodge. This might be considered a slightly unusual location, given that it was a Bomber Command airfield and that No. 60 Group was part of Fighter Command, but one reason may have been that No. 60 Group had a special section devoted to radar navigational aids that was based in Cambridge.

We are fortunate that the flying log books of Wing Commander Edwards survive, as they give some rare hard evidence of the dates when the R.C.A.S.U. was operating at Gransden Lodge. The logbook's Record of Service pages show that he was serving with the R.C.A.S.U. in August 1945 at Defford, and from 3rd October 1945 at Gransden Lodge, though Edwards had been commuting regularly between Defford and Gransden Lodge from the beginning of September 1945 onwards. From this we can deduce that the unit was at least partially in place at Gransden Lodge from early September 1945.

AFTER THE BOMBERS

In the following months the crews of the R.C.A.S.U. were busy training and perfecting their survey techniques. This led to an accident on 10th November 1945, when a Mosquito from the unit crashed near Wolverhampton, killing the pilot, Pilot Officer Vander Heyden, and injuring his navigator. A reminder, if any were needed, that aviation of any kind carries with it its risks.

Later in the month a high-level meeting was held regarding the R.C.A.S.U. The attendees at this meeting were drawn from many areas, including the Air Ministry, the Admiralty, the War Office, Bomber and Coastal Commands, the Ordnance Survey, and Australian, New Zealand, Canadian and South African forces. The invitation to the meeting set out succinctly the reason for the creation of the R.C.A.S.U., its composition and the equipment it used, and underlined that the intention was that the unit was to be sent to South East Asia in the very near future. This meeting was set to take place at Gransden Lodge on 21st November 1945, in order to allow all the interested parties to inspect the unit before it left the U.K. From the directions supplied to delegates, we can also glean the fact that the R.C.A.S.U. had set up home in the hangar and offices on the south side of the airfield.

Within days of this meeting, it became clear that there were differing opinions as to what should be done with the unit. On one hand, there were requests to expedite its departure for South East Asia, on the basis that the weather in the area would soon start to deteriorate and the political situation might prevent a long stay. However, a convincing case was also made that the unit should not be sent to South East Asia at all. Even though there was still a perceived need for photographic mapping of the area, despite the war having ended, various delays had meant that the entire unit would have to be despatched by air in order for it to arrive in time to be of use before the weather closed in. This would have caused disruption to the trooping operations, which

TRIALS AND TRIBULATION

were of high priority, so the Air Staff asked that the program be reconsidered, and that unit might instead be sent to the Gold Coast to carry out survey operations there.

While these debates were going on, on 28th November 1945 there was a change of 'station master' at Gransden Lodge when Group Captain Forbes took over command from Group Captain Womersley.

A week or so later a recommendation as to the fate of the R.C.A.S.U. was made, suggesting the immediate dispatch of the unit to the Gold Coast, where a significant air survey had to be undertaken by the end of February 1946. The unit would soon be ready for such a deployment, as by mid-December 1945 it was recorded that its operational trials were complete. The Record of Service of Wing Commander Edwards tells us that from 20th December 1945 he was serving with the R.C.A.S.U. at Watton in Norfolk, and his logbook records that he flew a Mosquito there from Gransden Lodge two days later, so the unit must have moved to Watton by that date.

Watton was a much more sensible base for the unit, as in October 1945 the station had been transferred to No. 60 Group, and was the home of the R.A.F.'s Radio Warfare Establishment (later the Central Signals Establishment), whose Flying and Servicing Wings had been formed from our old friends No. 192 Squadron. Later logbook entries by Wing Commander Edwards indicate that the survey work in the Gold Coast did go ahead, as by April 1946 he was undertaking survey flights with No. 541 Squadron in Ghana.

Even as the R.C.A.S.U. was preparing to leave Gransden Lodge, a new unit had begun arriving on the station on 8th December 1945, with the appearance of the first aircraft from No. 53 Squadron, which was moving in from Merryfield. This marked the beginning of a new role for Gransden Lodge - to be a fairly short-lived one, as it would turn out - as a Transport Command station.

AFTER THE BOMBERS

No. 53 Squadron, at the time flying Liberator bombers converted for troop transport, had been based at Merryfield airfield in Somerset, a few miles south-east of Taunton, since September 1945. Like No. 142 Squadron, No. 53 Squadron had a history dating back to the Great War, having been formed in 1916, seen service in Flanders, then disbanding in 1919. It was re-formed in 1938 and for most of the war flew with Coastal Command on maritime reconnaissance duties, including stints based in America, Trinidad and Iceland. The squadron was transferred to Transport Command in June 1945 and began flying trooping operations, being initially based at St. David's in Wales before transferring to Merryfield. To handle the maintenance of the squadron's Liberators, No. 4053 Servicing Echelon also moved with it to Gransden Lodge.

The summary in No. 53 Squadron's O.R.B. for December 1945 gives some indication that its members were not best pleased with the move from Somerset to the relative bleakness of an East Anglian winter:

> MOVE OF UNIT. The move, intimated in November's summary, commenced on December 3rd. It was unfortunate that after all arrangements had been made and the advance party, which included the orderly room staff and equipment, had been dispatched from MERRYFIELD, that instructions were received to delay the move until 9th.... It was found that the new station was in no way ready to accommodate an operational Squadron and for the first two weeks acute discomfort was experienced by all....
>
> MORALE Morale which was not good in November did not improve after the Squadron transferred to this new Station which in itself tends by virtue of its vastly dispersed sections and domestic sites and the almost total unpreparedness of the station to discourage a very high standard. It

> must be hoped that when the Squadron finally
> settles down there will be a much more cheerful
> atmosphere showing an improvement in morale.
>
> [AIR 27/507]

We see here once again the common complaint that the way that the station's sites were dispersed made living and working there something of a test of stamina.

The assertion that 'the new station was in no way ready to accommodate an operational Squadron' is interesting, in that it was only a matter of a few months since two bomber squadrons had been operating there. Another entry in the same summary gives a hint as to the cause:

> Almost immediately after its arrival at GRANSDEN
> LODGE the Navigation Section under the leadership
> of Flight Lieutenant D.J. Norton began organising
> its quarters. As the station had been in the
> process of closing down it was found that little
> or no equipment was available but there were
> good sites.
>
> [AIR 27/507]

So even though we know that, behind the scenes, Gransden Lodge was under consideration for future use as an active station, it appears that facilities there were being run down anyway, but that it had been pressed back into service to accommodate the squadron. In addition to this, it is likely that the requirements of a squadron ferrying large numbers of troops to and fro were different from those of a bomber squadron. In fact, there are signs that (some weeks later) works were under way to improve the lot of those based at the airfield, as the Station Sick Quarters were being spruced up with a new lick of paint.

Despite these irritations, No. 53 Squadron was soon back in

business flying trooping operations, mainly to Mauripur in India (now in Pakistan), Istres in France and Castel Benito airfield in Libya. Around 15th December 1945 the first flights departed from Gransden Lodge, but because of the lack of facilities these initial departures were routed *via* Tempsford, where the passengers could more easily be embarked and disembarked. The tempo of operations then picked up, with an arrival or departure most days in December 1945 when the weather permitted, and sometimes two or three.

By the end of December 1945, No. 53 Squadron had 301 members based at the airfield, and, as might be expected, the change of status back to an active flying station caused a flurry of postings of flying control and engineering personnel into Gransden Lodge to replace those recently posted out. At this same date, an entry in the Gransden Lodge O.R.B. shows that the irritation with the new situation was not felt exclusively on the part of No. 53 Squadron, as it noted a complaint that a great deal of extra work had been required by the sick quarters staff due to the state of the documentation sent from Merryfield. As an aside, the same entry shows that the previously mentioned unofficial methods of improving the heating in buildings on the airfield may have claimed a victim:

```
Cpl. Berrill was burnt by flaming petrol, whilst
involved in a fire inside a hut situated near
Flying Control. Patient was given emergency
treatment and then transferred to R.A.F.
Hospital, Ely.
```

[AIR 28/318]

The route flying continued in January 1946 to the same destinations, and more flying training was done, but both were hampered by the winter weather. The increase in training was mandated from above by the Air Council, which was concerned

TRIALS AND TRIBULATION

about the high fatality rate being experienced, even in peacetime, by units undertaking trooping operations.

On 28th January 1946 the first direct departure from Gransden Lodge for 'the route' was able to take place, as a Passenger and Freight Section had now been established at the airfield. The reversal in the reduction in numbers on the station continued, with an acceleration in the number of postings in. These included more flying control and technical staff, but also personnel to fill meteorological, operations and administrative posts.

Ironically, this increase in staff was unnecessary. On the very day after the first direct route flight, No. 53 Squadron learned that it was to be reduced to 'number' basis. This meant that it would exist solely as a squadron with a number, until such time as it was disbanded and the number could then be transferred to another unit. Whether it was a cause or consequence of this, Gransden Lodge's life as an operational airfield was shortly to come to an end, as No. 53 Squadron's records note that the airfield was to be reduced to 'care and maintenance' status.

A few route flights were carried out in the first days of February 1946, but the majority of the flying was to deliver the squadron's aircraft to other airfields. The itinerary for the last of these route flights, which began on 7th February 1946, gives an interesting insight into the distances covered in one of these operations. The route followed was Gransden Lodge – Castel Benito – Cairo West (Egypt) – Wadi Halfa (Sudan) – Aden (Yemen) – Mesira (probably actually Masirah, Oman) – Mauripur – Shaibah (Iraq) – Lydda (Palestine, now Israel) – Castel Benito – Istres – Rennes – Gransden Lodge, where the Liberator arrived back on 21st February 1946.

The end for No. 53 Squadron came on 28th February 1946, when, as feared, the squadron number was transferred to the existing No. 102 Squadron, and the ex-No. 53 Squadron was disbanded. The majority of the squadron personnel had already been sent on indefinite leave, and the aircrew had been posted to other squadrons before the axe fell. The juggernaut that had been set in motion to bring Gransden Lodge up to strength to support No. 53 Squadron's activities was now thrown into reverse, as during February the postings were again almost entirely away from the station.

In March 1946 there was still flying at the airfield, but it almost exclusively took the form of the departure of Liberators to their new locations, either for further service or to be scrapped. The station's new lowly status is indicated by the fact that by the end of March 1946, though the change in command is not recorded, the Station Commander was a Flight Lieutenant Williams (three ranks lower than a Group Captain), and the flow of postings out was continuing.

The final entry in Gransden Lodge's O.R.B. was made at the end of March 1946, by the station's medical officer, and reads:

```
Station Sick Quarters and Dental Centre have
been closed, leaving an M.I. Room under control
and supervision of S.M.O., R.A.F. Station, Bourn.
```
[AIR 28/318]

With the closing of the station's O.R.B., we now, once more, have to resort to examining a number of sources to piece together its history in its later years. We saw that the assumption was that Gransden Lodge was being closed down when No. 53 Squadron arrived, but in fact we find that by mid-July 1946 Gransden Lodge had, indeed, been listed among those airfields that had been placed under 'care and maintenance' so that they could be brought back into use in time of war. It had not escaped the notice of the planners that not only would it take a considerable time to build new airfields were they to be needed, but that it was also unlikely that the funds and manpower to do so would be available in the straitened post-war years.

TRIALS AND TRIBULATION

At this point the airfield was still allocated to Transport Command, but its 488 acres (about 197 hectares), all of which had by now been purchased by the government, were earmarked for return to Bomber Command. The fact that it had hard runways, and a relatively long (6,000 ft./over 1,800 m) main runway, was one reason for it being of interest for further use by the R.A.F.

A few weeks before this, those runways had been used for a very different purpose, when the Cambridge University Automobile Club arranged for the first U.K. motor racing meeting after the war to be held at Gransden Lodge. A circuit of just over two miles (3.4 km) in length was laid out using parts of the runways and perimeter track, and a dozen or so races were held on 15th June 1946. These races were limited to only three laps of the circuit, since petrol was still rationed, so they were short compared to today's races. The winner of one of these was George Abecassis, who had been a special duties pilot at Tempsford during the war, and amongst the other competitors was Alec Issigonis, later to become famous as the designer of the iconic Mini.

Edith Heap's record of her nocturnal encounter with an Italian has told us that prisoners of war were in the Gransden Lodge area. Evidence of a more official nature can be found when in February 1947 the Ministry of Works was being asked to foot the bill for the use of P.O.W.s for the removal of defences and restoration of the land on the airfield so that it could be prepared for a return to agriculture. Perhaps unsurprisingly, the answer was in the negative.

Gransden Lodge was again used for motor racing later in 1947, when the Cambridge University Automobile Club once more arranged a meeting, in association with the Vintage Sports-Car Club, to take place in July of that year.

As *'The Bulletin of the Vintage Sports-Car Club'* recorded, preparations for the race did not go smoothly, since numerous hurdles were put in the way of the organisers, mainly in the form of resistance on the part of some in the hierarchy of the R.A.F. These latter delivered what they thought would be a decisive blow to prevent the race by stating that the owners of the land on which the airfield had been built had not consented to racing, and might have a legal case against the Air Ministry were the event to go ahead. Not to be outdone, the organisers decided to set about getting the signatures of the six landowners for permission to hold the race. This cross-country pursuit, reminiscent of the days of silent cinema, was carried out in a vintage Bugatti racer:

> "It was, therefore, 2 p.m. at the Caxton Gibbet Hotel before the autograph-hunt actually started. On the whole, quite amazing luck attended the chase, although the Clutton Bugatti had in one case to carry out a ding-dong pursuit of a farmer on his Fordson tractor, over country which placed the Fordson at a distinct advantage. The last owner of all looked like sinking the ship; his large mansion appeared completely void, and the impressive door-bell evoked nothing more than a derisive echo down the empty corridors. The next hope seemed to be his agents in Cambridge, but enquiry there revealed that the only person capable of taking authority was conducting an auction sale in St. Neots. Rapid action got the party to St. Neots just as the valuable property was withdrawn, not having reached its reserve price. The Auctioneer - understandably, perhaps - was not in the best of tempers. But he signed. In two-and-a-half hours all the signatures had been obtained."

The way was now clear for the race to go ahead, and the next few days were taken up in frantic preparation, with some of the organisers actually living in the old control tower in order to be on site. They were not aided in their efforts when at one point the Clerk of the Works at the airfield cut off the electricity and water supplies. In

TRIALS AND TRIBULATION

spite of all this, by 13th July 1947 all was prepared, practices had been carried out the previous day, and the racing commenced.

These stills from a newsreel film shot on the day, unfortunately not of the highest quality, show that the Gransden Lodge buildings were still in good repair at this date and, if nothing else, give testimony to the quality of wartime roof construction!

The M.T. workshop (large building top left centre), which still exists, and various contractors' and other buildings (British Pathé)

The finish line showing three flight offices (left) and locker/drying room (centre) with squadron offices just visible behind (British Pathé)

AFTER THE BOMBERS

According to reports of the time, the meeting was well attended and was deemed a success:

> "The takings were disappointing in that experienced judges put the number of spectators at ten to fifteen thousand, whereas the paid admissions recorded by National Car Parks amounted only to five thousand. We were, nevertheless, able to send five hundred guineas to the Flood Victims' Relief Fund, which was the Charity selected by R.A.F. Bomber Command to benefit from the meeting."

This marked the end of Gransden Lodge's brief career as a motor racing circuit, but the trail blazed there in using airfields for motor racing (road racing being banned) was followed at many other ex-airfields including Goodwood and, most famously today, Silverstone.

In his book *Action Stations*, author Michael Bowyer recalls that a display of a different type took place on the airfield at around the same time, when a small air show was held. These motor races and flying displays must have been, for some, a welcome relief from the austerity of wartime, but that austerity was not yet over. From 1946 to 1948 bread rationing was introduced in the U.K., ostensibly as a response to worldwide food shortages. It has been suggested that this was, in fact, mainly a political gesture intended to put pressure on the U.S. to provide food to the inhabitants of the British Zone in occupied Germany, where shortages were very real, and actually there was no need for bread rationing in the U.K. Be that as it may, there was certainly a move to bring as much land as possible into agricultural production, and this land naturally included airfields, even those that were still active.

Each airfield was allocated a category that defined the agricultural activities that were allowed, and where, and by

TRIALS AND TRIBULATION

September 1947 Gransden Lodge had been classified by the Ministry of Agriculture and Fisheries (M.A.F.) as being in 'Category 4 – Airfields not likely to be required for some time'. Unrestricted agriculture was allowed on most parts of airfields in this category, apart from in some areas alongside the runways and perimeter tracks. Agricultural production was already taking place on the airfield though, as at the end of October 1947 the M.A.F. representative in Cambridge was able to report Gransden Lodge's 'surplus areas already under cultivation'.

For the remainder of the 1940s the airfield was retained by the R.A.F. on a care and maintenance basis, since no decision had yet been made about what use, if any, could be made of those long, extensible runways.

The return of the airfield to food production did not mean that the future of Gransden Lodge as a flying station was no longer being deliberated upon. In a document written in July 1951 one use for dormant airfields, as bases for the R.A.F.'s medium bomber force, was being considered, and contained in this document there was a recommendation for the airfields that might be used in this role. Two, Marham and Wittering, had already been decided upon, and Gransden Lodge featured in the list of other inactive airfields that were viewed as particularly suitable.

At about the same time the station was also listed as a candidate for a home of one of the R.A.F.'s medium bomber Operational Conversion Units; it was, however, last on that list, probably for the reasons noted, namely the poor gradient on the main runway and the limited space available for dispersal areas. The comment on the gradient of the main runway was justified, as there was a noticeable slope to the north-eastern end of main runway, and if that runway had been extended further to the north-east, as would probably have been the intention, that slope would have become marked indeed. In fact, the view of the airfield's suitability for medium bomber deployment changed rapidly, as by August 1951 Gransden Lodge was now on the 'doubtful' list. A hint as to another possible use appeared in a note in a slightly later document – 'U.S.A.F. War'; that is, as a base for U.S. forces in a future conflict.

Within a few months the airfield would become a serious contender for use by the Americans, but before that, by the end of February 1952 at the latest, Gransden Lodge had finally become a satellite of Bassingbourn, as had been intended ten years before, and was recorded at that date as being among those airfields still suitable for emergency use. Bassingbourn was to become a base for training crews on the R.A.F.'s Canberra jet medium bomber, so (as would be noted a little later in the year), having another useable airfield close by would have been convenient.

As is well known, by the end of the war it had become clear that the Russians, while still allies at that time, were likely to be the enemy in any future conflict. By the early 1950s that conflict seemed possible, if not probable, given that the Korean War was currently being waged with Russian support. Both the U.S. and U.K. governments were formulating plans for how such a war, probably involving nuclear weapons, could be carried out and the facilities that would be required to wage it. Two separate plans, known as GALLOPER on the U.K. side and OFF-TACKLE in the U.S., were concerned with how U.S. air forces would be deployed at bases in the U.K. A document issued by the Air Council on 9th April 1952 lists the works required to provide these bases for U.S. units. These included long range bomber groups, long range strategic reconnaissance groups, tanker squadrons, defensive and escort fighter groups among others, plus two troop carrier groups. Previous plans had only called for one of these latter units, but now there was a need for an additional troop carrier base, and Gransden Lodge was nominated for the job. Thus the plan was now for the airfield to revert to another of its previous roles, that of an air transport base. The U.S. forces would also have needed hospital facilities, and the wartime hospital at Wimpole Park, in the grounds of Wimpole Hall close to Gransden Lodge, was earmarked as one of the three that would be provided. The deliberations as to who should pay for all these facilities makes interesting reading.

By August 1952 no start had yet been made on building work, but then, as now, the opinion of the neighbours and how they might react to the new use of the airfield was being actively considered. The Director of Administrative Plans at the Air Ministry wrote that:

> ... I am therefore to request that you will arrange for Station Commanders, responsible for the airfields shown in Appendix 'A' which are likely to be extended or reconstructed in the future, to consider possible causes for objection by any important person or persons with interests within 5 miles radius of the airfields concerned, and for any relevant reports thereon, together with a list of any members of the Royal Family and such other local residents who might be deemed in the category of "Very Important People" to be forwarded to Air Ministry (D.D.O.(P)).
>
> [AIR 20/7716]

Gransden Lodge was named in the appendix, and soon the reply came that there were indeed two people considered 'Very Important' in the local area, to wit: Lord Huntingfield of Croxton Estates and Captain Briscoe, M.C., the Lord Lieutenant of Cambridgeshire, who lived at Longstowe Hall. In the end their acquiescence would not be required, but their reaction, and that of the other locals, to such a potentially large upheaval in their midst would have been interesting to observe. The Lord Lieutenant in particular would have had to endure even noisier occupants of the airfield just over his back fence.

Perhaps one reason for the lack of movement on the building front was that, despite the discussions that had been going on for months, the best use to which the airfield could be put was still undecided. Notwithstanding any other plans being made for its future, the proximity of Gransden Lodge to the Canberras at Bassingbourn made it a natural location for a Relief Landing Ground (R.L.G.) for the tyro crews learning their trade at the O.C.U. This was confirmed in a letter written in December 1952, in which it was indicated that the fact that the airfield was intended to become a troop carrier base for the American forces meant that it would be developed to a standard suitable for use by Canberras.

And there, for some years, matters appear to have rested, with the airfield remaining in 'full agricultural use'. The large B1 hangar on the airfield had been loaned to the Ministry of Works by the Air Ministry for use by the Ministry of Food for the storage of emergency food stocks – a common post-war use for hangars on disused airfields – but by early 1955 the situation was about to change once more, and the Ministry of Works was to vacate the site. The reason for this was that the American forces still had their eye on Gransden Lodge, and in January 1955, in a letter from the headquarters of the American Third Air Force relating to the U.S.A.F.'s wartime hospital requirements in the U.K., another use for the airfield was mooted as:

> ... The USAF has proposed to establish in wartime thousand bed hospitals at several sites in the United Kingdom. These are in addition to existing facilities in operation by or under control of the USAF. The sites which have been tentatively selected are Prestwick (Heathfield), Gransden Lodge, Babdown Farms and Doncaster. (Secret)

> 3. The basic concept in establishing each of the wartime hospitals is as follows: In the first phase, in peace, a hospital nucleus would be constructed on each site to provide the basic facilities required for a surgery, pharmacy, laboratory, X-ray room, administrative space, 200 ward beds and dead storage for essential hospital equipment to permit the immediate establishment of a 200 bed hospital upon declaration of war. After war had started, the hospitals would be expanded through four additional phases to meet the full one thousand bed requirement. Normally, phase one would require about three acres of ground, and phases two through five would require an additional twenty-seven acres. (Unclassified)
>
> [AIR 2/13657]

The fact that the Wimpole Park hospital would be close at hand may have been a factor in proposing the airfield as a future hospital site. Further surveys of Gransden Lodge and (one assumes) R.A.F. Babdown Farm in Gloucestershire were then carried out, but it would be several months before the results were available.

In the meantime, the Air Ministry had convened the Inactive Airfields Working Party to review the status and future of the many remaining disused airfields in the U.K. Data sheets were created for these airfields as reference material for the new working party, and in April 1955 the data sheet for Gransden Lodge showed it as a 'State owned Air Ministry airfield', and under 'Present use' it was noted that the Ministry of Works still occupied the B1 hangar to house food stocks. This data sheet would have been considered later in the month, as Gransden Lodge was one of the airfields under examination at the first meeting of the working party, whose decision was that the airfield should be retained. This decision was underlined in June 1955 in

AFTER THE BOMBERS

correspondence with the Ministry of Works questioning the state of the electricity supply to the B1 hangar. In this letter it was clearly stated that Gransden Lodge was one of a number of inactive airfields that the government had firmly decided to retain against future R.A.F. requirements.

By early August 1955 the results of the surveys of Gransden Lodge and Babdown Farm were in, and had been considered by the American Third Air Force. It seems that Gransden Lodge met with their approval and so would feature in their Emergency War Plan (E.W.P.):

```
1. As a result of a survey by this headquarters
of RAF Gransden Lodge, it was determined that
this base is suitable for the establishment of a
1000 bed EWP hospital. (Secret)

2. It is planned to construct the hospital
nucleus and access road during peace, for which
funds are held by higher headquarters and will
be released upon availability of land. (Secret)

3. The establishment of this hospital will require
seven (7) acres of land, and utilization of one
(1) hangar during peacetime, expandable to 35
acres during war. It will therefore be appreciated
if Air Ministry will make the following areas of
land available to the USAF: (Secret)

a. Peacetime:
(1)    Approximately seven (7) acres of land as
       indicated outlined in blue on attached
       drawing. (Uncl)
(2)    Strip of land, outlined in blue for
       construction of access road. (Uncl)
(3)    One (1) hangar, preferably, that marked
       "A" and outlined in blue. If this hangar
       cannot be made available, the alternative
       choice is that marked "B". (Uncl)
```

b. <u>Wartime</u>:
(1) The area outlined in red, on drawing, approximately 35 acres. (Secret)

[AIR 2/13657]

For whatever reason, the access roads and nucleus buildings were never built, and, thank goodness, the need for another wartime hospital never arose. A hospital was later built at the large U.S.A.F. base at Lakenheath, so perhaps that filled the requirement for which Gransden Lodge was originally proposed. Unfortunately the drawings referred to in the document seem to have been lost, but aerial photographs taken in October 1955 show that at least the southern T2 hangar was still standing at this point, though the other T2 had probably been removed. In fact, these photographs show that a substantial number of the airfield buildings had survived until this date, the most notable exceptions being the station sick quarters and one of the smaller outlying domestic sites.

The years rolled past, and Gransden Lodge remained on the Air Ministry's list of retained airfields, but time was taking its toll. With the passing years the buildings that still existed on the airfield were becoming more dilapidated, as can be seen from the photograph, below, of the control tower taken in 1960, complete with the windows through which we glimpsed the staff at work. Whatever the state of the runways, the care and maintenance policy obviously did not extend in any large measure to the buildings on the airfield. Some of them still existed, at least, and so they could have been refurbished if they were needed again, but it would have been an uphill job.

Finally, by the middle of 1961 a decision had been reached on the future of Gransden Lodge and a number of other redundant airfields. In a letter written in June of that year the Air Ministry acknowledged that, given the planned size and shape of the R.A.F. over the next ten years or so, and the fact that a number of

AFTER THE BOMBERS

The Flying Control Tower, 1960 (Bill Brown)

currently-active airfields would no longer be needed, the government was 'over-insuring' its future airfield needs. The author then went on to name thirteen airfields that the R.A.F. recommended should be put up for disposal, and the fifth on the list was Gransden Lodge.

There was still some way to go between the decision and its implementation, though. In February 1962 the airfield was still listed as being suitable for emergency landings, but the process of removing or re-using the airfield's facilities was underway. Local lore has it that the runways at Gransden Lodge were excavated and the concrete used as foundations for building the M1 motorway, and a further tale holds that the concrete went to construct a by-pass around the nearby town of Biggleswade on the main A1 road. That may or may not have been the case (the dates make it seem a bit unlikely), but an aerial photograph taken in May 1962 apparently shows all the runways, perimeter tracks and hardstandings still in place, and there is evidence from a newsreel film of land yacht racing on the airfield that at least the main runway was still intact in the summer of 1963.

By June 1969, when there was further aerial photography coverage, the reclamation of the airfield was definitely well advanced, as the runways (apart from a small strip along the edge of two of them), all the hardstandings apart from one, and the majority of the buildings had been removed, and most of the perimeter track had been much reduced in width, although its circuit was still complete. On further photographs taken in July 1972 the airfield appears in roughly the state in which it would stay for almost the next two decades, except that one stretch of perimeter track that would be completely removed at some later date still remained.

Another activity for which the chronology is uncertain is the use of the airfield for automotive trials; not for racing this time, but for engineering tests. At some point in the post-war period the car manufacturer Vauxhall used the runways at Gransden Lodge for aerodynamic testing of new vehicle designs. This involved, among other things, sticking wool tufts to a car and observing the effects of the airflow on these tufts as it was driven at speed along the runways. These trials must have taken place sometime before the late 1960s, since in 1968 the company constructed the Millbrook Proving Ground near Bedford to undertake such testing.

And so, by the closing years of the twentieth century, the land once occupied by this busy airfield had returned to agriculture, the remaining perimeter tracks were being put to good use by local teenagers learning to drive, and the only flying being done was by the skylarks. In the late 1980s, however, plans were being hatched to give the airfield a new lease of life and enable aviation to take place there again. The Cambridge University Gliding Club was flying from the Imperial War Museum's airfield at Duxford, but it

AFTER THE BOMBERS

The first day's flying at Gransden Lodge by the Cambridge University Gliding Club, 16th September 1990 (Andrew Hulme)

was becoming increasingly difficult to operate alongside the high performance 'warbirds' such as Spitfires and Mustangs that were based there. There was also little scope to expand the club's facilities and operations, so the search was on for a new home. Many sites in the Cambridge area were considered, but Gransden Lodge was always one of the favourites. After an extended period of negotiations with the various interested parties and planning authorities, on 16th September 1990, after many years of inactivity, aircraft once more took off from Gransden Lodge.

Even though the former runways were still under stubble from the previous summer's crop, an advance guard of the gliding club brought a few gliders over to the airfield from Duxford and flew from what was to be the club's new home. There was still much work to be done to get the airfield ready for serious flying – including removing the remaining debris of the old concrete runways so that new grass ones could be laid – but to paraphrase the splendid '*1066 And All That*', on that date history came to a stop and the present day began.

Over the decades since those first flights from what was still effectively a farmer's field, Gransden Lodge has matured to become one of the foremost soaring centres in the U.K. Once more flyers, including world-class competition pilots, take off from the airfield to fly long distances, pitting their wits against the weather, but now with nothing more than pleasure in mind.

Long may it continue.

EPILOGUE

Little physical evidence remains of the once-bustling airfield that was Gransden Lodge. The most obvious buildings that still stand are the flying control tower, the B1 hangar and a number of the M.T. yard buildings, together with a workshop and the shell of the operations block. Some residential buildings and bomb shelters remain on the dispersed sites around the airfield's periphery, as do the filter beds of the troublesome sewage disposal plant, but most of the station's quickly-built infrastructure has now disappeared. Even some of these remaining buildings are being removed or are succumbing to the ravages of time and the weather.

Many hundreds of aircrew and ground personnel served at Gransden Lodge during its fairly brief operation life, and amongst these were Johnny Fauquier and Reg Lane, widely regarded as the two most outstanding Canadian bomber pilots of the war.

On leaving No. 405 Squadron in January 1944, Johnny Fauquier was posted No. 6 Group headquarters at Allerton Park, near Knaresborough in Yorkshire – often referred to by the expressive title of 'Castle Dismal'. Promoted to Air Commodore, he served as Senior Operations Staff Officer, then as commander of No. 62 'Beaver' Operational Base that controlled the Yorkshire R.C.A.F. stations of Linton-on-Ouse, East Moor and Tholthorpe. While serving in this capacity he set about improving, in his

TRIALS AND TRIBULATION

characteristically robust style, the standards of bombing accuracy of the squadrons on the stations under his command.

By late 1944 Fauquier was ready to get back to operational flying, and in December of that year he took a voluntary reduction in rank to Group Captain in order to assume command of No. 617 (The Dambusters) Squadron, in which post he served until the end of the war. It would be interesting to know the feelings of both Fauquier and his former comrades on this move, given the sometimes strained relations between No. 5 Group, of which No. 617 Squadron was the élite unit, and No. 8 Group. While with the squadron he managed the introduction to service of the huge 22,000lb (almost 10,000 kg) *Grand Slam* bomb and its use against strategic targets such as viaducts, canals and U-Boat pens. It was only mechanical failure of his aircraft that prevented him being the first pilot to drop a *Grand Slam* in anger.

At the end of the war, Fauquier was reinstated to his previous

Air Commodore Johnny Fauquier
(Bomber Command Museum of Canada)

EPILOGUE

rank and retired; in peacetime he took up a career in business. Air Commodore Fauquier, dubbed 'The King of the Pathfinders', died on 3rd April 1981.

After his own stint at 'Castle Dismal', Reg Lane was posted to H.Q. Tiger Force at Bushy Park, on the outskirts of London, as Group Captain (Ops). His role was to plan the operations that Tiger Force, which was to be based at airfields on the island of Okinawa, would carry out. After much frantic activity, Lane was nominated to head the second of the two advance parties (SNOWBALL 1 and SNOWBALL 2) that were to be sent to Okinawa to prepare for the arrival of the force's aircraft. The SNOWBALL 1 party set off, but the atomic bomb was dropped on Hiroshima the day before SNOWBALL 2 was due to leave. Lane was actually just about to board the bus for Hendon aerodrome to fly out when he was stopped and told that there was an indefinite delay, as the war might soon be over. In fact, Lane and SNOWBALL 2 never left the U.K. for the Far East, and the personnel of SNOWBALL 1 ended up serving in India.

Lieutenant-General Reg Lane
(Bomber Command Museum of Canada)

TRIALS AND TRIBULATION

This was by no means the end of Lane's air force career. Choosing to remain in the R.C.A.F. after the war, he eventually rose to the rank of Lieutenant-General, and became Deputy Commander in Chief at NORAD (North American Air Defence Command) before his retirement. After membership of the Consultative Group on Disarmament and Arms Control, in 1989 he became director of the Canadian Institute for International Peace and Security. Lieutenant-General Lane died on 2nd October 2003.

The ending of the war also marked the end for some of the units that had been based at the airfield, but some continued in action for many years.

No. 192 Squadron was disbanded in 1945, but formed, as we have seen, the nucleus of the Central Signals Establishment. In 1951 the squadron was re-formed to carry on in its previous role as a signals intelligence unit, until it was re-numbered as No. 51 Squadron in 1958. This squadron is still flying, operating electronic reconnaissance aircraft and so carrying on a long tradition.

No. 405 Squadron was disbanded in Canada in September 1945. It was re-formed briefly in 1947, then in 1950 it was reborn as No. 405 (Eagle) Squadron – no longer No. 405 (Vancouver) Squadron – based at Greenwood, Nova Scotia, as a maritime reconnaissance unit, a role that it continues to fulfil today. This again harks back to the squadron's wartime operations when it was similarly engaged in maritime patrols with R.A.F. Coastal Command.

Of the two Light Night Striking Force squadrons, No. 692 Squadron was never re-formed. The other, No. 142 Squadron, was re-formed in Kenya in February 1959, this time as a fighter-bomber unit, but it was re-numbered as No. 208 Squadron within a few months. It re-formed again in a very different guise in July

EPILOGUE

1959 as a Thor strategic missile unit; it was disbanded for the last time in 1963.

No. 53 Squadron underwent a number of amalgamations and re-numberings, but continued in existence (with a few short breaks) as a transport squadron, including taking part in the Berlin Airlift, until it was disbanded in September 1976.

The members of these squadrons who had been based at Gransden Lodge, and the relations of those who did not make it back there, still visit their old airfield from time to time. Sometimes they are accompanied by current members of No. 405 Squadron, one of only two of the Pathfinder squadrons still in existence, the other being No. 7 Squadron.

In 1989 a stained-glass window commemorating No. 405 Squadron was installed in St. Bartholomew's Church, Great Gransden, as a memorial to the 801 members of the squadron that lost their lives while in service during the war.

The visitors' book in the church still shows a steady stream of well-wishers from around the world, many, of course, from Canada, who come to admire the window and reflect upon the sacrifices made by their countrymen.

As 'Pee Wee' Phillips, the pilot who brought his aircraft back to Gransden Lodge aided only by his crew and a length of stout rope, said:

> "We were very much an isolated unit - a squadron was very much a bond of people together, and even after the war when we had a reunion, when they came across from Canada and we put up a memorial window in Gransden Lodge church it was still that bond there then. You could feel it."

TRIALS AND TRIBULATION

The commemorative window in St. Bartholomew's Church,
Great Gransden (Author)

ACKNOWLEDGEMENTS

Thanks are due to the following people for their help in the preparation of this book:

Mr. Bill Brown D.F.C. for sharing his memories of flying the Mosquito, and for his stories and photographs from his time at the airfield.

Mrs. Edith Kup and Mr. Angus Robb C.G.M. for kindly giving permission to use extracts from their respective memoirs.

Danielle Russell, John Frederick and their colleagues at the University of Victoria, British Columbia, for supplying copies of taped interviews with Reg Lane before they were available online, and for permission to use transcriptions of parts of them.

Alexandra Tichinoff of The Memory Project, Canada, for supplying the photograph of Mr. Ed Miller and his ground crew colleagues.

Liz Butler at The Australians at War Film Archive for generous permission to use extracts from Ian McLeod's interviews.

Lianne Smith at the Liddell Hart Centre for Military Archives, King's College, London, and Ellen Parton and Richard Hughes at

TRIALS AND TRIBULATION

the Imperial War Museum, London, for help with copyright clearances.

Tim Dutton for showing me around the Pathfinder Collection at the R.A.F. Wyton Heritage Centre, and for providing copies of photographs held there.

Dave Birrell of the Bomber Command Museum of Canada, Nanton, for supplying copies of some of the museum's photographs.

The team at the R.A.F. Museum, London, particularly Guy Revell and Andrew Dennis, for their assistance and sleuthing.

Richard Brickwood at the Cambridge Gliding Centre for access to airfield maps, plans and other information.

Jennifer Parkerson for giving permission to use copies of maps held at the National Library of Scotland.

Jennie Gray for arranging permission to use the photograph of the 'Black Thursday' funerals.

Derek Daniels for his reminiscences.

Cecil Payne for memories of his brothers.

Ian Ferguson for permission to use the extract from *'The Bulletin of the Vintage Sports-Car Club'*.

Ian Coomber for information on Vauxhall's aerodynamic testing program.

ACKNOWLEDGEMENTS

Andrew Hulme for the photograph of the first day's gliding at the airfield (and sound accountancy advice!).

The ever-helpful staff at the National Archives, Kew, the Cambridge and Huntingdon offices of the Cambridgeshire Archives, Cambridge University Library, the English Heritage National Monuments Record, Swindon and the R.A.F. Signals Museum, R.A.F. Henlow.

and

Tim Hutchinson for his father's recollections - and also for humouring me when I was banging on about Gransden Lodge over a beer.

GLOSSARY

A.A.	Anti-Aircraft.
A.A.A.	Amateur Athletics Association.
A/C	Aircraft.
ACH/GD	Aircraft Hand/General Duties. A rank held by both men and women, indicating that they were trained in no particular trade.
A.F.C.	Air Force Cross. A decoration awarded to officers and warrant officers for courage or devotion to duty while flying, though not in active operations against the enemy.
A.O.C.	Air Officer Commanding. An officer of the rank of Air Commodore or higher who holds a command appointment (for example, who commands a Group).
A.P.I.	Air Position Indicator. A device that calculated an aircraft's position in the air, based on a known starting point and the aircraft's airspeed and heading.
B.D.U.	Bombing Development Unit. A unit within Bomber Command that carried out tests on new devices designed to aid bombing, and their operational application.
Boffins	Scientists engaged in developing new devices and techniques for use on operations.

GLOSSARY

Boozer	A radar receiver system designed to warn when an aircraft was being tracked by air- or ground-based radars.
Carpet	A electronic countermeasure used to jam the *Würzburg* radar system.
C.G.M.	Conspicuous Gallantry Medal. The other ranks' equivalent of the Distinguished Service Order, awarded for conspicuous gallantry in action against the enemy at sea or in the air.
Coned	Held in the beam of one or more searchlights.
Dad's Army	The title of a well-loved B.B.C. television comedy series depicting the antics of a fictional Home Guard platoon.
D.F.C.	Distinguished Flying Cross. A decoration awarded to officers and warrant officers who displayed courage or devotion to duty whilst flying in active operations.
D.F.M.	Distinguished Flying Medal. A decoration awarded to N.C.O.s and men for bravery whilst flying on operations against the enemy.
D.R.	Dead Reckoning. Calculating a current position based on a previously known position and elapsed time, winds, airspeed etc.
D.S.O.	Distinguished Service Order. A decoration awarded for highly successful command and leadership during active operations.
Düppel	A German radar jamming system similar to *Window*.
E.N.S.A.	Entertainments National Service Association. An organisation set up to provide entertainment for British armed forces personnel. The abbreviation was popularly believed to stand for 'Every Night Something Awful'.

F.I.D.O.	Fog Investigation and Dispersal Operation. A system for clearing fog from runways using heat from petrol burners.
Fishpond	A radar system designed to give warning of attack by a nightfighter approaching a bomber from below, using a signal derived from the bomber's *H2S* ground mapping radar.
Flak	From the German *Fliegerabwehrkanone*. Ground-based anti-aircraft artillery.
Flensburg	A German tracking system designed to allow nightfighters to home onto the emissions from *Monica*.
GAF	German Air Force.
Gee	A navigation system that used three or more ground stations transmitting coordinated radio pulses that enabled an aircraft's location to be calculated with fair accuracy.
Gee-H	A system somewhat similar to *Oboe*, but using *Gee* transmitters and with control systems located in the aircraft, not on the ground. Sometimes known as *G-H*.
G.P.I.	Ground Position Indicator. A navigational aid that calculated an aircraft's position on the ground, based on a known starting point, the aircraft's airspeed and heading and the wind speed and direction.
H2S	A ground mapping radar system used for navigation and target identification, operating at 10 cm wavelengths.
H2X	Similar to *H2S*, but operating at a wavelength of 3 cm for higher resolution.
Home Guard	A volunteer organisation within the British Army that carried out secondary defence duties.

GLOSSARY

	Members were normally too young or old for regular army service, or in reserved occupations.
Klystron	An electronic vacuum tube (valve) that can be used as a microwave amplifier in radar systems.
L.D.A.	Local Defence Advisor. An Army officer attached to an R.A.F. airfield to give advice on its defence.
L.N.S.F.	Light Night Striking Force. A force within No. 8 Group R.A.F. that used Mosquito aircraft for bombing, marking and meteorological operations.
M.A.F.	Ministry of Agriculture and Fisheries. A U.K. government department.
Magnetron	An electronic device capable of producing high power microwave radio energy. Used to generate the signals used in the *H2S* radar system.
Monica	A radar system fitted to the tail of bomber aircraft to warn of approaching nightfighters.
M.T.	Motor Transport.
N.A.A.F.I.	Navy, Army and Air Force Institutes. An organisation created to run recreational establishments for the British Armed Forces, and to sell goods to servicemen and their families.
Naxos	A system similar to *Flensburg* that homed onto the emissions from *H2S*.
N.C.O.	Non-Commissioned Officer. An enlisted member of the R.A.F. who has been delegated leadership or command authority by a commissioned officer.
Oboe	A radar device that allow ground-based controllers to determine the location of an aircraft with great accuracy and direct the aircraft's crew when to drop munitions in order to bomb or mark a target.
O.C.	Officer Commanding.

O.R.	Other Ranks. Personnel who were neither an officer nor an N.C.O.
O.R.B.	Operations Record Book. A record kept both by individual units and operational stations, intended to form a historical document.
O.C.U.	Operational Conversion Unit. A unit where new crews were trained before being sent to their operational squadrons.
O.T.U.	Operational Training Unit. See O.C.U.
P.F.F.	Path Finder Force. No. 8 Group R.A.F., whose role was to mark and illuminate targets for the Main Force of Bomber Command's aircraft.
R.A.A.F.	Royal Australian Air Force.
R.A.E.	Royal Aircraft Establishment. The British government aircraft research centre at Farnborough in Hampshire.
R.A.F.R.	Royal Air Force Regiment. A unit within the R.A.F. tasked with defending airfields from attack.
R.C.A.F.	Royal Canadian Air Force.
R.C.A.S.U.	Radar Controlled Air Survey Unit. A unit that used aircraft controlled by *Gee-H* to assist in the production of maps.
R.N.Z.A.F.	Royal New Zealand Air Force.
S.B.A.	Standard Beam Approach. A blind landing aid/technique based on the use of radio beams aligned on a runway.
S.H.Q.	Station Headquarters.
Sky-marking	A P.F.F. marking technique in which parachute markers were dropped above cloud. These were positioned so that bombs falling through them would hit the target.
S.M.O.	Station Medical Officer.

GLOSSARY

S.P.	Service Police.
Spoof	A diversionary raid designed to draw defenders away from an attack on another target.
S.S.Q.	Station Sick Quarters.
Tinsel	A simple system used to jam radio communications between German controllers and nightfighters by broadcasting noise from a bomber's engines.
T.R.E	Telecommunications Research Establishment. A British research unit based at Malvern in Worcestershire, which specialised in research into radar systems. Now known as the Royal Radar Establishment.
U/S	Unserviceable.
U.S.A.A.F.	United States Army Air Force.
U/T	Under Training.
Village Inn	A radar system that enabled a bomber's gunners to engage an attacking fighter while it was still invisible in the darkness.
W.A.A.F.	Women's Auxiliary Air Force. The women's branch of the Royal Air Force.
W.E.F.	With Effect From.
Window	A method of jamming German radar systems by deploying very large numbers of tinfoil strips, each an efficient radar reflector.
W.T.	Wireless Telegraphy. A system used by aircraft to pass messages over long distances using Morse code.
Würzburg	A German ground-based radar system used to direct flak batteries and to track and control nightfighters.

REFERENCES

Some information in this book is derived from U.K. Government sources. It:
- Contains public sector information licensed under the Open Government Licence v2.0.
- Contains public sector information licensed under the Open Government Licence v3.0.

The National Archives, Kew, London

Planning of new airfields and Bomber Command Organisation, AIR 20/298
ROYAL AIR FORCE: Bomber Command (Code B, 67/9): Expansion, AIR 2/8069
Expansion scheme, AIR 14/2196
Target Force E: expansion, AIR 14/1113
Target Force E: expansion, AIR 4/2196
Bomber Command expansion, AIR 14/2631 and AIR 14/2632
Tempsford Operations Record Books, AIR 28/820
Oakington Operations Record Books, AIR 28/607
Specialist units at Tempsford Beds. and satellites location and administration, AIR 14/1120 and AIR 14/1121
Gransden Lodge Operations Record Books, AIR 28/317 to AIR 28/321 inclusive

REFERENCES

No. 1418 Flight, Marham and Gransden Lodge, AIR 29/868

Occupation of new aerodromes, AIR 14/1054

Expansion and re-equipment: operational Groups, AIR 14/1140

Bomber Development Unit: Formation, AIR 14/682 and AIR 14/683

Bomber Development Unit, Boscombe Down; formed November 1940, disbanded April 1941; Bombing Development Unit, formed Gransden Lodge July 1942, moved to Feltwell April 1943, then Newmarket September 1943 and Feltwell February 1945 (BDU UK), AIR 29/769

RAF Gransden and RAF Feltwell: B.D.U. reports, AIR 14/2588

RADAR AND RADIO COUNTERMEASURES (Code B, 61): Monica: installation policy in Bomber Command, AIR 2/5443

No 192 Squadron: Operations Record Book, AIR 27/1156 [includes No. 1474 Flight O.R.B. entries]

No 35 Squadron: Operations Record Book, AIR 27/380

Type: Stirling 1 (R-9265); Location: Gransden Bedfordshire; Report No.: W1401, AVIA 5/22 [report on the Stirling crash at Gransden Lodge, 19th December 1942]

No 169 Squadron: Operations Record Book, AIR 27/1094

No 421 Squadron RCAF (Royal Canadian Air Force): Operations Record Book, AIR 27/1827

Despatch on War Operations, Feb. 1942 - May 1945, by Air Chief Marshal Sir A.T. Harris, A.O.C. in C Bomber Command., AIR 16/487

No. 8 PathFinder Force Group: summary of events, AIR 14/539 and AIR 14/540

Pathfinder Navigation Training Unit, Gransden Lodge, Upwood and Warboys (UK), AIR 29/709

Beam approach training flight, AIR 14/1151

No 405 Squadron RCAF (Royal Canadian Air Force): Operations Record Book, AIR 27/1788 to AIR 27/1790 inclusive

No. 2708, AIR 29/74 [O.R.B. of No. 2708 Squadron R.A.F.R]

TRIALS AND TRIBULATION

No 97 Squadron: Operations Record Book, AIR 27/767
No. 7 Blind A.T.F., Finningley, later No. 1507 Beam A.T.F., Finningley, Warboys and Gransden Lodge, AIR 29/872
Miscellaneous papers on intelligence about pilotless aircraft (V1) and long range rockets (V2), DEFE 40/12
2955 Anti-Aircraft Squadron RAF Regiment. Formed at St Athan from 4154, 4158 and 4163 Anti-Aircraft Flights. Later moved to other UK locations including Davidstow Moor, Selsey and Snaith, AIR 29/136
LEEMING, AIR 28/451 [O.R.B. of R.A.F. Leeming]
Bomber defence training flights, AIR 14/1637
ROYAL AIR FORCE: Bomber Command (Code B, 67/9): Bomber Defence Training Flights: formation and disbandment, AIR 2/8259
Operation "Overlord": bomber forces, AIR 20/3223
No 142 Squadron: Operations Record Book, AIR 27/975 and AIR 27/976
AERODROMES (Code B, 3): Post-war Airfield Requirements Committee: agenda and minutes of meetings, AIR 2/8630
Bourn, AIR 28/94 [O.R.B. of R.A.F. Bourn]
WOODBRIDGE, AIR 28/954 [O.R.B. of R.A.F. Woodbridge]
Operations record book, AIR 25/130 [O.R.B. of No. 6 Group R.C.A.F.]
No 692 Squadron: Operations Record Book, AIR 27/2216
South East Asia and India: need for radar controlled air survey, AIR 20/906
RADAR AND RADIO COUNTERMEASURES (Code B, 61): Radar and photographic methods for air survey, AIR 2/5635
Photo-Reconnaissance and Air Survey Units: establishments, AIR 20/3387
Air Ministry and Ministry of Defence: Operations Record Books, Miscellaneous Units. AIR MINISTRY EXPERIMENTAL STATIONS. Radio Warfare Establishment, Watton, AIR 29/141
No 53 Squadron: Operations Record Book, AIR 27/507
ROYAL AIR FORCE: General (Code 67/1): Use of RAF airfields consolidated statements, Feb-Apr 1946: May-June 1946 and amendments lists 1946, AIR 20/7261

REFERENCES

Inactive airfields in UK: safeguarding policy, AIR 2/17402
AERODROMES (Code 3): Airfields: policy, AIR 20/7716
AERODROMES (Code B, 3): Airfields: policy, AIR 2/11362
Restoration to agricultural use of airfields, MAF 140/26
Agricultural operations at RAF airfields, MAF 105/70
USAF: airfield and land requirements and works services, AIR 8/1804
AERODROMES (Code 3): Airfield requirements: general policy, working party papers, minutes of meetings of Air Chiefs, etc., AIR 20/7589
USAF hospitals in the UK: policy, AIR 2/13657
Inactive airfields working party, AIR 2/14492
AERODROMES (Code B, 3): Security of tenure of airfield accommodation, AIR 2/11808
Agricultural use of airfields surplus to R.A.F. requirements, MAF 48/679
Disposal of concrete runways from former airfields, MAF 142/416

University of Victoria Digital Collections, Canadian Military Oral History

Lane, Reginald J.: my Air Force recollections, interview with Lieutenant-General R.J. Lane by R.H. Roy and C.D. Main, identifier SC104_LRJ_228

The Liddell Hart Centre for Military Archives, King's College, London

The papers of Wing Commander E.P.M. Fernbank, reference code GB99 KCLMA Fernbank.

Extracts used by permission of The Trustees of the Liddell Hart Centre for Military Archives

TRIALS AND TRIBULATION

The Royal Air Force Museum, Hendon, London

Gransden Lodge Record Site Plan Site No. 1 [Airfield Site], Air Ministry drawing 4400/44, MFC 78/24/531

RAF Days: My life and times in the Royal Air Force 1941-1946 by Angus Robb, object number X001-3517/001 [No. 405 Squadron]

Wireless operator's flying log book of Sgt R.G. Henderson, 21 April 1941- 9 September 1946, object number X003-6153 [No. 405 Squadron]

Pilot's flying log book of Flt Lt G.F. Barton, 7 December 1942-9 May 1946, object number MF10060/9 [No. 53 Squadron]

The Imperial War Museum, London

Phillips, John Alwyn 'Pee Wee' [taped interview], Imperial War Museum sound archive, accession number 17685/3

Private Papers of Mrs E M Kup, catalogue number Documents.507

Private Papers of Wing Commander R S J Edwards DFC, catalogue number Documents.17086

The Australians at War Film Archive

Ian McLeod [filmed interview], archive number 0105

REFERENCES

The English Heritage National Monuments Record, Swindon

The aerial photographs mentioned in the text are held at the N.M.R., Swindon, as follows:

Date	Sortie number	Library number	Frame numbers
22nd June 1942	RAF/FNO/1	8770	6025, 6056, 6057, 6058
7th March 1943	RAF/AC276	8670	5090, 5091, 5092, 5093
17th October 1955	RAF/58/1900	3880	23, 24
23rd May 1962	RAF/58/5135	2446	69
8th June 1969	MAL/69053	5415	133, 134, 135
16th July 1972	OS/72233	10304	104, 105, 106, 107

Aerial photographs showing prehistoric settlement in the area of the airfield were taken by the author, and copies are lodged with the Cambridgeshire Historic Environment Record.

Other original sources

Gransden Lodge airfield hangar plans, Reference No. 4436, Huntingdonshire Archives, Huntingdon [Hangar sale, 1963]

Gransden Lodge Runways and Tracks Layout, Air Ministry drawing 17096/40, via Cambridge Gliding Centre archives

Gransden Lodge Runways & Tracks Extension of N.E. and S.W. & Revised Position of N.W. and S.E. Runways, Air Ministry drawing 1999/41, via Cambridge Gliding Centre archives

TRIALS AND TRIBULATION

Published material

Archaeology of Cambridgeshire, Vol 1: South West Cambridgeshire by Alison Taylor, Cambridgeshire County Council, 1997

A History of the County of Cambridge and the Isle of Ely: Volume 5 by C.R. Elrington (editor) and others, Oxford University Press, 1973

Works and Buildings by C.M. Kohan O.B.E., M.A., Her Majesty's Stationary Office and Longmans, Green and Co., London, 1952

A King's Heritage: The memoirs of King Peter II of Yugoslavia by King Peter II of Yugoslavia, Cassell and Company Ltd., 1955

Bomber Command by Max Hastings, Michael Joseph, 1979

Espionage in the Ether by William J. and John E. Rees, Compaid Graphics, 1999

Most Secret War by R.V. Jones, Penguin Books, 2009

March of Technology: Closing the Radar Gap by Norm Shannon, Ésprit de Corps magazine (on the Web), January 2007

Instruments of Darkness: The History of Electronic Warfare by Alfred Price, Panther Books, 1979

Reap the Whirlwind: The Untold Story of 6 Group, Canada's Bomber Force of World War II by Spencer Dunmore and William Carter, Crécy Books, 1992

The Bomber Command Handbook 1939-1945 by Jonathan Falconer, Sutton Publishing, 1998

The Bomber's Eye by Group Captain Dudley Saward, O.B.E., Cassell, 1959

Echoes of War: The Story of H2S Radar by Sir Bernard Lovell, Taylor and Francis, 1991

Pathfinder Force: A History of 8 Group by Gordon Musgrove, Crécy Books, 1992

Pathfinder by Air Vice-Marshal Donald Bennett CB CBE DSO, Goodall, 1998

Above and Beyond: The Canadian's War in the Air, 1939-45 by

REFERENCES

Spencer Dunmore, McClelland & Stewart Inc., 1996

Royal Air Force Bomber Command Squadron Profiles No. 84: 405 (Vancouver) Squadron Royal Canadian Air Force by Chris Ward, Chris Ward, 2000

The Berlin Raids: R.A.F. Bomber Command Winter 1943-44 by Martin Middlebrook, Penguin, 1990

Target Berlin, The National Film Board of Canada, 1944, from *Target Germany*, DD Home Entertainment, 2006

Flying Through Fire: FIDO - The Fog Buster of World War Two by Geoffrey Williams, Sutton Publishing Ltd., 1995

Through Adversity: The History of the Royal Air Force Regiment by Kingsley M. Oliver, Forces & Corporate Publishing Ltd., 1997

Black Night for Bomber Command: The Tragedy of 16 December 1943 by Richard Knott, Pen And Sword Aviation, 2007

Avro Lancaster: The Definitive Record: Second Edition by Harry Holmes, The Crowood Press Ltd., 2001

142 Mosquito Bomber Squadron by Barry Blunt, Barry Blunt, 2001

Path Finders at War by Chaz Bowyer, Ian Allan Ltd., 1977

Archive of War - Night Bombers Oracle Home Entertainment, 2004 [commercial version of the film *Prelude to Victory*]

British Aircraft Armament Volume 1: RAF Gun Turrets From 1914 to the Present Day by R. Wallace Clarke, Patrick Stephens Ltd., 1993

Lancaster Down!: The Extraordinary Tale of Seven Young Airmen at War by Stephen Darlow, Grub Street Publishing, 2000

Bomber Crew, Channel 4 Television, 2004

The Royal Air Force Medical Services, Volume II, Commands edited by Squadron Leader S.C. Rexford-Welch M.A., M.R.C.S., L.R.C.P., R.A.F., Her Majesty's Stationary Office, 1955

Action Stations 1: Wartime Military Airfields of East Anglia 1939-1945 by Michael J.F. Bowyer, Patrick Stephens Ltd, 1979

The Bulletin of the Vintage Sports-Car Club, Vol. VI., No. 3, September 1947

TRIALS AND TRIBULATION

Car Racing Comes Back at Cambridge, British Pathé, 1947
Land Yachts Race, British Pathé, 1963
1066 and All That by W.C. Sellar and R.J. Yeatman, Methuen and Co. Ltd., 1930
The Dam Busters by Paul Brickhill, Pan Books, 1954

Web resources

In addition to the original and published material mentioned above, some information was obtained from resources on the Web, including Wikipedia and Google Maps for general background information. Links to resources on specific subjects, correct at the time of writing, are given below.

The link to the resource containing the photograph showing the funeral procession of those members of No. 405 Squadron killed on 'Black Thursday' is part of an article by William Francis (Bill) Bessent, Jane Pilling-Cormick and Jennie Gray. The resource in which Arthur Bonikowsky's recollections were found appears no longer to exist. Arthur died on 2nd January 2011.

Subject	Link
The Open Government Licence	http://www.nationalarchives.gov.uk/doc/open-government-licence/version/3/
Front cover photograph	http://www.defenceimagery.mod.uk/fotoweb/Grid.fwx?archiveId=5042&search=45154145.jpg
Bomber Command campaign diaries	http://webarchive.nationalarchives.gov.uk/20070706011932/http://raf.mod.uk/bombercommand/diary.html

REFERENCES

Currency conversions	http://www.measuringworth.com/index.php
Derek Daniels' recollections	http://www.bbc.co.uk/history/ww2peopleswar/stories/99/a7941099.shtml
Photograph of Ed Miller	http://www.thememoryproject.com/stories/917:ed-stanley-miller/
P.F.F. roles	http://www.raf.mod.uk/rafbramptonwyton/history/avrolancastercont.cfm
Exercise SPARTAN	http://www.cmp-cpm.forces.gc.ca/dhh-dhp/his/rep-rap/doc/cmhq/cmhq094.pdf
1943 weekly rations	http://www.cooksinfo.com/british-wartime-food
Operation STARKEY	http://www.combinedops.com/Operation%20Starkey.htm
Modane (in French)	http://www.modane.fr/Centre-d-Exposition-Lyon-Turin.html
'Black Thursday' funerals	http://www.ww2-pathfinders.co.uk/Bessent%20Twins.html
Analysis of the Battle of Berlin	http://www.technologyreview.com/article/406789/a-failure-of-intelligence/

TRIALS AND TRIBULATION

'Teddy' Blenkinsop	http://www.bombercommandmuseum.ca/s,blenkinsop.html
Monument to the Coldrey crew (in French)	http://aerosteles.net/fiche.php?code=charmoie-lancaster&type=nd&valeur=78&lang=en
Monument to the Gray crew	http://www.wingsofmemory.be/Engels/StHubert.html
MANNA and CHOWHOUND	http://militaryhistory.about.com/od/aerialcampaigns/p/manna.htm
Mr. N.J.R. Empson's recollections	http://www.gamlingay.org/irember.htm
Post-war bread rationing	http://howitreallywas.typepad.com/how_it_really_was/bread_rationing/
Edwin Horner's recollections	http://www.bbc.co.uk/history/ww2peopleswar/stories/54/a4674954.shtml
Roy Simmons's recollections	http://www.bbc.co.uk/ww2peopleswar/stories/59/a7031459.shtml
No. 60 Group history	http://www.rquirk.com/cdnradar/cor/chapter12.pdf

REFERENCES

R.A.F. Watton	http://www.rafwatton.info
1946 motor race report	http://archive.motorsportmagazine.com/page/july-1946/5
1947 motor race report	http://archive.motorsportmagazine.com/page/august-1947/1
Newsreel of the 1947 race	http://www.britishpathe.com/video/car-racing-comes-back-at-cambridge
Johnny Fauquier	http://www.bombercommandmuseum.ca/s,fauquier.html
Reg Lane	http://www.bombercommandmuseum.ca/s,reglane.html

APPENDIX: THE UNITS

The units listed below are known to have served at Gransden Lodge, and, where available, the dates when they served there are included. This is probably not a complete list, as some units will undoubtedly have served at the airfield, perhaps for quite a short period, and left no trace of their passing.

Unit	Dates
No. 816 Defence Squadron (later No. 2816 Squadron R.A.F.R.)	1st December 1941 – ?before April 1942
No. 4265 Anti-Aircraft Flight R.A.F.R.	?before April 1942 – ?7th July 1943
No. 1418 Flight	8th April 1942 – 20th July 1942
No. 1474 Flight	10th July 1942 – 4th January 1943
Bombing Development Unit	20th July 1942 – 6th April 1943
No. 192 Squadron	4th January 1943 – 7th April 1943

APPENDIX: THE UNITS

No. 169 Squadron	5th March 1943 – 10th March 1943
No. 421 Squadron R.C.A.F.	5th March 1943 – 10th March 1943
Path Finder Force Navigation Training Unit	10th April 1943 – 19th June 1943
No. 405 Squadron R.C.A.F.	17th April 1943 – 26th May 1945
No. 9405 Servicing Echelon	?17th April 1943 – ?26th May 1945
No. 1507 Beam Approach Training Flight	17th June 1943 – ?31st December 1943
No. 2708 Anti-Aircraft Squadron R.A.F.R.	7th July 1943 – ?8th December 1943
No. 97 Squadron (one Flight thereof)	29th August 1943 – 3rd September 1943
No. 2955 Anti-Aircraft Squadron R.A.F.R.	13th October 1943 – 8th November 1943 & 8th December 1943 – ?March 1944
No. 2784 Anti-Aircraft Squadron R.A.F.R.	?March 1944 – ?December 1944 or later
No. 1696 Bomber (Defence) Training Flight	21st March 1944 – 28th October 1944
No. 142 Squadron	25th October 1944 – 28th September 1945

TRIALS AND TRIBULATION

No. 6 Group Diversion Unit	? – 28th November 1944
No. 692 Squadron	4th June 1945 – 20th September 1945
Radar Controlled Air Survey Unit	?5th September 1945 – ?20th December 1945
No. 53 Squadron	8th December 1945 – 28th February 1946
No. 4053 Servicing Echelon	8th December 1945 – ?28th February 1946

INDEX

A.P.I. 19, 21, 31, 33
Allerton Park 269
Avro Lancaster Mk. VI. 139-140
Avro Lincoln 140, 220, 229, 238
B.D.U. 27-29, 31-35, 37, 41-48, 50-52, 54-57, 73, 77, 133, 137, 175, 215-216
Baldwin, J.E.A. 11-12, 18, 47
Barry, W. 23, 27, 39
Bennett, D.C.T. 60-61, 66-67, 79, 87, 92, 99, 103, 123-124, 134, 144, 175-176, 230, 233
Black Thursday 109, 112-113, 168, 191
Blenkinsop, E 138-139
Boozer 52, 216
Brain, W.H. 90, 96
Brookes, G. 73
Brown, W. 198
Browne, J. 121
Butt Report 58, 61
Cambridge University Automobile Club 254
Cambridge University Gliding Club 266-267
Carpet 157

Castle Dismal 269, 271
Cochrane, The Hon. R. A. 47, 49, 51, 67-68
Cribb, P.H. 46
Dodwell, T.E. 149
Dunlop, G.P. 93, 116, 124, 208
Düppel 55
Edwards, R.S.J. 246, 248
Emergency War Plan 263
Exercise POST MORTEM 234
Exercise SPARTAN 52
Exercise UMBRELLA 100
F.I.D.O. 103, 111, 182, 191, 198
Fauquier, J.E. 64, 68, 81-82, 85, 88, 91, 93, 118, 120, 163, 236-237, 269-271
Fernbank, E.P.M. 23-24, 56
Fishpond 98
Flensburg 43, 49
Forbes, Group Captain 248
G.P.I. 33, 55
GALLOPER Plan 259
Gee 16-22, 24, 29, 33-35, 40, 42, 52, 59, 75, 89, 146, 234, 246
Gee-H 42, 245-246
Grand Slam 270

Gray, K. 238
H2S 31-34, 44, 47, 49, 55-57, 59, 62, 73, 75, 77, 89, 94, 97-99, 102, 137-138, 173, 183
H2X 137-138
Hannah, H. 178-179, 204
Harris, Sir Arthur 58-60, 89, 105, 122, 130-132, 134-135, 155, 162, 172
Harrison, R. 51
Jay 18, 37, 40
Jones, R.V. 17-18, 37-40, 43, 146
Jordan, H. 39
Killip, L. 20, 56-57, 137
King George VI 9, 68, 124
King Peter II of Yugoslavia 8-9, 124
Knickebein 39-40, 72
Kup, E. (née Heap) 236-237, 254
L.N.S.F. 175-176, 195, 213
Lane, R.J. 47, 94-95, 98-99, 104, 110, 120-122, 124, 129-130, 138, 141, 144, 163, 170-171, 229, 269, 271-272
Lichtenstein 37-40, 43-44, 49
LORAN 42, 181, 206
Lorenz 71-72
Lovell, Sir Bernard 31-32, 34, 57
Ludlow-Hewitt, E. 51
Lynch, A. 149
Martin, G. 178-179
McEwan, C.M. 133
McLeod, I. 194, 213, 226

Medhurst, C. 11-12
Menaul, S.W.B. 70, 93
Monica 43, 49, 51-52, 54-56
Morrison, H.A. 167, 170
Nathan, B.G.D. 177, 238
Naxos 49
Newson, W. 173-174
No. 102 Squadron 252
No. 105 Squadron 175, 236
No. 109 Squadron 11, 14, 22, 24, 26, 40, 100, 175
No. 115 Squadron 17, 243
No. 139 Squadron 175, 208
No. 1418 Flight 14, 16, 18-19, 21-22, 25-28
No. 142 Squadron 175-185, 187-211, 213-222, 224, 226, 228-229, 231-235, 238-239, 241, 243, 249, 272
No. 1507 Flight 71-72, 100, 102, 109, 117, 242
No. 169 Squadron 52-53
No. 1696 Flight 128, 136, 149, 155, 166, 174, 176
No. 192 Squadron 44-50, 52, 54, 56-57, 72, 174, 210, 235, 248, 272
No. 2708 Squadron R.A.F.R. 75, 90, 96, 106, 108-109
No. 2784 Squadron R.A.F.R. 126, 178, 186
No. 2955 Squadron R.A.F.R. 96, 98, 100-101, 109, 126
No. 3 Group 3, 11, 14, 30, 47, 51, 60-61, 68

INDEX

No. 35 Squadron 44, 47, 56-57, 94, 232
No. 405 Squadron 62-70, 72-73, 75-80, 82, 84, 86-93, 96-99, 101-102, 105-109, 111-113, 115-126, 128-129, 133-138, 140-141, 143-144, 146-153, 156-157, 159-161, 163-173, 176-185, 187-197, 199-211, 214-221, 224-231, 236, 269, 272-273
No. 421 Squadron 53
No. 4265 Flight R.A.F.R. 40-41, 74
No. 5 Group 51, 67-68, 123, 138, 168, 200, 233, 270
No. 53 Squadron 248-253, 273
No. 6 Group 63, 73, 83, 118, 120, 122, 133, 163, 165, 170, 172, 184, 230, 269
No. 60 Group 246, 248
No. 617 Squadron 67, 90, 123, 155, 187, 270
No. 692 Squadron 232-233, 237, 241-242, 272
No. 8 Group 56, 60-61, 67, 69, 76, 90, 100, 102, 117, 125, 128, 137-138, 152, 174-175, 183, 187, 190, 201, 208, 230, 241, 270
No. 816 Defence Squadron R.A.F.R. 10, 40
No. 97 Squadron 29, 86-88, 112, 138, 149
Oboe 24-25, 42, 59, 65, 77, 156-157, 175, 188-189, 246

Operation CHASTISE 67
Operation EXODUS 226-228
Operation GOMORRAH 77-79
Operation HURRICANE 172
Operation MANNA 223-224
Operation OVERLORD 132
Operation SPASM 243
Operation STARKEY 89, 132
Operation THUNDERCLAP 207
Operation TOTALISE 159-160
Operation TRACTABLE 161
Operation UNDERGO 169-170
P.F.F.N.T.U. 61-62, 64, 69-71, 94, 98
Palmer, C.W. 163, 170
Paulton, E. 39, 49
Peenemünde 82-83, 88, 150
Phillips, J.A. 'Pee Wee' 74, 79, 144, 273
Queen Marie of Yugoslavia 8, 201
R.A.F. Babdown Farm 261-263
R.A.F. Bassingbourn 3, 5, 10, 12, 73, 77, 259, 261
R.A.F. Bourn 61, 66, 86, 88, 107, 111-112, 118, 123, 128, 138, 176, 236, 253
R.A.F. Coltishall 122
R.A.F. Davidstow Moor 101, 109
R.A.F. Defford 43, 246
R.A.F. Downham Market 190-191, 194, 200, 213
R.A.F. East Moor 269
R.A.F. Graveley 3, 12, 44, 61,

66-67, 86, 93-94, 103, 111, 118, 190, 232, 243-244
R.A.F. Linton-on-Ouse 93, 230-231, 269
R.A.F. Marham 16, 43, 111, 118, 258
R.A.F. Merryfield 248-249, 251
R.A.F. Oakington 44, 61, 66, 75-76, 78, 86, 91-92, 107, 113, 118, 149, 186
R.A.F. Stradishall 14, 22
R.A.F. Tempsford 3-5, 10-14, 16, 41, 47-48, 50-51, 53, 61, 70, 241, 251, 254
R.A.F. Tholthorpe 269
R.A.F. Upwood 69-71, 98, 118, 221, 234
R.A.F. Warboys 61, 69-71, 111, 190, 241
R.A.F. Watton 182, 248
R.A.F. West Raynham 119
R.A.F. Woodbridge 116, 168, 182, 184, 198, 200, 204, 218
R.A.F. Wyton 24, 43, 61, 68, 70, 118, 136, 242
R.C.A.S.U. 245-248
Robb, A. 84, 173, 185, 225
S.B.A. 71-72
Saundby, R.H.M. 38
Saye, G.I.L. 22, 31
Schräge Musik 83, 143
SHORAN 42
Simpson, G.W. 91
St. Bartholomew's Church 273-274

T.R.E. 16, 31-32, 137-138
Tallboy 155
The 'Ruhr Express' 93-94, 99-100, 105, 196-197
The Fellowship of the Bellows 232
The Night of the Strong Winds 129
Tiger Force 229, 232, 238-239, 241, 271
Tinsel 66
Tizard, Sir Henry 21, 25
U.S. Third Air Force 261, 263
V.E. Day 224-226, 229, 235, 237
V.J. Day 240
V-1 150, 165, 172, 189
V-2 82, 84, 150, 152, 165, 216
Vasse, G.H. 41
Vauxhall Motors 266
Vielle, E.E. 22
Village Inn 157
Vintage Sports-Car Club 254
Webster, P.F. 46
Whitley, J. 230
Willis, C.V.D. 56
Wimpole Park 260, 262
Window 54-55, 77-78, 182, 204-205
Womersley, G.H. 208, 248
Würzburg 157
Young, F.C. 242